An Angel for Detroit

SANDRA BRAHAM, Ed.D

Bible verses reference the following translations, NIV, King James, ESV

Publish@nowscpress.com
www.PublishWithNOW.com
@nowscpress

Ordering Information:

    Quantity sales. Special discounts are available on quantity purchases by corporations, associations, and others. For details, contact the publisher at the address above.

    Orders by U.S. trade bookstores and wholesalers. Please contact: NOW SC Press: Tel: (813) 970-8470 or visit www.PublishWithNOW.com

Printed in the United States of America

First Printing 2022

ISBN: 979-8-9870349-9-6

Dedication

An Angel for Detroit is dedicated to the memory of Doris Rice (Boyd) Edmond, my mother, who has earned her wings as a woman who loved God and humanity, and to my sisters, Lorie and Lacy. To my husband Eric, I love you to the end of time. Thank you for your never-ending encouragement and for giving me the greatest gift of all, my three beautiful children.

As much as the book honors God and His creations and gifts, An Angel for Detroit honors all persons who live with mental illness or who are raising children with mental illness, and for children and teens who find themselves in our nation's foster care system.

This body of work would not be possible without the contributions of so many who gave of their time, possessions and talents. Special thanks to:

Deborah Benedict
Kimberly Bishop-Jones and Vincent Jones
Samuel Boyd, Sr.
Katherine Brennand and Chris Cummings
Dr. Maceo C. Dailey*
Etta Dortch
The Driemeier Family
Doris Rice (Boyd) Edmond*
Ryan Griffith
Lucille Mongo
David Rice, Sr.
Walter Rice
Dede Rogers*
Jody and Jonathan Schwartz

I hope this book and the years of research that went into its production are seen as an ultimate gift, capturing aspects of my family's history and America's Black experience, to be shared for generations to come.

*deceased

Contents

Preface

I am driving over the Belleair Causeway, a short but amazing bridge that connects the City of Belleair in Pinellas County, Florida, to the island of Sand Key. The Belleair Bridge crosses the Intercoastal Waterway, a passage for boats and water vehicles that provides launch sites and access to the Gulf of Mexico. When a person reaches the peak of the Belleair Causeway, there is a surprise for the first-time crosser – the Gulf of Mexico appears, stretching endlessly beyond Sand Key. When crossing the bridge at sunset, the view is even more breathtaking as the sun reflects off the waterways, which sandwich the island. I slowed down (as most people do for those views) and took a deep breath as I reveled in the majesty of God's handiwork. I exhaled and thought, *Life has not always been this good.*

Sand Key is about a mile and a half south of Clearwater Beach, "America's #1 Beach," according to *USA Today* in 2010 and *TripAdvisor* in 2018. *TripAdvisor* also rated Clearwater Beach the "7th Most Wonderful Beach in the World." A 2010 marquis welcomes visitors who exit the Causeway and drive a few miles down the Key after crossing the Sand Key Bridge. I was visiting Sand Key to pick up the keys to the condominium my husband Eric and I had rented to get a taste of what life would be like living in a beach community.

A search firm contacted me in 2015, looking to hire the next president and chief executive officer of a large non-profit based in Clearwater, Florida. After twenty-four years of living and working in El Paso, Texas, I had never considered that Florida might be my next career move. The more I thought about it, the more I realized that God certainly has a sense of humor. An African American, Christian female—chosen to lead one of the largest Jewish organizations in the country. It all seemed quite extraordinary, especially up to that point in my life.

As I crossed the bridge, I thought, *But for the Grace of God, I am here, in this place, at this time.* What else but by grace does a young girl born into a poor, humble family with a mother diagnosed with schizophrenia find herself living on Gulf Boulevard in one of the most desired areas of the country? How else, if not for grace, did I survive foster care and graduate from high school, even though I was on the verge of homelessness? My story is of God's Grace — how it manifests and acts as the medium through which faith, hope and love deliver God's abundant blessings. As I reflect upon my life, I see those moments when grace rescued, protected, clothed and gave me a warm, clean place to call home. Grace made me grab hold of the right people amongst a crowd of a hundred "wrongs" — people who sowed seeds into my soul. Those seeds would sprout when the time was right, and those same seeds would eventually yield a testimony that I have longed to share since my seventeenth birthday.

Introduction

It was November 4th, 1981 — my seventeenth birthday. I sat glumly in the McCluer North High School counseling office, anxiously awaiting a meeting with my counselor. I needed immediate help because the anticipated day was finally here after weeks of planning. That morning I had woken up and thought, *Today I will be free. I will never again return to this self-worth-draining, verbally and physically abusive place.* I had retrieved my bag of clothes and personal items that I'd slowly packed weeks prior and had hidden in the back of the closet in the bedroom I shared with my foster sister.

I left for school and went about my day as usual, and near the last class, I went to the counselor's office. I insisted on waiting until she could assist me. While waiting, I reflected upon my life over the preceding two years. My life had been a mess. I thought, *Mine is a great story. I have gone through so much. I will write a book. Perhaps Alex Haley might be interested in my story. Perhaps he might think it is worthy of being a movie. However, perhaps seventeen years is not long enough to have sufficient experiences to be the basis of a book. I will write it when I have more to tell, when the time is right, and when I am older.*

Decades have passed, and time has pressed me to complete the project I envisioned so many years ago. Life has been no less interesting, and I realize I must tell my story. Teens in foster care need to read this book because they need to know that there is life after foster care, which can be amazingly beautiful. People must read this book if they have experienced living and engaging with the twists and turns brought on by the mental illness of a close family member. Little girls who are impoverished and daily wonder how they will ever reach their goals and achieve their dreams will be inspired to stay the course and see life through its many adventures. And those who have struggled with forgiveness of others who have hurt them deeply must read this book, as one cannot live wholly and fully while harboring hate.

Chapter One

THE FAMILY TREE
AND EARLY LIFE

"Everybody back up! Give Momma some room. Sit her in the chair over here."

My aunts and uncles huddled in the living room, desperately trying to help. Big Daddy stood over the chair, holding Big Momma's hand.

"The ambulance is here! Move the table out the way so they can get in."

The paramedics entered, and I sat on the couch across from Big Momma, watching the chaos but without knowing what it meant. This was my first memory. I was eleven months old. An ambulance took Big Momma away, and others in the room followed. My grandma never returned home. She died sometime during the early morning hours on October 6, 1965.

My mother often told me I was in bed with Big Momma that night. I was grandma's baby, and she called me "Honeybunch." I am the only one of my siblings to have a nickname. On the night Big Momma died, momma told me she came into the room to get me because Big Momma was sick.

"Momma, I'm taking Honeybunch."

To which grandma replied, "Don't you take my baby."

"But, Momma, you're sick."

Then, sometime later, I sat on the couch, observing Big Momma's last moments.

Background: Rice Family History

I was born Sandra Elaine Boyd, the second daughter of my mother, Doris Delaine (Rice) Boyd and my father, Samuel Dale Boyd. On the maternal side, Momma was the youngest of twelve children born to Earnest Rice, Sr. and Dora McDonald-Rice. Earnest and Dora's first child, Cora, lived only four days and Mary, their fourth child, died at birth. The seventh child, my Aunt Sallie, died at age twenty-five, leaving behind six young children, including a six-week-old baby girl. Sallie's boyfriend brutally murdered her. My grandfather and my aunts and uncles raised Sallie's kids. All of Momma's siblings, including four girls and five boys, were active parts of my life growing up, and all of them had nicknames except Aunt Lucille. There was also Aunt Honey (the oldest), Aunt Bay, Aunt Dean (short for Dora Dean), Uncle Biggon, Uncle Hut, Uncle Buddy, Uncle Sammy and Uncle Shug.

My grandfather, Earnest Rice, Sr., or "Big Daddy" (as we fondly knew him), was born February 28, 1895, in Belmont, Alabama, and raised nearby in Coatopa. He was the son of Nancy Johnson and Thomas Rice, or "Tom," as his family and community knew him. Tom's parents were Leach Rice and Ellen Hobbs (Crenshaw) Rice. Leach's mother was Jennie Rice, a slave on the Rice plantation in Green County, Alabama. Jennie was born in 1805 to John Rice and Rachel Hopkins Rice, a slave in North Carolina, born in 1770. Tom and Nancy were farmers. Nancy gave birth to five sons, including Walter, Robert, Earnest (my grandfather), Alonzo and Katie. She also had one "very beautiful daughter," Mabel. Because of Nancy's sudden death in 1901 at age twenty-six and Mabel being the only daughter, the community grew to love her. Most residents welcomed the opportunity to invite her into their homes, feed her and do other nice things for her. Sadly, Mabel died before her thirteenth birthday, and the family's account is that her young death resulted from food poisoning. She ate old cabbage from a neighbor, which caused a violent convulsion of the intestines. They had left the cooked cabbage covered on the stove for at least the full day and night before.

Tom Rice was a known ladies' man; according to family accounts, he had multiple relationships outside his marriage to Nancy. Nancy died when Earnest was only six years of age. Sometime after Nancy's death, Tom hooked up with Mariah Winston. Mariah was married to John Inge, and, according to the 1900 census, she and John had been married for five years, though the census indicated he was not living in the home then. Mariah was the head of the household. Mariah and John had two daughters, Elvira Inge and Ruby Inge. The 1910 census listed Mariah as widowed, though John did not die until 1928. This same census indicated that Mariah had four children in the home: two teenage girls, Elvira and Ruby Rice and two boys — Roosevelt Rice, age seven, and Willie Rice, age six. Though Tom was not living in the home with Mariah in 1910, he was the known father of Mariah's two sons.

Tom was rumored to have had two wives, one on each side of town, in two houses between which he lived, and, as if that was not enough to manage, he routinely met a third mistress in the cotton patch. The 1920 census bears out some of this rumor as one report showed fifty-six-year-old Tom married to twenty-seven-year-old Rosa (Rose) Rice, with whom he resided. A second 1920 census account showed Mariah "Rice" with two children living in the home, fifteen-year-old Roosevelt and thirteen-year-old Willie. In this same census, Mariah identified herself as a widow and head of household, though John Inge did not die until 1928. Tom Rice was also very much alive, living with his wife, Rosa, and sons Willie (a second one) and Sam.

Tom's first wife, Nancy, had a brother, Ernest Johnson, who was married to Alberta Shaw-Johnson. Alberta had a younger sister, Rose Ann Shaw. Even though Tom was in a relationship with Mariah, Tom and Rose ran off together and married in 1911. The 1920 census confirmed Tom and Rose were married and lived together with two sons, Willie (eight years old) and Sam (seven years old).

Despite Tom's lifestyle and Earnest (my Big Daddy) being very young at the time of his mother's death, many believed that Earnest was blessed by God and may have been "born to preach." He reported to have accepted Jesus Christ at a young age, and by the age of twenty, he began spreading the Gospel as a traveling evangelist. Through Earnest's travels, he met Dora McDonald of Coatopa, Alabama. In 1917, at twenty-two, Earnest entered the United States Army to serve in World War I. Save for the 369th, 92nd and 93rd Infantry Divisions, Black soldiers were mainly relegated to cooking and digging ditches and graves for fallen White soldiers. Big Daddy was a cook. After serving his country for several years, the Army honorably discharged Earnest. After returning to Alabama, Earnest lived with his brother Walter and Walter's wife in Belmont for a short while. Earnest later returned to Coatopa, where he reconnected with Dora. Dora was six years younger than Earnest, and his time in the service gave her additional time to develop as a young woman. Earnest and Dora were reportedly married on Christmas Day in 1921.

The 1910 census listed Dora McDonald as the five-year-old niece of Frank and Cora Amos. Frank and Cora were cotton farmers. Though it is not clear if there was a blood relationship between Dora and the Amoses, they raised Dora as their child after her mother died during a shootout between Dora's father and another man. It is also not clear what happened to Dora's father.

Frank said that he and Cora found Dora alone in a sandstorm, partially buried, with sand covering her face and caked in her hair and on her little hands. It is hard to imagine how and why Dora came to be abandoned, but the storm prompted Frank and Cora to go and check on the family.

Cora was an incredible cook, and Dora was an excellent student. She learned to cook, bake and manage a home, thanks to Cora's teaching. After Dora's marriage to Earnest, her Aunt Cora and Uncle Frank routinely visited them. It became a loving tradition for Dora to make homemade biscuits. Cora and Frank considered Dora a gift from God, as they had no other children.

Dora loved her Aunt Cora, who became her mother for all practical purposes. Dora honored Cora by naming her first baby, a little girl, after her. Baby Cora was born in 1922, shortly after Dora married Earnest. However, the honor and celebration were short-lived, as Baby Cora died four days later. It was not long before Dora was pregnant again, and in 1924 she gave birth to Mamie, whom she nicknamed "Honey." Following Honey was Willie (Buddy) and then Mary, who was stillborn. Then came Magnolia (Bay), Earnest Jr. (Shug), Sallie and Lucille.

During these years, Dora and Earnest left Coatopa. They moved to the rural town of Brewersville in Sumter County, Alabama, where they worked as farmers, following the tradition of Dora's Uncle Frank. Farming was a means to feed their growing family. Earnest also continued to preach the Gospel. Dora cooked, cleaned and ensured Earnest and the children were well-dressed for church services and school. She continued to bear children and gave birth to Samuel (Sammy) and Walter (Biggon), both born in Brewersville. As the family grew, so did their financial pressures. Earnest held several jobs to earn money. He worked as a cotton picker, foreman, lumberjack and coal miner while also preaching and farming to feed the family.

After some time, Earnest moved the family to Demopolis, Alabama. His brother lived there and provided the opportunity for added support. While in Demopolis, Dora had additional children, including Dora Dean (Dean), David (Hut) and her youngest child, my mother, Doris. Doris' birth was a challenging one. Dora's older children believed that Dora was going through something, perhaps a deep depression, as she denied she was pregnant. According to my aunts, Big Mama insisted that there was "no baby," even throughout her labor, until Doris was finally born.

Life in Demopolis was a challenge for such a large low-income family. The oldest children began to make their way out into the world, starting with Honey, who married and moved to St. Louis, Missouri, with her husband, Frank. Buddy, Bay and Sallie followed Honey, leaving Dora and Earnest with the remaining children in Demopolis.

Answers to Life's Mysteries

Times were hard for the Rice family. They usually ran low on certain necessities. On one occasion, Dora sent Lucille to a neighbor's home for a glass of milk. Dora drank some of the milk and became ill. The family tried hard to make her well, but she continued to worsen. In those days, it was common for people who had fallen ill or experienced misfortune to seek remedies or solutions from "Hoo-doo" or "root workers." These individuals used pagan methods for healing or connecting with the spirit world, where guidance might be obtained and passed on to those who sought deeper insight into their current or future circumstances. My Aunt Lucille described Hoo-doo workers as "two-headed people." The family advised Dora to seek assistance as her health had not improved.

Dora visited one such two-headed man who confirmed that a woman had poisoned her, and she knew exactly who that woman was. According to Aunt Lucille, the neighbor who sent the milk had eyes for Earnest, and they believed she poisoned Dora out of jealousy. The two-headed person gave Dora a special tea and advice for healing, but her health continued to fail. By this time, Honey was married and living in St. Louis. Honey communicated with her mother that the two-headed people in St. Louis were more skilled than in the rural south, and she recommended Dora go there to consult with one of them. Dora had an enormous responsibility to care for her home and children and being sickly weighed heavily on her ability to manage day-to-day duties. She took Honey's advice, left Demopolis with her two smallest children, Hut and Doris, and traveled by train to St. Louis. While there, her health started to improve.

Lucille remained in Demopolis to care for her remaining siblings and father. She took care of the home, cooked, cleaned, maintained her sister Dean's hair and prepared her father's clothes for preaching and church activities. All the while, she attended school Monday through Friday. When her grades began to drop, the teacher requested a meeting with Earnest, who explained the family's predicament. They agreed that Lucille could skip school on Fridays. Her teacher sent her work home on Thursdays and made it due Mondays. This allowed Lucille more time to manage the needs of her father and siblings. As months passed, Lucille continued in the roles of student and homemaker.

Earnest was a quiet man who loved his family. He took time to talk with his children and to understand their wishes and concerns. During one such conversation, Lucille told her father that she "felt like a lady." Earnest asked Lucille for clarification regarding her feelings. She explained that she did everything a lady does—cook, clean, comb hair, launder clothes, iron, etc., and that she was worn out. Earnest was very understanding and agreed that this was a large responsibility for her to shoulder. He asked her in what other ways she felt like a woman, and Lucille explained that she had a boyfriend. Earnest asked her to bring him for a visit, which she did. The two explained that they were in love, and even though Lucille was not of marrying age, Earnest agreed to sign his consent allowing the two to be married. Lucille and her fiancé agreed to wait a period because the matter of the family's care needed resolution if she would no longer be there.

Earnest wrote to Honey and explained the situation. It was agreed that the remaining children would be sent to Honey. That was except for Sammy, who was rebellious and too much of a burden to be without his father. Dean and Biggon went to St. Louis by train, with youth "tags" that hung around their necks because of their age. They traveled with a large trunk containing their clothing and other items needed for the family in their new home. Lucille married and left Demopolis, Alabama, leaving behind Sammy and Earnest.

In 1948, with Dora and most of the Rice kids living in St. Louis, Earnest decided to join the family in Kinloch in St. Louis County. The family lived in a small, cramped apartment with issues and vermin located on the east side of Carson Road. Children from Kinloch families who lived on the east side of Carson attended Vernon School for Blacks in Ferguson. Children from families on the west side of Carson attended Kinloch Schools, including Kinloch Elementary and Dunbar High School. Biggon had started at Vernon school in 1948. After completing the eighth grade, Vernon students attended the segregated school in Webster Groves, Missouri.

In 1954, The Supreme Court decision in Brown versus Board of Education made segregation illegal, and Missouri was among the early implementers of integration. Biggon left Webster Groves and enrolled in Ferguson High School, walking six miles roundtrip to school. The "Carson Road Gang" was formed to protect students like Biggon who attended school in Ferguson, as the Kinloch boys did not like the Ferguson boys (even though they all lived in Kinloch). Sammy belonged to a *real* gang, one that carried knives and guns. Years passed, and the older Rice children began to have their own children. During this time, Dora and Earnest became "Big Momma" and "Big Daddy."

By 1957, Earnest had saved enough money to purchase a small "shotgun" house on Scott Street, west of Carson in Kinloch. Shotgun homes were popular in the South. They were typically one room wide and up to four rooms deep and were called shotgun houses because the front and rear doors were aligned so that a gunshot could pass from the front to the back of the house. "Another theory of the shotgun house is that its name derived from the African word "to-gun," which means a place of assembly."[1] The Rice's Kinloch home was four rooms deep, including the kitchen. There was no indoor plumbing for many years, so an outhouse served the family for several decades.

Earnest joined a small church where he could continue to share the Word of God and raise his family in the ministry. In addition to his work as a preacher, Earnest worked at a chemical plant in Ferguson making matches. He found land surrounding his house and farmed it, raising vegetables and planting fruit trees for the family. With the entire family together again, Earnest focused on ensuring they continued to grow in their relationship with Christ. Earnest later became an active member of the clergy at Solid Rock Missionary Baptist Church in Kinloch, where he continued to preach until shortly before his death at age ninety-one.

My mother, Doris, was very smart and beautiful. While attending Dunbar Grade School in Kinloch, she attracted the attention of Samuel Boyd, my father. Samuel was the second youngest child of eight born to Carliena (McQueen) Boyd. Samuel's father was Reverend James J. (J.J.) Boyd. The Boyd family was financially "well-off" by the day's standards. J.J. Boyd owned several businesses and served as pastor of another Kinloch church. According to my father, Grandpa Boyd:

> "Was an iceman in the summer to help families stay cool, and he was a coal man in the winter, helping families stay warm. JJ Boyd had a fillin' station where he sold gas to folks with cars, and he had a taxi stand for providing transportation to those who didn't have cars. He owned a small grocery store and a restaurant to serve folks who didn't want to buy groceries and cook at home. He owned apartments that he built himself and rented and a couple of houses, which he made available for rent to larger families. He was chair of the Board of Education for Kinloch schools and a truant school officer. He was a bail bondsman, and he preached on Sunday mornings. Seasonally, he used his limousine service to transport workers to Sikeston, Missouri, to pick cotton. During their stay, he served as the foreman and prepared meals for the workers, receiving a 'cut' from their pay when the work was completed."

With so many vocations, it was no surprise that the Boyd family was financially stable. In contrast, the Rice family was impoverished.

---

1   Taken from the displayed description of "shotgun houses" which are across the street from Martin Luther King Jr.'s childhood home in Atlanta, GA.

The McQueens

Carliena McQueen Boyd was the eleventh child born to Richard and Edna Bell Adams McQueen of Louisville, Mississippi. Richard was the son of Susan Anderson and Hugh McQueen, the brother-in-law of a plantation owner for whom Susan was a house servant. The 1910 census lists Richard's race as "mulatto", noting his half-white ancestry. According to the McQueen family account, Richard married "the blackest woman he could find," Edna Bell McQueen. To their union, eleven children were born, including my paternal grandmother, Carliena. Since 1976, the McQueen family has hosted a reunion every two years. This tradition has been a significant factor in passing the family's history to younger generations and has played a decisive role in maintaining the family's connections, which stem from the original family tree.

Before My Birth

The Boyd and Rice families were generally close, and Big Daddy and Grandpa Boyd even preached and traveled together to various regional churches. Sam's relationship with Doris continued. At sixteen, she became pregnant and gave birth to my older sister, Lorie, by cesarean section on May 14, 1962. Doris had her seventeenth birthday about two months later, on July 22nd. Doris was about three months older than Sam, who turned seventeen on November 3rd. Lorie was born with the last name Rice, as at the time of her birth, Momma and Daddy had not married. Their parents insisted the two marry, and the families agreed that the marriage was in the best interest of everyone in light of their commitment to one another and the new baby. Sam and Doris were married shortly after that at Big Daddy's house and the two moved into a second-floor apartment in St. Louis. Doris was immediately pregnant again and suffered a miscarriage of their second child. After a year or so of living in their apartment, Momma became pregnant again, this time with me.

Big Mama was very protective of Doris, her baby girl. She was a major influence on the young couple's marriage. When she learned that Momma was pregnant again, Big Mama began to exert her influence. She expressed concern that Momma could not climb the flight of stairs at the apartment and should, therefore, return home where she could benefit from the support of Big Mama. Convinced this was best, Doris left the apartment (and my father) to return to her mother. Daddy pleaded with Momma to come home, but this was to no avail. His future and fate would unfold in Daddy's self-described loneliness and sense of abandonment. He began to see another woman, Ernestine.

Daddy had his nineteenth birthday on November 3, 1964, and I was born the next day on November 4th. Momma named me Sandra, as she thought it was close enough to Samuel, which is what they had planned if I'd been a boy. With another cesarean section and a toddler needing care, Momma needed her mother's assistance and did not return to the apartment. Just shy of a year after I was born, Ernestine gave birth to a baby girl. Daddy suggested the name Sandra. Ernestine had no idea he had another daughter named Sandra, so she agreed. Daddy continued the relationship, and Sam Jr. was born to Ernestine a little over a year later. Four weeks after that, Lacy was born to Doris in the same hospital as Sam Jr.

Daddy was very talented and played the flute. He formed a band with friends, and they performed throughout the city and parts of Illinois. During Daddy's many performances with his band, he met Blanche. Blanche became pregnant and gave birth to Lynnette early in 1968. Then there was another Doris. Doris number two gave birth to Lorenzo about two and a half years later. Then there was Annette, who gave birth to Brian a little over a year after that. At some point during these relationships, my father and mother divorced and he married Ernestine. He and Ernestine had one more child, Keith, born in 1974. Keith is the youngest of Daddy's nine children.

Chasing dollars to meet the needs of five women and nine children would become a way of life for Daddy. Having nine children by the age of twenty-five forced him to find ways to care for them all. So many men father children and walk away. Certainly, the thought of providing for nine by multiple women might break the *average* man — Daddy was far from average. Daddy tried, dedicating himself to three jobs to make ends meet. He maintained his gigs with the band, learned to do routine maintenance on apartments and houses, and worked nights as an aircraftsman for McDonnell Douglas. He had a challenging and stress-filled life.

Mom's One Job

We lived in the Boaz Apartments in Kinloch. The Boaz Apartments were government subsidized but nice. They were newly constructed in the early 1960s when we lived there (the first time). My older teenage cousin and her friends would babysit us when Momma went to work. She worked evenings until about ten o'clock at a sandwich shop. I liked being around my teenage cousins. They were nice, liked to comb my hair and their conversations were always interesting. Of course, some of these conversations were about boyfriends, so they routinely excused Lorie and me during these juicy talks.

Though we did not have lots of money, life seemed good. We always had a nice breakfast with rice or grits, eggs and occasionally bacon or sausage. The eggs were usually powdered, as we could not afford real eggs. Over time, the eggs became less of a favorite. Mom was a good cook and liked to make dishes like spaghetti, fried chicken, greens (a combination of mustards, turnips, and spinach), corn, pork chops and other foods you would typically find on an African American dinner table. Mom taught us to clean and pick up after ourselves and I washed dishes while standing in a chair over the kitchen sink. Times were good.

"*Train up a child in the way he should go: even when he is old he will not depart from it.*"

— PROVERBS 22:6

One evening, my aunts and uncles came for Momma. They told her she was sick and needed to go to the hospital. Momma argued that she was not sick, but they took her against her will. The cousins and friends stayed with us for about a month, and Momma eventually returned. I did not know what was wrong with her. She did not appear to be sick to me, so I never understood her reason for going to the hospital.

The Road to Motown

It was 1969. Momma allowed our cousin to make our hair into afros. There was so much fuss about how we looked. I loved my afro, which was big and thick. A couple of days after getting our afros, Momma gathered a few things together — we were going somewhere, but we were not to tell anyone. We got dressed, picked out our afros and took a taxi to pick up Lorie from school. Then, it was on to the Greyhound bus station. We wore our new white capes. Momma bought the tickets and later, we boarded the bus. I had never experienced a trip by bus, and I was excited to see all the people.

We found seats near the back, on the left. Several nice white women sat across from us. They commented on how well they liked our hair. I asked Momma where we were going.

"To Detroit," she replied.

I then asked, "Why are we going to Detroit?"

She answered, "Because Stevie Wonder sent for me."

I thought, wow, Stevie Wonder, this will be some kind of trip. Even at four years old, I knew who "Little Stevie Wonder" was. We saw him on the big black and white console TV in the living room at Big Daddy's house. Momma loved to listen to and dance to his music. She loved "My Cherie Amor," a song that takes me back to many of my childhood memories. I wondered what it would be like in Detroit to meet Stevie Wonder.

I was excited to be on the bus. We settled in for the ride, not knowing how long the trip would take. There we were, Momma and Lacy sat in front of Lorie and me, all of us looking hip and on our way to the Motor City. Once we arrived in Detroit, we went to a hotel for the night. It had one big bed and lots of red velvet, from the blanket to the lampshades. It seemed like a nice enough place. Of course, I had never been in a hotel room, and this was part of the adventure. There was a television, and Momma let us turn it on.

Morning came, and we waited for Stevie Wonder. Momma argued with the hotel operator, who kept calling, insisting that we check out. Stevie Wonder never came. We remained in the hotel, and management forced us to leave against my mother's wishes. A car picked us up, and I thought we would finally meet Stevie Wonder. The driver took us to another place. It looked like a hotel also, but older. After spending time in the office, the staff showed us our living quarters. There was one large room with mattresses and cots, and we shared the space with two to three other families. It was all a bit strange. We would remain in this place until they could find us an apartment.

It had been a long day without a meal. Eventually, the people in the office gave Momma meal tickets and instructed us to go to the restaurant across the street. It was an Italian restaurant, and we all had spaghetti with a giant meatball. I had never seen such a large meatball — it was the size of a baseball. It was a delicious meal. We still had no idea that Stevie Wonder was not coming. After our dinner, we made our way back to our shared quarters. We slept in our makeshift beds alongside the other families who found themselves in our same predicament. The following day, Momma returned to the office, and they gave her breakfast tickets; later, lunch

> *"And my God will meet all your needs according to the riches of his glory in Christ Jesus."*
>
> — PHILIPPIANS 4:19

and as the evening approached, we received more dinner vouchers. This became the daily routine — waiting to hear if we had our place to live, getting meal tickets for breakfast, lunch and dinner, and trying as much as possible to stay out of the way of the others in our shared quarters. We took short trips to big offices where we waited with Momma to meet people to "take care of business." Momma said she had to transfer her food stamps and welfare.

After a few days, we moved into our permanent housing. It was a run-down apartment in a large, old multistory building. An older white woman, the apparent manager or owner of the place, welcomed us. She showed us to our third-floor apartment. Our apartment had two bedrooms, a living area, a kitchen and a bathroom. Though it was furnished, the furnishings were minimal and old. The living room was inside when one entered the apartment from the hallway. There was a bedroom on the right where no one slept. When you passed into the living area, there was a set of double doors with square windows toward the front and left side of the apartment. These doors led to what was a second bedroom. To reach the kitchen from the apartment's entrance, one would go left toward the bathroom, walk a few steps and take another left, which opened to a relatively spacious area. There was a small table with chairs in front of the window and a refrigerator and stove. One could see an apartment in the building next to ours through the kitchen window.

Momma immediately redecorated. She moved the couch in the living room back to make space for a mattress she took from the main bedroom. This became her bedroom, right in the middle of the living room floor. We girls all slept in the room with the double doors. Momma hung a bed sheet to create privacy. The window in our bedroom was on the front side of the building and drew my attention. I liked looking outside at the neighborhood and the people passing below. When peering off into the distance, we could see a school. Lorie was to start in the fall. We thought this would be her school. Just across the street and to the right was a corner store.

We settled into our apartment, and our routine began. The woman in the office would personally deliver any mail or messages daily. There were no phones in the apartment, so whenever Momma needed to make a call, she would go downstairs and request to use the phone in the office. This was not a problem as her phone usage was rare. There was no television, so my sisters and I made up games and diversions to keep ourselves occupied. We spent hours every day looking out onto the street and listening to the sounds of people passing and talking on the sidewalk below. Going outside to play was not an option, as Momma said it was too dangerous. Therefore, we rarely left the apartment, and only then if Momma chose to take us with her when she left, for whatever reason.

We dreamed about the school Lorie would be attending. When not looking out the front window, we would peer through the sheet over the double doors to check on Momma. There were periods when Momma relegated us to our room to give her privacy. During these times, she would lie half-dressed, often smoking cigarettes. Momma had never smoked before, but the woman she had become in Detroit was a smoker. Watching Momma smoke became a natural pastime for us little spies. Watching the man in the apartment building next door became another. Lorie and I would make our way to the kitchen window each night to spy on him. He was white and usually naked. We had never seen a naked man. Nightly, he walked about his apartment, room to room, drinking, sitting here and there, unaware of our observations.

Some days, there was a knock at the door, and the woman from the office would deliver the mail or other messages. She never spoke to us kids and never stayed for any length of time. Momma would occasionally come and go, forbidding us from leaving the apartment. Monthly, Momma would go out and return with large amounts of groceries. After Momma stocked the refrigerator monthly, we had the fortune of experiencing meals we liked. I do not recall Momma cooking when we were in Detroit, but we ate spam sandwiches and whatever else we could find—that is, until month's end. The end of the month was horrible. There was typically no food, so we would make do with sugar sandwiches made with the ends of the bread or wilted lettuce with ketchup salads. Whatever we could find, we ate, but often went without.

As the months passed, our afros deteriorated into something else. The bugs and mice multiplied in the apartment, and Momma continually neglected our hygiene and her own. Still, we maintained our routine. We looked outside the windows, listened to the sounds of people and music from the street below, watched the naked man next door, waited for school to start and wondered if we would ever see Big Daddy and our relatives in St. Louis. By now, the rats and mice had overtaken the apartment. We could not go to the bathroom without the creatures harassing us.

Since the mice liked to hang out in the cool bathtub, I had the brilliant idea that we could drown them. Lorie and I put this plan in motion. First, we would need to plug the tub. Risking a mouse attack, we were finally able to plug the tub after days of gaining courage. We waited for the right time when some would be in the tub. Then, the hot water went on. We may have caught a couple. Of course, we did not win the war. The bathroom was a very nasty and scary place. Over time, the toilet clogged, and no one came to fix it. Still, we had to go there to relieve ourselves. After holding it for as long as we could, we resorted to urinating and defecating over the side of the bathtub. As children, we did what we needed to do to make things work. There was no adult to tell us otherwise, and the toilet was not functional. This practice continued throughout the rest of our stay in Detroit.

School started, but Lorie never attended. We watched from afar as students came and went and hung about the school grounds. We told Momma that school had started, and she insisted that Lorie's school had not started. Not much else changed in Detroit.

Chapter Two

DESTINED TO BE AN INDEPENDENT WOMAN

My Plan to Escape

I knew the situation in Detroit was not right, even at four years old. I devised a plan to get back to St. Louis. I figured we came here on the bus; I could get back on the bus. I knew that I needed money to buy a bus ticket. Thus, I needed a job to earn money to purchase the ticket. I decided that once I left, I was never coming back. I told Lorie that once I got back to St. Louis, I would tell the family where they were so they could be brought back home as well. I packed a small pink suitcase (I have no idea what I planned to take). I knew I could not simply walk past my mother with the suitcase. That would seem strange. I would be discovered and foil the plan. I would have to sneak it out. I decided to drop the suitcase out the third-floor bedroom window. I watched it fall and made my quiet exit past Momma, who was in her typical position

— somewhere between sleep and no man's land on the mattress in the living room. Lorie was well aware of my plan and helped me to sneak past Momma.

I made my way down the flights of stairs to the front entrance of the building. My suitcase was right where it fell. I picked it up and set out to find a job. My first stop was the corner store across the street. I had seen this man, the owner, from our bedroom window. I walked inside. He asked what he could do for me. I explained that I needed a job.

"Why do you need a job? You're too young to work," he replied.

I told him I needed the money to buy a bus ticket to get home to St. Louis. He explained that he did not have a job for me. I insisted I could be helpful and needed the money to buy a bus ticket. Frustrated, he went to the door and pointed up to a window on the side of the building across the street.

"Isn't that your momma hanging out the window?" he sneered. "She's looking for you."

I looked up and across the street. This woman hanging out the window did not appear to be my mother. I told him the woman in the window was not my mother.

"Sure, that's yo' momma," the man replied. He then told me, "Go home to your crazy momma."

I did not think my plan through beyond securing a job at the store across the street. I had no choice but to return to the apartment, pink suitcase in hand. When I walked in, Momma was furious. She beat me with a wooden rod from the retractable blinds. It did not last long, but that would be my last attempt to escape.

> "*Behold, I am sending you out as sheep in the midst of wolves, so be wise as serpents and innocent as doves.*"
>
> MATTHEW 10:16

The routine did not change much after that. Momma went out monthly to stock the house with groceries; by each month's end, there was no food for what seemed like days. We routinely scavenged whatever meal we could. We prayed for food. We had become accustomed to Momma's response to our question about food and meat, "You want food, ain't no food, pray to God and ask for food. You want meat? Meet Jesus!" Despite the lack of food at the end of the month, more always came, and we learned to adjust to our moments of famine.

The Cigarette Run

One evening after dark, Momma decided to send Lorie and me out to purchase more cigarettes. There was a store around the corner, about a block away. They were open until 10:00 pm, and she asked us to buy her a pack of Cool Cigarettes. We did not question her. Momma gave Lorie some money, and we left the apartment. We made it to the store around the corner, but the owner had locked the doors. A man inside was mopping the floor and yelled, "We're closed." Lorie and I agreed that we should not return home without cigarettes, and we set out to find another open store. We walked and walked and finally encountered an open store. We went inside, and the clerk shouted, "We're closing."

Lorie explained, "But we have to get cigarettes for our Momma, and the other store was closed."

The man said in a mean tone, "Well, come on, hurry it up!"

We bought the cigarettes and started back home. We soon realized that we were lost and had no idea which way we had come to find this store. We were afraid. There was a large crowd gathered across the street. We had become accustomed to seeing groups of people outside our window on the street, meeting for various purposes. This was like a rally or protest of some sort. I suggested that we make our way across the street, as perhaps someone would be able to help us. We walked into the crowd, not knowing where to begin to seek help. A tall white man appeared and asked us if we were okay. We explained that we were lost and did not know our way back home. He asked us for the name of our street. We did not know. We explained that we lived in an old apartment building (which could have described most any building in that area of Detroit). We also mentioned the school off in the distance. He took us by the hands and told us he would help us get home.

We began walking with the stranger. We walked and talked for a while. He then somehow walked us directly to the front door of our building.

The man asked, "Is this where you live?" We said yes, and he replied, "Go on upstairs. Your mother is waiting." We were so thankful to make it home. We went upstairs and the man did not follow but left us at the front of the building upon entering.

"For he will command his angels concerning you to guard you in all your ways."

PSALM 91:11

The next day we went back to our everyday lives, looking at the naked man in the next building after dark, listening to the people passing on the street below, dodging mice in the bathroom, watching Momma and being thankful when groceries arrived. Perhaps the most exciting thing that happened was a light bulb breaking in Lorie's hand while she was attempting to change it. I worked to stop the bleeding and bandaged it with a cloth. She never went to the doctor, but it seemed to heal okay.

We Have Visitors

There was a knock at the door.

Momma asked, "Who is it?"

The woman from downstairs answered. Momma would only answer the door for her. Momma opened the door, and there was my Aunt Dean, Uncle Sammy and my father. Momma was very surprised, as were we. I was so happy that they had finally found us. As Daddy and my aunt and uncle surveyed the situation, Daddy could not hold back the tears, realizing the horrid and unsanitary conditions we were living in. They told Momma that they were taking us back to St. Louis. They smelled and commented on the stench of the bathroom and spent a great deal of time trying to keep Momma calm. Despite Momma's erratic state, the elder siblings made no bones about the fact that we were returning to St. Louis. They looked through the refrigerator and found a freezer full of meat and other perishable items.

Momma was very argumentative. She argued that she would not return and that they could not force her. She argued that she would not leave all of her stuff behind. There was no "stuff" that she owned, only food from a recent grocery trip. After much wrangling, they agreed to load and carry as much as possible to appease Momma and calm her. The adults spent the day packing what they could and what they felt was worth trying to salvage. They lectured Momma incessantly. My Aunt questioned Lorie and me about what we did in Detroit, and Lorie explained that she did not attend school. We did not realize the dire nature of the situation in which the family found us. After loading the car, Momma's siblings forced her to get into the car to return to St. Louis. Somewhere between Detroit and St. Louis, my uncle decided to get rid of some meat and food items. Momma was very angry when they stopped to throw the meat away. After what seemed like forever, we made it back to St. Louis.

Our first stop was the bathtub. We three girls shared a bath in the same tub at the same time, and several aunts were in the bathroom with us, working to scrub our bodies and wash our hair. They talked about how bad we looked. The afros we left St. Louis with were now matted messes. We went through several water tubs to return to our fresh, sparkling selves. The next day, the family had Momma admitted into the hospital, and we girls remained in the care of my older cousins at Big Daddy's house. A short time later, while awaiting Momma's return, we moved to Wellston, where my Uncle Sammy and his family lived. My cousin, Twinnette, had a small apartment nearby. We girls were safe between Twinnette and Uncle Sammy's family sharing duties. Things seemed to be getting back to normal.

Jonathan Rogers, the Traveling Evangelist

Years later, I asked my father about the Detroit experience. Daddy explained his version of the story of Momma's disappearance. The family's first inclination was that Momma had run off to follow Jonathan Rogers. Rogers was a traveling evangelist who annually brought his Christian tent revival to Kinloch and set it up on a large vacant lot on Martin Luther King, Jr. Avenue and Scott Street, a stone's throw from Big Daddy's house. One could sit on the front porch and hear the choir singing and praising. Momma was very drawn to Rogers' charismatic preaching and looked forward to his summer visits. When Rogers came to Kinloch, Momma always wore her best attire and forced us to do the same. We attended the revival as a family, whether we girls wanted to or not. Revivals lasted a full week, and we were there every night.

Momma was very enamored with Rogers, though he was married. I do not know if Evangelist Rogers realized how much Momma liked him. He traveled with an entourage, and his followers hailed him as a faith healer. The entire family, including my father, knew about Momma's obsession with Jonathan Rogers. It was not surprising that his ministry would be a good place to begin the search for Momma and her missing daughters. Daddy contacted Rogers' ministry to inquire about Momma's whereabouts, and he received disturbing news that they had no idea of her whereabouts.

Daddy then turned his search to the welfare department, anticipating that Momma needed money and food stamps and that she had likely transferred these services to a new address. He tried desperately to have the Department of Family Services in St. Louis release information about where the checks were going. According to my father, welfare officials told him Momma was a "ward of the state" (as were we girls). As she was a state ward, officials had no obligation to release Momma's (or the children's) whereabouts, despite Daddy having paid child support. He explained that Momma was unstable and likely unable to care for us girls properly. Through these continued efforts, he eventually obtained the information about our whereabouts. This information led to the family finding us and our eventual return to St. Louis.

A *Changed* Man

Daddy would never be the same after this. He admittedly cried for months, recalling the conditions he found us in, the scene of junk throughout the apartment and the smell of human sewage in the bathtub. Daddy told me I was the worst of all. He vowed to stay closer to us and to keep a better eye on things. After the Detroit incident, Daddy said he made a pact with Big Daddy. If Big Daddy allowed us to stay with him in Kinloch, Daddy would assist by financially supporting the household. Therefore, it began. Whenever Daddy visited us, he slipped money into Big Daddy's hands. I never understood this as a child — I only thought it was his way of being nice to Big Daddy.

Head Start Dropout

We learned of a new program in the community, Head Start, shortly after returning to St. Louis and Momma's return home after a stay in a mental institution. Momma said Head Start was a "special program for smart kids" to help them prepare for school. Head Start was a new federal program, and Kinloch was among the first communities in the nation to have a Head Start center. Momma was thrilled that I would go to school with this opportunity.

I started the program with a small group of children. After a very short time, we learned that our Head Start would be closing. The staff gave families the option of attending the Head Start program in the neighboring community of Ferguson, just across the creek from Kinloch. Even though residents of Kinloch and Ferguson were literally "back-door" neighbors, the communities remained racially divided, and communication across the small creek was not common. Despite Ferguson's proximity, my Head Start center would still have been about four miles from Big Daddy's house; thus, they offered transportation. My mother agreed, and soon after that, a van arrived daily to pick me up and transport me to the new program.

There were already children in the van by the time the driver picked me up, including a nice White boy. I did not know where he had come from nor where the van stopped before picking me up. I was happy to take this daily ride and looked forward to the adventures in my new school. My new Head Start group was quite large and racially mixed. Most of the teachers were White, though there was one Black teacher who moved with the program from Kinloch. I enjoyed the program and my daily routine, including group play, reading, singing and snacks. I liked coming home as much as going to Head Start because of the time I would spend doing all sorts of projects around the house with Big Daddy.

One morning, Momma woke me for school. The weather was terrible. A winter storm had passed the night before, leaving a sheet of ice on the streets. As was typical every morning, I woke up, dressed and waited for the van. The van arrived, and I got in. We headed slowly down Scott Street. There was a stop sign down the road just before the big hill that led down to Scudder Ave. When we reached the stop sign, the van did not stop. We slid into the stop sign, slightly damaging the front of the van. I was distraught. The little White boy tried to comfort me and explained that everything would be okay. The van driver was able to use a neighbor's phone and called for assistance; she also called my house to have someone come for me. My cousin came and walked me back home.

I did not realize how deeply the accident affected me. Every school morning that followed found me begging not to go. I cried and screamed not to get back in that van. Momma tried to help me understand that it was safe and that there would not be an accident, but I threw a fit every day. She eventually informed the van driver that I would not be returning to Head Start.

My real education began when I dropped out of Head Start. I became Big Daddy's sidekick, and we did everything together. We rode the city buses everywhere. We shopped at hardware and garden stores, where we bought seeds for planting. Big Daddy had a large vacant lot next to his home on Scott Street, and he plowed the fields and planted his garden every year. Our mornings would begin with coffee, a small cup for me, with milk and sugar. Before working in the field, Big Daddy would cook breakfast. He was an excellent cook and routinely made biscuits from scratch. His homemade apple butter, jelly and preserves went well with his biscuits that melted in your mouth.

It was usually over breakfast that Big Daddy would speak of his Native American heritage. He talked about his grandfather being an Indian Chief. After our meal and coffee, he gave instructions on how to end breakfast.

Accordingly, we would state, "That was *gu!*"

He said this is what the Indians would say. I enjoyed his Native American stories. Big Daddy never spoke of his mother or father but routinely exchanged letters with his brothers in Mississippi and Alabama.

After breakfast, our work began. Big Daddy made rows for planting yellow and white corn, squash, black-eyed peas, tomatoes, butter beans, cucumbers, onions, bell peppers and various greens, including cabbage, collards, mustards and turnips. He also had a peach tree, an apple tree and grape vines. Every fall, we would work the fields, picking all the vegetables in preparation for the winter season.

Big Daddy was not only an excellent cook but an expert canner as well. He canned homemade vegetable soup, fruits and other items from the garden for food throughout the winter months. After weeks of canning, Big Daddy stored the food jars in the cool basement. Vegetable soup was always available and welcomed during the cold winter months. I simply went to the basement, grabbed a large mason jar of soup and heated it atop the stove. One of my favorite dishes was Big Daddy's fried corn. After cleaning the ears, we would grate the corn on the back of a large, perforated metal tray.

We spent hours laughing and talking around tubs and bowls of corn as we grated the ears. This resulted in a liquid mixture of corn and its natural milky juices. After heating a large pan with lard, he seasoned the corn and fried it slowly for hours. This was a favorite dish among the family. Cobblers, peaches and apples were also favorites, and Big Daddy made all his desserts and other meals from scratch. There were the southern favorites: black-eyed peas and neck bones, fried okra and collard greens with the best homemade cornbread, turkey and dressing. Needless to say, we were never hungry at Big Daddy's house.

Once we finished planting the garden, I helped Big Daddy with his seasonal work around the house. This included planting roses and pruning bushes, replacing roof shingles and working in the shed. I often climbed the ladder to the roof to bring my grandfather tools and brushes for prepping and tarring the roof. I was his regular little helper, and it was a great experience. There was always work to do at Big Daddy's house, and work was the priority, then play.

Big Daddy was an assistant pastor at Solid Rock Missionary Baptist Church. As we lived with Big Daddy on and off for most of our lives, we attended his church, and he saw us baptized there. Sunday mornings were routine; everyone got up, ate breakfast, dressed for church, and piled into my Uncle Shug's car. Uncle Shug usually made multiple trips on Sunday mornings as Big Daddy never drove, and we could not all fit in his car. Uncle Shug's children visited overnight on some weekends and attended church too. We attended Sunday School at about 9:00 am and learned age-specific Bible lessons.

After Sunday school, Big Daddy or Uncle Shug would give us twenty-five to fifty cents. There was about a fifteen-minute break before the Devotional began for regular church service. During the break, we headed immediately to the store up the street and purchased enough candy and gum to keep us satisfied during the preacher's message. This was a weekly ritual. Back in service, the ushers routinely tapped us on the shoulder, as they did not tolerate gum chewing. Ushers were quite intimidating in their all-white uniforms, badges, white head coverings and white gloves. If the usher caught us chewing gum, she reached her hand over the pew and we knew to spit the gum out into the glove.

First Sundays were more formal, as this was the day when church leaders served *The Lord's Supper*. Before serving, there was the washing of feet for one of the ministers. This ritual reminded the congregation of the spirit of service, love and humiliation that Jesus demonstrated and desired of His disciples. The Lord's Supper reminds Christians of the sacrifice Jesus made by dying on the cross in payment for the world's sins. Solid Rock's Deacons wore white gloves and passed tiny crackers and vials of grape juice, representing the Body and Blood of Jesus, which the Lord commanded His disciples to eat, drink, and remember. As a child, I was able to partake in the Lord's Supper after my profession of faith and baptism.

> "And he took bread, and when he had given thanks, he broke it and gave it to them, saying, 'This is my body, which is given for you. Do this in remembrance of me.'"
>
> LUKE 22:1

After church, we returned to Big Daddy's house for a large Sunday dinner that the family typically prepared on Saturday evenings; thus, we only needed to heat things. In addition to Uncle Shug, Aunt Sallie's kids (including the ones who took care of us during our days at the Boaz Apartments) lived with Big Daddy. Though Big Daddy's house was always full of people, we all managed to find a space to sleep. As my cousins entered their teenage years, Big Daddy struggled with the girls and felt he could no longer take care of them or manage their comings and goings. He enlisted the help of his daughter, my Aunt Bay, to take the girls. Joe eventually went into the Air Force, and Gubba remained behind, living most of his early adult life with Big Daddy, except when he got married and moved away.

Chapter Three

HOUSING AND EDUCATION

Big Daddy's House

In the original design of Big Daddy's house, there was no bathroom, but the family utilized an outhouse just a short way off the back of the kitchen. Years later, Big Daddy added rooms to the left side of the house, including a new entrance to what became a family living room, a bathroom and a private bedroom (the only private bedroom with a door) that became Big Daddy's room. This is the version of the house in which I grew up. Years later, the outhouse remained and all the family used it when necessary — especially when cousins and relatives would visit.

There was also a smaller two-room shotgun house on the property with a kitchen. This was my Uncle Shug's house. He was divorced, and his four children often visited, including two boys and two girls, who were my and Lorie's ages. When visiting my uncle, the girls stayed with us in Big Daddy's house, while the boys stayed with their father in the small house. We were very close throughout our childhood and teen years. Their primary home was with their mother in East St. Louis, Illinois, some twenty miles from Big Daddy's house. The youngest girl became pregnant at a young age. In addition to her first child, she and the baby's father had two more children. She had her third child at age seventeen and died during childbirth due to uncontrollable bleeding. This was devastating for the entire family; my uncle was emotionally wrecked upon losing his youngest child. I did not attend the funeral. I could not bear the thought of seeing her in a casket. I had never experienced the death of a cousin so young, and I wanted to remember her before she had children.

Back to the Boaz

Momma moved a lot during our childhood. She routinely complained of her siblings and others "being in her business" or her lack of privacy at Big Daddy's house. Momma was also concerned about my father, who came and went as he pleased. We lived in at least eleven places before I left home at age fifteen. Though we spent a lot of time living at Big Daddy's house, things would get a bit tense between him and Momma after certain periods, and he made it clear that she needed her own place. Thus, she would find a place, and we moved.

I was in the third grade when we moved back to the Boaz Apartments. Being older, we girls had many friends and enjoyed playing in the grassed areas between the buildings, sometimes until well after dark in the summer months. The Boaz Apartments were St. Louis County's first rent-subsidized apartments, erected on Mable Avenue alongside the creek that separated Black Kinloch from White Ferguson. The creek flowed into a sizeable quarry-like area with trees and hidden places where we could disappear, play imaginative games and be kids. After a good rain, we could walk to the canyon area and dig through its thick, red clay ground.

My best friend Precious lived in the apartment on the first floor, directly under ours. Precious was a lovely girl and lived with her mother, an older sister and a brother. I loved playing with Precious because she had so many toys and games we never had nor could we afford, including a Light Bright and an Easy Bake Oven. Her mom would make pizza from a box. I had never eaten pizza before. Precious loved pickle slices, and her mom would let her eat as many as she liked. We often sat inside the enclosed stairwell of our apartment building, talking, dreaming and eating salted pickle slices.

Church attendance remained a big part of our life. We maintained our membership in Big Daddy's church. Still, whenever Momma lived in her apartment, she preferred to attend churches affiliated with the Church of God in Christ (COGIC) tradition. According to the COGIC historical accounts[2], the church was born out of revivals held in 1896 in Jackson, Mississippi. During these revivals, many accepted Jesus Christ under the teachings of Elders Charles Harrison Mason, C.P. Jones, J.E. Jeter, and W.S. Pleasant. Many considered these Gospel preachers militant, and their revivals included faith healings and focused on the doctrine of sanctification. As a result, the Baptist church closed its doors to Elder Mason and all of those persons who believed in his teachings.

Mason became the founding Bishop of the Church of God in Christ. Some refer to the members of this faith as "holy rollers," as there was a great deal of shouting and speaking in tongues and rolling on the floor after being "filled with the Holy Spirit." With such a strong Baptist tradition in my family's history, I am unsure how or why Momma broke from it and favored the COGIC.

We attended several COGIC assemblies, including one in Kinloch, another in Wellston, and one in Faith Temple, which we attended during our extended second stay in the Boaz Apartments. This was a small congregation of about fifty, including children. At Faith Temple, we were in services all day, from the morning Sunday school classes to the evening worship services that usually ended at about 9:00 pm to 10:00 pm.

Most of the congregation would meet at a member's house for dinner and fellowship between the Sunday morning and evening services. We never hosted the group as we lived far away from the church. The church was in the city, about a thirty-minute drive from Kinloch. A Deacon and his family picked us up for every worship service. They drove a large station wagon, and the four of us would pile in along with their other children. In hindsight, it had to be a tremendous sacrifice to make this trip a couple of times each day. During revivals, we made the trip daily, for a week at a time. There were routine Friday night services, and we kids made the most of these.

Even though Big Daddy baptized me, and I was a member of his church, it was at Faith Temple where I began to make a concerted effort to have a stronger relationship with God. I joined the church and sang in the youth choir. Speaking in tongues was a big part of this church, so the "experienced" members spent time trying to push new members along in gaining this gift. I thought the process of "training" was strange. If this unique language were a

2   *The Church of God in Christ*, retrieved June 3, 2013, from http://www.cogic.org/our-foundation/the-founder-church-history/

gift to one personally from God, why would the common person have to train you for it? Just watching people was interesting. They tried hard to obtain the gift, foaming at the mouth in the process, with one of the recognized leaders pushing to "stay with it." While there was a COGIC national doctrine, teachings and hierarchy, the smaller churches often did things differently and were not as strict, in my experience.

Momma had diametric views and representations of religion and manifested these views with pretty far-out notions. She often described how blessed we girls were, emphatically telling us of our futures.

In her discussions, she insisted that we would be wealthy, "Ooh, you girls are gonna have so much money! God has shown me that you're gonna be rich." When questioned how she could know such things, Momma replied, "Because I am God." She believed that she was God at times. When challenged by Lorie or me, she became upset. We learned to live with her insanity and insistence that she was God. Of course, she never shared these thoughts with others in the church. Church attendance generally represented the "balanced" periods in her life.

At some point during our years at Faith Temple, we moved into the home of one of the church members. She had a large house on Adelaide Avenue in St. Louis City, where she resided with her husband and children. This made church attendance much easier as we lived within a short drive. Though most were relatives, this family became one of the many families who took Momma in with her three girls. Momma contributed money for rent. We attended school not far from this house, but it was not long before forced bussing required us to transfer to a school on St. Louis' south side. This was almost a thirty-minute drive each way. I do not know why families took us in nor the reasoning Momma provided for needing a place to stay. We moved a lot, with most moves lasting no more than one to two years.

The Fight to Survive

For third grade, I attended Kinloch Elementary School. I loved school and had great teachers like Mrs. Price and Ms. Harris. They worked well with the students, and I excelled. In Ms. Harris' class, some of my classmates called me the teacher's pet. This was likely because she always called on me to answer questions when other students could not, and she selected me for involvement in special projects. On one occasion, another female classmate and I had the opportunity to stay overnight at Ms. Harris' house. Ms. Harris wanted help with a project and chose us to help her prepare.

In the 1970s, education was very different. Today, one cannot imagine teachers asking parents' permission to have their children stay overnight in the teacher's home. It is simply unthinkable with today's school rules, countless stories about sexual misconduct between teachers and students, and educators' fear of chastisement from school officials. As I think about my educational experience and that of children today, teachers must work extra hard to find creative ways to empower students and make them feel special, both in and outside the classroom. Coming from my humble surroundings at Big Daddy's house, staying with Ms. Harris was outstanding. She had a lovely apartment, and I felt exceptional that she chose me. My mother had no problem with my going, and the experience made me even more excited about school and doing well.

As the school year ended and summer came and went, discussion began about the fourth grade. The Boaz Apartment complex was a target area in Kinloch and was chosen to participate in a voluntary busing program for an elementary school in the Ferguson-Florissant School District. The Lee Hamilton Elementary School was only about eight miles from Kinloch but a twenty-minute drive by bus. Life in Ferguson, compared to Kinloch, seemed like night and day. There was deep racial division; thus, many viewed the busing pilot for integration purposes as a bold step. Momma broke the news to us girls that she had volunteered to participate in the busing pilot and that we would be changing schools with the start of the new school year. My teachers in the Kinloch schools had been very nurturing, and they validated my hard work and efforts to make straight As. I wondered what school would be like with many white teachers and students. I was unhappy about the new busing plan but had no choice.

On the first day of school, I was happy to see a full busload of some twenty-five kids from the Boaz waiting to get on the bus. We boarded the bus, made our way to the new school, and found ourselves immediately immersed in new classes with unfamiliar teachers. There were lots of students and few Blacks in any of my classes. Recess was perhaps the best part of the day, so I initially thought. The large playground allowed groups of students to separate for a period while attempting to avoid the obvious racial tension prevalent in the school hallways (name-calling, pulling white girls' ponytails and running, and other tit-for-tat actions).

Issues in the neighborhood spilled over into the school. Bridgette, a neighbor from the Boaz, repeatedly threatened Lorie. Lorie had a crush on a boy who lived in the apartment in front of ours, and the girl who made the threats liked the same boy. He did not seem to notice that either of them had eyes for him, but this did not stop the girl's threats and interest in fighting. One weekend, Lorie and Bridgette began fighting in the grassy area in front of Precious's apartment, and Bridgette's younger brother jumped in. They were beating up on Lorie, forcing me to jump in and help. The four of us fought in front of our apartment building until someone broke us up.

The fight did not end before I bit the brother's arm. It simply was not a fair fight, a boy versus a girl, so I took measures to protect myself as much as possible. The following week in school, the situation was still raw. Bridgette taunted Lorie for some time before the school bell rang, and Lorie decided that she had had enough. Lorie invited Bridgette to hit her, which Bridgette did. The fight began again. The brother and I started fighting again as well, and school officials suspended all of us from school. Lorie and I had reputations of being good students, not prone to trouble; thus, the school gave us some benefit of the doubt. Eventually, both girls realized the boy they were fighting about had another girlfriend who did not even live in the apartments. This realization helped ease tensions, and we collectively avoided the peer pressure to fight. Lorie and Bridgette eventually became friends, putting a permanent stop to the fighting between the brother and me.

Though things settled for Lorie, I was continually taunted by a kid new to the neighborhood—another boy! I could not understand what was behind his ongoing harassment and bullying. He teased me on the bus, shoved and pushed me, called me names and simply made it his life's cause to ruin mine. I tried to ignore him without success. I had to fight him. In preparation, I decided that it would be a fight he would not forget and one that would keep him from ever bothering me again. Still, I prayed that I would not have to fight this boy as it would be awful for him. I told my friend Precious of my plan to scratch his eyes with Christmas tree ornament hooks. My pocket was full of them, and I was ready. All he needed to do was mess with me one more time, which would be his last. I got on the bus — he was not there! This was good. The ride home after school would be the fateful time. I boarded the bus home. He boarded the bus, walked past me, never said a word and we had a peaceful ride home. The day was uneventful, and I thanked God as I breathed a sigh of relief. I never had to fight this young man; he left me alone from that point forward.

> *"Do not be anxious about anything, but in every situation, by prayer and petition, with thanksgiving, present your requests to God."*
>
> PHILIPPIANS 4:6

Another Move

Momma decided to move into a small mobile home park about two miles down the road. I did not understand why we left the Boaz to move into a much smaller place — a trailer. It had a small kitchen with a table against the window, close to the front door. To the right was a small living room, which led to a small room where we girls slept. Momma's room was on the other side of the kitchen, and there was a bathroom near the front door. Like during the Detroit days, Momma did things we were not accustomed to. While she did not smoke, she frequented the nightclub scene. Momma would go to Kinloch's favorite *Thread N' Needle*, the local hotspot. Over the years, I realized that my mother was either in the church or the street, doing those "worldly" things not viewed well by Christians. Momma was either heavy into the church or heavy into the club scene. We would go for years attending church. Then, almost overnight, we would not participate in church and Momma was part of the nightclub scene. Momma's regular nightclub attendance coincided with her mental instability. There were always men willing to hook up and take advantage of her relative innocence — a church girl at heart and a welcome, fresh, beautiful face at the club.

During one visit to the club, mom hooked up with a man who would become one of Kinloch's most notorious criminals, Rayfield Newlon. Rayfield was a known bad boy with a long list of criminal activity. Because of Kinloch's small-town nature, even we kids knew that Newlon was bad news. He was a terrifying character, and the tales that followed him were even scarier. Momma was supposedly *dating* Rayfield, though he was never part of our lives. It did not take long for Momma to see his bad side, and she eventually tried to distance herself from him. One night, Rayfield arrived at our trailer with a couple of friends.

Momma ignored the knock on the door. We girls had gotten ready for bed and were wearing dress slips.

As the knocks grew stronger, Rayfield's voice began to rise, and he yelled, "Doris, open up the door; I know you're in there!" Momma told us to remain quiet. "I'm gonna break this damn door down," he continued.

We were terrified. Momma finally yelled that she was trying to sleep, the girls were in bed and she was not up for company. He continued to insist that she open the door. She gave in, opened the door, and he forced his way inside. He shoved Momma onto the bed. We girls began to scream, and Momma yelled for us to get help. The other men were just observing the situation. My sisters and I ran out of the house to the trailer across the lot, and the woman who lived there answered the door. We explained that the men in our house were trying to harm our mother, and she called the police. They left before the police arrived, and Momma gave a statement. Rayfield did not return.

Back to Big Daddy's House

Shortly after this incident, we moved back into Big Daddy's house. We were so happy to feel safe again. I had nightmares about Rayfield Newlon for many years, always afraid he would break into our home again. Years later, Rayfield made headlines — police arrested him for the murder of a Kinloch storeowner. This was the same man, Mr. Dave, who would sell us candy on Sundays after the morning service at Big Daddy's church. Rayfield and his accomplices stood trial, and Rayfield, nailed as the "trigger-man," was found guilty. Rayfield received the death penalty for his brutal murder of Mr. Dave, whom he had robbed at gunpoint and shot to death. Mr. Dave was very friendly, well-liked and respected in the community. When people learned of his death at the hands of Newlon, the community mourned the loss of one of its long-time business leaders.

My nightmares increased after this, as I was worried that Rayfield would return to harm our family, even though he was in jail. I feared he would break out and try to finish what he started that night with my Momma in the trailer. Newlon's trial and subsequent appeals made headlines, and legal scholars still reference his case in courtrooms and classrooms. The case has been a precedent for similar trials because of how the prosecutor pleaded with the jury to "Kill him now. I've been a prosecutor for ten years, and I've never asked a jury for a death penalty, but I can tell you honestly, I've never seen a man who deserved it more than Rayfield Newlon."[3]

The court reversed Rayfield's original death penalty sentence because the prosecutor's closing argument violated Newlon's due process by comparing him to Charles Manson and other mass murderers. As of the time of publishing, Rayfield remained imprisoned, serving a life sentence without parole in a State of Missouri correctional facility.

I began to understand the nightclub was not a good place because whenever momma frequented the club, she walked away from the church and was less and less likely to focus on her children. I hated the *Thread N' Needle* and was never surprised to hear about fights, shootings, stabbings and other troubles

---

3   (Daryl Shurn v. Paul Delo, 1999)

which seemed to plague it. As much as I grew tired of being in church three or four days a week, I longed to attend with Momma, at least on Sundays, because it became clearer as the years passed that if she attended church, she did not frequent the nightclub.

Room for all at Big Daddy's house

My Uncle Hut had moved into Big Daddy's house with his wife (Aunt Wilatrel) and their children for a brief period. Uncle Hut was also a preacher and attended school to better prepare for the ministry. Living with everyone under the same roof was great while it lasted. There were always cousins present for playing games, bigger holiday dinners and a larger circle group for praying each New Year.

Aunt Wilatrel's sister is Jenifer Lewis. Jenifer always had the theater bug and planned local talent shows where she performed great skits and sang. We had the opportunity to be a part of them by singing, dancing, or acting. Jenifer usually hosted her shows in the Holy Angels Catholic Church fellowship hall, down the street from Big Daddy's house.

Jenifer surprised everyone when she announced her plans to move to New York to pursue her dream of an acting career. Everyone was very excited for her, and we were thrilled to hear of her success. She was cast in 1979 as "Eubie," a small role in a musical based on the musical works of Eubie Blake, and later, she landed the role of "Effie White," a character in the musical workshop *Dreamgirls*. When *Dreamgirls* moved to Broadway, Jennifer Holliday was cast in the role of Effie[4]. Jenifer later became a backup singer for Bette Midler and had a small role in the movie, *Beaches*. Jenifer eventually moved to California in 1992 and became a very successful actor, having appeared in many productions on stage and on the big screen where she portrayed someone's mother or aunt. She played Will Smith's aunt in *The Fresh Prince of Bel Air*, Tina Turner's mother in the story of Tina's career, *What's Love Got to Do with It*, Tyler Perry's *Meet the Browns* and *Madea's Family Reunion* and the aunt of *Jewanna Man* in that movie, to name a few. She landed roles in animated films, including *Cars* and *Shark Tales*. Jenifer's success affirmed that I could do anything I dreamed of doing. I spent a lot of time dreaming about being famous, having an acting career, and marrying Michael Jackson.

---

4   Retrieved on June 6, 2013, from the World Wide Web: http://en.wikipedia.org/wiki/Jenifer_Lewis

Uncle Hut eventually moved his family into a new home in Kinloch. He began church services in the basement, and Momma decided we would attend this church. At the basement church, we received personal Bibles and learned to recite all the books in The Old and New Testaments. Uncle Hut was always very good to his baby sister, Doris and her girls. He later became the pastor of First Baptist Church in Kinloch, where he served for many years. As Uncle Hut's ministry grew, he eventually relocated and opened a church in Meacham Park in St. Louis County.

Life in the City of St. Louis

As was typical, we would eventually wear out our welcome at Big Daddy's house. Perhaps we kids were too noisy. Maybe the expense of caring for us was a burden, or Momma's case was simply too much to be managed by a senior citizen. Whatever the underlying reasons, we found ourselves living with my Aunt Lucille back in the City of St. Louis. Aunt Lucille had a large, Victorian home near St. Louis' Forest Park, just off Skinker Blvd. Aunt Lucille was a widow then, but she and her husband had raised several children. She seemed happy to take her baby sister Doris in to give Big Daddy a break.

Living with my cousins Rodia and Felicia was great as we were all about the same age. We grew very close because they would spend nights and weekends with us at Big Daddy's house and living with them allowed us to enjoy what seemed like one big sleepover. Momma's furniture was stored in the basement as there was no room for it in the main portion of the house. The basement became our hideaway and preferred play place when not outside, walking the neighborhood or playing games on the steps like "rock school." In this game, everyone started at the bottom of the stairs, and the person playing the teacher had a small rock. With hands behind her back, the teacher hid the rock in one of her hands, bringing closed fists to the front with one wrist crossed over the other. The first student would pick one of the fists. If it contained the rock, she would proceed to the next grade or step in this case. Each step represented a grade. The turn would move to the second student, who had one chance per round. The games ended when one of the students reached the top staircase—graduating at the top of the class.

Another favorite game was "house." Here we would arrange Momma's furniture in the basement, build a fort with sheets and blankets for cover and assume our various identities. We pretended that we were having a good time, smoking and drinking like the adults, though no one in this home was a serious smoker or drinker. We simply used our imagination to do what we saw other adults doing. We tore brown paper bags into pieces that we twisted into pretend cigarettes. We lit our pretend cigarettes with butane lighters and attempted to smoke them. To cover the smell of our breath, we used Scope from the main bathroom and watered it down to hide its disappearance. Aunt Lucille discovered our antics after a few weeks of this game because of our having watered down the Scope. Aunt Lucille thought we were drinking it — we knew better than that. We kept our breath fresh and covered the smell of our paper smokes. We never admitted to twisting the brown bags and smoking them because we were in enough trouble for just using the Scope.

Several adults went to the basement to check out our little hideaway. We were in bigger trouble because we had broken Momma's table, unbeknownst to us. Aunt Lucille called us individually for our chastisement, followed by several slaps on the rear end. Everyone cried except for me. I was determined not to show weakness. It was a well-known fact among my sisters and cousins that I would not cry during spankings. Some attributed this to my strong will and others to my being stubborn. I simply was determined not to show weakness by giving the adults the satisfaction of being able to break my spirit.

As my cousins peeked around the corner, Aunt Lucille and Momma insisted they'd spank me until I cried. I refused, not saying a word, and they became more frustrated by the minute. My cousins began pleading with me, "Just cry, Honeybunch." I did not care. I truly wanted their feelings to be hurt, for them to feel bad about spanking me—sort of a test of wills, I suppose. After a bit, I faked some tears and sobbing to satisfy everyone and end the ordeal. I was not a crier, at least not for those things. One would rarely see me cry. I only cried when I had unsettled emotions. This was usually the case when things in my life were terrible and uncertain, and I had no control over my circumstances. I was always quick on my feet relative to solving everyday issues and challenges. In such cases, I would dig in my heels and do what I needed to fix things—much like when we lived in Detroit when I set out to get a job to earn money for a return bus ticket to St. Louis. I cried at the funerals of loved ones and when seeing others I loved, I wept.

After living with Aunt Lucille for a period, it was time to move again. I hated moving. We never seemed to settle, and it was as though moving was simply our way of life. This time, we moved in with my Aunt Dean for a spell. This did not last long. Aunt Dean's house was a party house. There were always people coming and going. During our time at Aunt Dean's house, Momma was very different. She routinely talked of being God, did not manage her hygiene, and once tore up a Bible, according to my aunt. Her bedroom was a mess of clothes and other items piled everywhere. Momma was a different person. We moved back to Kinloch, and Big Daddy had Momma committed to Malcolm Bliss[5].

The Missouri Department of Mental Health dedicated Malcolm Bliss Mental Health Center in 1964. Malcolm Bliss Mental Health Center succeeded the Malcolm Bliss Psychopathic Institute, founded in 1938 as a St. Louis City Hospital System hospital. We girls understood that Malcolm Bliss was the hospital where Momma always went when she was "sick." Momma never considered herself sick—this determination was always the function of her older siblings and Big Daddy. Whenever Momma was in the hospital, there was a care plan for us. We never worried about a place to stay and never understood that these care plans must have been determined well before each intervention with Momma. In this case, my cousin Twinnette watched us while Momma was in the hospital.

Cabanne Courts

Although Kinloch was in St. Louis County, it had a reputation for being as tough as any neighborhood in the urban corridor of the City of St. Louis. Most people in Kinloch knew of the town's major families, and residents recognized one another when they walked about the community. We grew up a couple of houses down from the Clay family. The Clays had a lovely home and were one of Kinloch's prominent families. The children were all well-educated young adults. Mrs. Clay worked at the Kinloch Post Office for her entire life and later became its Postmaster. The family was always kind to "Doris' girls." Momma and Big Daddy raised us to honor and respect our elders and senior citizens. We met many of them through Big Daddy and felt comfortable visiting these families' homes without adult family members during our long walks throughout the community. We could stop at any of their homes without an invitation and get water to drink if we were thirsty or to use their bathroom. It was always a practice for us girls to let certain families know we were back in the community after leaving Kinloch for periods to live with aunts and others. This latest return to Kinloch was short-lived as Momma was frustrated with her family's interference in her life, including forcing her into Malcolm Bliss against her will. She never trusted her siblings relative to their motives. Momma always believed they were trying to have her institutionalized. Thus,

---

5   History of Malcolm Bliss retrieved June 9, 2013, from http://dmh.mo.gov/mpc/history.htm

as soon as she could, Momma found an apartment far from Big Daddy, back in the City of St. Louis.

It was midyear, and I was in the fifth grade. Momma moved into an apartment in the city. It was a low-income complex, as were all of the places we lived outside the homes of family members and friends from church. Cabanne Courts, as they were named, was a series of apartment buildings located on Vernon and Cabanne Streets. Like many low-income housing projects, there was one way into the u-shaped series of buildings and one way out. We lived near the front of the building on the first floor. The door to the apartment opened directly to the outside (unlike the Boaz in Kinloch). Making friends was a bit harder because we could not go inside others' apartments. Playing outside in the square did not feel safe.

Momma enrolled Lorie and me in Mitchell School, across the street and one block from our apartment. Lacy, being younger, enrolled in Mitchell Branch School, located a bit further than Mitchell School. Being new to the class was no fun.

When the teacher introduced me to the class, another Sandra commented, "Well, if her name is Sandra, then you can call me Penelope." I thought it was interesting that I would have issues over the name "Sandra." Daddy named my sister from his second marriage Sandra, and we learned to live with it without fighting over who had it first.

Other girls in the class did not receive me well, and my teacher was the most unprofessional teacher I had ever encountered. In between smoke breaks, she gossiped and taunted the students. She ignored me during most of the classroom time and seemed to dislike me, and I could not understand why. All of my prior teachers loved me, supported and encouraged me. I was an excellent student. Despite my efforts to demonstrate that I was smart by participating in class and doing everything my teacher asked of me, when I received my first report card, it had Cs on it. Momma immediately went to the school to complain because I had never brought home a grade less than a "B." School officials reassigned this teacher shortly after she changed my grade to a "B." Mr. Haymon became my new teacher. He was very professional and kind. He liked Momma, and she liked him. We girls continued the struggle of making friends in the neighborhood.

Momma allowed me to have a birthday sleepover and Rodia and Felicia came. These girls, my first cousins, were beautiful with long, "good hair," and the girls from the neighborhood were jealous of them. Having good hair was a big deal in the Black community. Loosely described, good hair was not kinky but long, most times straight and easy to manage. Good hair could usually be styled by simply adding water and a bit of hair oil.

On the other hand, bad hair was kinky, hard to manage and typically straightened with a pressing comb—a metal, thick-toothed comb introduced in the United States by Madam CJ Walker, an entrepreneur who was America's first self-made female millionaire. Water only made bad hair kinkier. The good hair/bad hair drama is a major source of controversy within the Black community. Some believe by straightening one's hair, Blacks buy into America's White image of what it means to be beautiful. At the same time, straightening one's hair destroyed a major aspect of Black culture—Black hair itself, with its kinks and twists, afros, braids and natural styles.

Today, more than a hundred years after the introduction of the pressing comb, the good and bad hair controversy continues. Chemicals have become widely used for Black hair straightening, and hair weaves have become a primary way to cover and change original hair to appear "good," giving African American women access to the same lengths and styles worn by White women. Comedian Chris Rock documented issues surrounding Black hair in a 2009 Documentary, *Good Hair*. In the early 21st Century, there was a renewed effort by African American women to return to their natural hairstyles, and one can now see these styles worn by Black women commentators and national news and academic figures.

It was not long before other neighborhood girls began targeting my sisters and me. They bullied us as we walked to school, and Lorie had at least one fight in the neighborhood. They threatened to hurt us regularly. Things got so bad for us that Daddy started the routine of picking us up in the morning to take us to school after he completed the graveyard shift at McDonnell Douglas. Yes, he would drive miles to take us to school…across the street. Mr. Haymon would walk or drive us home after school, and we spent most of our time indoors.

We were afraid of our neighbors. One day while in the house watching TV, we heard a commotion in the courtyard. There was yelling, cursing and threats. Then we heard a loud banging sound. We peered out the curtains and saw a man using a metal closet door to ram a neighbor's front door. He was trying to knock it down to get inside. This was a horrible place to live. We called the police but asked that they not speak to us or knock on our door, as Momma was afraid that if the neighbors knew we called, they would come after us. We were always terrified. My only bright spot was being in Mr. Haymon's class.

Now that I had a teacher who cared about all students equally and appreciated my intellectual capacity, I was back to learning and embracing academic challenges. It was nice to have Mr. Haymon appreciate and praise my work. He allowed me to enter a self-paced math program pilot. Here, I would go to the main academic office and work at my own pace on math modules.

At the end of each module, I completed a test to progress to the next module. I was highly motivated by the idea of learning as much as I wanted. I loved the challenge of seeing just how far and how fast I could progress. Little did I know that this work would significantly impact my future.

We completed a timed, standardized test during the school year, The California Test of Basic Skills or CTBS Test. Students took the CTBS Test annually to ensure we were on track and ready to move to the next grade. I finished taking my test long before the other students in the class. Months later, our scores arrived toward the end of the school year. I should score a minimum of five to six points in the fifth grade, indicating the grade level. My results ranged from seven to nine point something, raising the attention of other teachers, counselors and the principal. My teacher explained that because my scores were so high, there was much discussion about where I should start the next school year, whether as a sixth or seventh grader. Mr. Haymon requested a meeting with Momma to present their recommendation—that I skip the sixth grade and move to grade seven. Momma was very proud of my performance and asked me how I felt about being with older kids. I was very excited. She agreed that I should start the next school year as a seventh grader. With the decision made regarding my grade promotion, we received even better news. Momma decided to move back to Big Daddy's house. I was so excited. Not only would I return to school in the Ferguson-Florissant School District, but I would also re-enter school a year ahead of my old classmates! I could not wait to share the news of my double promotion.

Chapter Four

TEEN LIFE, SPIRITUAL AWAKENING AND DEINSTITUTIONALIZATION

I Become an Unlikely Activist

During our time in the city, Momma had found a COGIC in Wellston, near my Uncle Sammy's house and not too far from the Cabanne Courts apartments. This church was very strict and interpreted the Bible very conservatively.

According to the pastor, the Bible commanded, "Men are not to wear women's clothing, and neither are women to put on a man's garments." The preacher often reminded us of this, and it was his basis for not allowing women to wear pants—considered by the church to be men's garments. Another rule was that we could not play card games, as he considered gambling a sin. To be sure that our baptism was *real*, the preacher insisted that he baptize us, even though Big Daddy baptized us years prior at his church. Momma did not question our need to be "re-baptized." Therefore, we joined a long line of others at the pool in front of the church for baptism again by the COGIC minister.

"*A woman must not put on men's clothing, and a man must not wear women's clothing. Anyone who does this is detestable in the sight of the Lord your God.*"

DEUTERONOMY 22:5

We were back living with Big Daddy in time for the start of the new school year. We were back to busing from Kinloch to the Ferguson-Florissant District schools. Being a seventh grader as the result of my double promotion, I did not return to Lee Hamilton but to Florissant Junior High School on Waterford Drive. I did not like doing the yellow bus thing again. School buses were always a problem. "Playing the Dozens," or "joning," as we knew it, was a favorite pastime during our extended bus rides. Then there were the infamous "yo-mama" jokes. With the dozens, the object was to put the victim down with verbal insults so nasty that he would simply give up trying to think of a worse putdown. I avoided being involved in this craziness and hurtful play for most of the year. I tried never to get in on yo-momma jokes, as I never wanted to bring negative attention to my mother.

One of my classes was physical education or "PE." For PE class, girls wore a striped, one-piece short suit. Since attending a strict and conservative COGIC assembly, I could not wear the required shorts (or pants) to comply with the PE dress code. I explained this to my teacher several times, and she sent me to the principal's office. This was not something she had ever encountered. I spent a few days in the principal's office until they could figure out what to do with me. I had no idea at the time that this was a major religious freedom issue. The principal conferred with District officials, eventually contacting my mother. Momma put the principal in touch with the church pastor, who affirmed the church's position of no shorts or pants. This forced school officials to find me an alternative class. The list of options was limited; thus, woodworking replaced physical education. We started with bud vases and ended the course with individual lamps.

I did not realize the significance of my actions, proclaiming my religious beliefs in the seventh grade, because the church forbade women and girls to wear pants/shorts as required by school dress codes. It was 1976, and I knew nothing about legal rights regarding the freedom of religion. In this case, the school could make accommodations, and they did. I guess I was a pioneer as my actions forced school and District officials to address a civil rights issue for a topic never previously encountered. I fought this battle, for the most part, alone. Momma did not raise the issue, but I did. Not wearing the mandatory dress uniform of shorts was undoubtedly a matter of conviction. I believed the Pastor's teachings. I was young and lacked the experience and knowledge to question COGIC interpretations of Biblical commands.

I enjoyed the woodworking class and working with the machinery so much that I decided to continue this training and joined the skateboarding club, which met after school. We learned to design and build skateboards. Skateboarding was a new trend; I could build my own with this opportunity, as we could not afford to buy a skateboard. Each student needed to raise about $35 to cover the materials costs. We could select the style, and mine would be made of plexiglass. After shaping, cutting and smoothing the sides, I anchored the wheelbases underneath.

My skateboard was unique when completed—see-through with orange wheels. I was even more proud to declare that I had made it myself. I learned to ride it up and down the street in front of Big Daddy's house. The Holy Angels Catholic Church, school playground and parking lot were my favorite locations for skateboarding. My family was impressed with my skateboarding skills, and I took excellent care of my skateboard. One day, Lacy begged me to ride the skateboard, and I refused. She kept pressuring me to let her ride, and I eventually gave in, despite a deep sense that I should not allow it. Off she rode down the street. When she did not immediately return, I took off down the street to find her. I located her just past Holy Angels, walking with my skateboard now in two halves. I could not believe it! I had ridden this skateboard the entire summer with no problems. In one short moment, my prized possession was gone - irreparable. That would be my first and last skateboard. I knew I should have followed my *first* mind and not let her ride it that day.

"Whatever is good and perfect is a gift coming down to us from God our Father, who created all the lights in the heavens. He never changes or casts a shifting shadow."

JAMES 1:17

My First Mind

Following my "first mind" is a term I have lived with my entire life. I always could sense the right decision first. My first mind usually comes into play when meeting someone new or responding to controversial matters. In describing my first mind, it comes from deep within, like a gut feeling. It is a quick read of a person's demeanor, which often instructs me to engage neither nor trust an individual and to keep that person at a distance. My first mind is not always about people but also situations. I found that whenever I second-guessed that first, top-of-mind thought, things didn't go as well as they might have. Through the years, I have learned from experience that my first mind never fails, leading to a better choice. I imagine the first mind impulse is not unique to me, but I wonder why, if folks have it, they continue to make bad decisions.

"Good and upright is the LORD: therefore he instructs sinners in his ways. He guides the humble in what is right and teaches them his way."

PSALM 25:8-9

I asked myself, "Why didn't I follow my first mind?"

There are countless examples of first-mind experiences in my life—the broken skateboard is just one of them. I have learned not to question how or why when following my first mind. I have simply grown to accept it as a fact, and it has not failed me.

Girl Fights

Growing up in Kinloch, opportunities to fight came as often as the sun rose and set. I tried to pick my friends carefully. They were never the popular kids, nor were they kids who were "wild," kids who talked back, disrespected their parents, or had bad habits of teasing others. My friends were never looking for trouble and were not prone to stealing and cussing. I worked to avoid those kids in the neighborhood whom trouble seemed to follow. I also tried to avoid making eye contact with others.

Eye contact with troublemakers usually prompted the question, "Who are you looking at?"

This question opened the door to a host of responses, none very good. Bullies considered those who ignored the question weak. Ignoring the question could then lead to being called names or having rocks tossed in your direction. I hated fighting, but it was a part of my childhood, primarily because of poverty and living in and around low-income housing projects for most of my younger years. I never picked a fight but always defended my sisters (and myself) when necessary. If ever I had to fight, it was never my intention to lose; thus, I always responded very hard and aggressively, using all the strength I could muster to send a message that one would not want to fight me again.

The summer following my eighth-grade year was a memorable one. My cousins, Rodia and Felicia, came to spend two weeks with us at Big Daddy's house. Our favorite pastime was sitting on the front porch and admiring the handsome young trainees who worked during the summer at the firehouse across the street. We were comfortable watching from afar but soon realized we were not their only admirers. We observed a couple of girls coming out of the firehouse. They were giggling, pulling up tube tops and simply behaving in a manner we considered "loose." After several days, it became evident to the girls that we were watching them, and one of them pointed in our direction. We were at the Catholic school down the street sometime later that week. As we neared the educational center behind the church, we encountered the girls from the firehouse.

One of them yelled to Felicia, "What you lookin' at, bitch?"

This prompted a verbal confrontation, "Who you callin' a bitch?" I urged Felicia to let it go. We turned to go back toward the street—wrong move.

The girls interpreted our retreat as our being afraid, prompting the firehouse girls to follow. "Hey, you bald headed bitch, you scared? Why are you running?"

Now, Felicia and Rodia were anything but bald. These girls were beautiful, and their hair was equally lovely.

Lacy jumped in and, grabbing a piece of her hair for demonstration, added emphasis and yelled back, "Bald? I got more hair than you'll *ever* have." Then came threats to "kick Lacy's ass," and all I could do was sigh — I knew this was now my fight, as were most fights that involved either of my sisters. I hoped I could stay out of it, thinking this was between the firehouse girl and Felicia.

As the girl continued to engage Lacy, I felt pressure to step in, as Lacy was the baby. I responded, "You'll have to kick my ass to get to hers."

The next thing I knew, we were on the playground and I was engaged in the fight of my life. She was tough, and I was in a dress. I grabbed her and began to get the best of her, slamming her into the monkey bars.

Strange onlookers, including her sister, egged her on, "Get her, Wanda!"

I continued to wear her out, and Wanda yelled for her sister, "Wendy, come help me!" Wendy then jumped in, pulling at my dress. I was now fighting Wanda *and* Wendy. Felicia tried to jump in, but the rest of Wanda's gang stopped them. I was now fighting two girls, and I was in a torn dress. This forced me to back away from the fight. It was a bit odd in that we just stopped. We took a time out. I told her that I was going to change and that I would be back. I went home to change clothes and explained that I had to finish the fight. Momma and others followed.

When I returned to the schoolyard, the sun was setting and Wanda and her entourage were on the other side of the fence, across the street, in the front yard of her apartment in the projects. I think she was surprised to see me. I yelled for her to come on over, and she asked that I come around to her yard, which I refused. She gave in and proceeded to the schoolyard, with many onlookers following, including several adults who ended up monitoring the match. Once Wanda reached me, she began to run her mouth as she had done all day. I wasted no time punching her as the crowd collectively said, "Ooh." I was glad to get the upper hand; this time, it was just Wanda and me, as the crowd prevented Wendy from helping.

One person said, "Ain't gone be no double-teaming." I was pleased with the way round two was progressing. It was a fair fight, and I made the most of this opportunity to prove my toughness.

As we continued to fight, we worked our way across the schoolyard, and I finally got a hold of Wanda's tube top, ripping it nicely. I could not believe she did not take the opportunity I took to change clothes. She must have thought I would not return. Wanda was so confident in her ability to win the fight that she did not worry I might win. I exposed Wanda's breast by ripping her top, forcing her to hold the top together with one hand while trying to fight with the other. She became desperate and ran to grab a stick from someone who had offered it to her. A kind man stopped her, reiterating that there would be no weapons. Her desperation prompted someone to end the fight by suggesting that others surround her to protect her "innocence." That was it. I won the fight, though somehow, I felt it would never be over.

The next day, Wanda and some of her friends were at the vacant lot across the street from Big Daddy's house. She called me out and attempted to coerce me into another fight. I told her it was over, and I continued ignoring her. I also kept my distance from the schoolyard to avoid the possibility of another fight. I hated fighting with a passion. I only did so in self-defense. I never wanted to become the neighborhood punching bag.

Felicia and Rodia eventually left, and summer vacation ended. I was starting the ninth grade at Florissant Junior High School. I boarded the bus at the usual location, across the field and on the next street where Wanda and Wendy lived. At the next stop, Wanda boarded the bus. I thought to myself, *Here we go again*. I ignored her as I had decided I would no longer fight. I turned fourteen years old and believed that young women should not fight. Even though I still had a couple of months before my birthday, I thought the new school year was a good time to start.

Wanda tried to bait me by making snide remarks, but she never touched me. I continued to ignore her. Then one Saturday morning, a couple of weeks later, there was a knock at Big Daddy's front door. I answered and was surprised to see Wanda bringing me some clothing items she had outgrown. She asked if I could fit them. I was shocked—she was trying to be my friend. I took the opportunity to move forward, to forgive her and let bygones be bygones, and I invited her in so that I could look at the items. They were adorable shorts and a shirt. By now, we were no longer attending the COGIC in Wellston, so I could wear pants and shorts again. I tried them on and thanked her, as they were a good fit. From that moment, we became friends. I never had any more problems with Wanda or Wendy.

Deinstitutionalization

My fourteenth birthday came and went. I was doing well in school, and life seemed to settle for a change. Still, something odd was happening. Momma stopped cooking, which she loved to do. Big Daddy was a great cook; we could always count on him for food from the garden, but daily meals prepared by Momma ended. We became accustomed to a diet consisting mainly of hot dogs and fries, which we cut and fried. The monthly trips to stock up on groceries ended, and Momma never seemed to have any money. Food stamps were in short supply as well. Lorie and I wondered what Momma was doing with her money and the food stamps and why she seemed to lack concern regarding meals.

Momma spent more time away from home in the evenings. After a while, she was rarely home at any time of the day or night. We knew that something was very wrong. Lorie took the initiative to share our concerns with my aunts and uncles and explained that Momma was not herself. They visited on various occasions and agreed that Momma displayed active signs of schizophrenia. We asked for their support in admitting her to the hospital, as they had done on numerous occasions during our childhood. The more the aunts and uncles explored these options, the more roadblocks they encountered. Lorie called the hospital to find out about admitting mom. Times had changed, and so had the rules regarding mental illness. We learned that family members could no longer commit relatives due to mental illness, and Momma would have to admit herself to the hospital. The only exceptions were if the individual was doing bodily harm to herself or someone else.

We learned a new term, "deinstitutionalization," and that President Jimmy Carter played a major role in ensuring that the mentally ill would have access to a better life with dignity outside the walls of mental institutions. According to the PBS website promotion for its Frontline Documentary, *Out of the Shadows*[6] :

> Deinstitutionalization was based on the principle that severe mental illness should be treated in the least restrictive setting. As further defined by President Jimmy Carter's Commission on Mental Health, this ideology rested on the objective of maintaining the greatest degree of freedom, self-determination, autonomy, dignity and integrity of body, mind and spirit for the individual while he or she participates in treatment or receives services.

More than fifty to sixty percent of persons released from mental institutions had a diagnosis of schizophrenia. My mother was one of them. We could do nothing to help her, to help herself. Months passed, Momma was now walking the streets, wholly detached and strangely dressed. She wore layers of clothing in the mid-summer heat, boots and a coat occasionally, and nothing matched.

School started, and I was now in the tenth grade—Lorie was a senior. My new school was McCluer North High; as in prior years, we rode the school bus. High school kids were now meaner than ever while on the bus. They joked about Momma. Some of the boys talked about "having my mother last night." This was very painful; all Lorie and I could do was ignore it. We were miserable. The hot dogs kept coming to the point of making me sick at the thought of having to eat one. By now, Big Daddy was very frustrated with the situation, and he enlisted my father's help. Daddy began to visit more regularly to ensure we were okay.

I do not know what prompted visits from social workers, but we began receiving monthly visits from a white female social worker. We girls were required to meet with her whenever she came into Big Daddy's living room. She inquired as to how we were doing at home and school. We complained

---

6 Deinstitutionalization: A Psychiatric "Titanic". Retrieved June 10, 2013, from the World Wide Web: http://www.pbs.org/wgbh/pages/frontline/shows/asylums/special/excerpt.html

about the hot dog diet, and she responded that this was not a problem as long as we had food. We complained about mom's behavior and dress and her walking the streets. It seemed that this was not a problem as long as Big Daddy was available and provided us with a safe place to stay. Momma became progressively detached each month, and the social worker visited and presented the same questions. I was so frustrated with the lack of help from the social worker that I, too, became detached. I hated the visits and felt they were a waste of time. From my point of view, while she was checking off the little notes on her pad, I remained stuck. I felt she was doing nothing to improve my life, so I quit participating. I stopped contributing to the conversations and was annoyed during the visits. I resented what I envisioned: after visiting us poor Black kids and checking off her pad, she would return to her bright, cheery reality. I felt as though she was patronizing us. I was angry and hurt and could do nothing about it.

Escape to school

I threw myself into school activities, as many as possible, to leave home on the early bus and return on the evening athletic bus as late as possible. I participated in the Fellowship of Christian Athletes before school and the Pep Club, Dance Club and anything else I could do after school. I found engagement in school activities the only way to escape my home life, which was deteriorating rapidly because of Momma's condition. Through the dance club, I met Beverly and Leslie. Beverly and Leslie were excellent dancers, and Beverly performed a mean robot. Rimp and Deneen were in the dance club too. Beverly and Leslie lived in Florissant, within walking distance of McCluer North High School. Rimp, Deneen and I all lived in Kinloch. I did not know them before our meeting in the dance club. Outside the club, we ran in different circles and had very different interests.

One day while changing classes, I stopped at my locker, and Rimp confronted me. She was upset because I had given my freshly baked cake, prepared in my Home Economics class, to Pete, a new student who had recently relocated from Billings, Montana. I liked Pete, as did most of the girls in Kinloch. Pete lived in Kinloch with relatives but rode a different bus to school. Rimp was close with Debra who also liked Pete and was upset when she learned I was pursuing a relationship with him. Though I do not believe in dating friends' boyfriends, I thought Pete was different—he was not anyone's boyfriend, and many girls liked him. Thus, as far as I was concerned, I had as much a right to like him and try to gain his interest as anyone else. In addition, I was looking for something or perhaps someone to help me forget about my problems at home with Momma. Pete was of Mexican descent, and I was in my second year of Spanish, which also gave me an avenue for getting his attention.

Rimp confronted me at my locker about Pete. She began yelling and shoving and challenged me to fight. Having given up fighting, I refused to engage her. Not to mention, Rimp was twice my size. I continued to ignore her.

Suddenly Beverly appeared and questioned Rimp, "Why you messin' with Honeybunch? She is too small for you to be picking on. I'm not gone let you fight Honeybunch. You'll have to fight both of us." Beverly saved me as she had a reputation for fighting. Rimp did not want to fight Beverly as they had been friends for some time through the dance club. Even though Beverly was skinny, she was tough, and her sister Leslie was also a good fighter. Beverly and I became the best of friends. Our dance club continued to meet, and Rimp no longer bothered me. We all became good friends from that point on. Again, God rescued me from having to fight or even defend myself.

> *"The LORD will fight for you, and you have only to be silent."*
>
> EXODUS 14:14

School officials announced the annual homecoming talent show, and the five of us decided to put together a routine for the competition. We spent a lot of time practicing, so I began spending more time on the weekends at Leslie and Beverly's house, as did Rimp and Deneen. As the talent show neared, we decided on our dress. We selected silver shirts with black satin slacks. To add flair, we collected bottle tops, connected them in long strands, and sewed them to the sides of our pant legs. We looked great. We performed the song "Shake Your Pants" by Cameo. The crowd loved us! It was amazing. The crowd liked us so much that the dance club sponsor asked us to perform during our school's Black History Month program. We continued our weekend practices and came up with a different routine.

Members of Beverly's family began making connections for us to perform at other venues, including nightclubs. Before the internet, iTunes and iPods, the radio was where one tuned in to learn about concerts, bands and city events of interest to the Black community. We often called the radio station to request songs. Every morning before school, we listened to the radio to hear shout-outs to various schools throughout the city and to see if we could get the DJ to play our requests. Folks who saw us perform received us well. We received bookings to perform here and there in the city, and one gig led to another. Beverly's aunt was a tailor and began making our performance outfits. In addition to performing at various nightclubs, we performed at neighborhood festivals and became very popular throughout the St. Louis metropolitan area.

As I spent more time with Beverly's family, my relationship with Daddy began to deteriorate. Momma continued to walk the streets in Kinloch. There was no sign that she would go to the hospital for treatment. Daddy's solution was for us to move in with him, back to the city. I hated this idea, not because of my father but because of the horrible memories of having to fight my way to school every day. I disliked the thought of mean-spirited kids who picked fights and threw rocks because I walked in front of their houses.

Daddy had divorced Ernestine and married Lorenzo's mother, Doris. What stuck out in my mind about my stepmother Doris was an incident that occurred years prior. Daddy made it a point to try to ensure that all of his children had not only relationships with him but with one another as well. To this end, there would be occasions where he would take all of us to Six Flags over Mid America, to Meremac Caverns, or simply to the drive-in for a movie or two. When we went to the drive-in, because there were so many of us, Daddy drove his van and hid most of us, kids, under blankets as we entered the property and neared its ticket window. Daddy instructed us to be very still and quiet, which we all did. On this occasion, once parked and settled, we went as a group to get enough popcorn to share. Doris gave little Lorenzo additional money to buy candy for himself. It seems silly that this stands out in my mind, but it simply did not seem fair that she singled out *her child* and not the rest of us. I decided that moving to Daddy's home was not an option, and I resisted any efforts toward that. I loved my school and all that I was doing there.

Tensions grew between my father and me primarily because I was the lone holdout in his plan for us girls to move with him. Lorie tried to convince me that I needed to say yes for things to move smoothly and quickly. To make matters worse, Daddy began to resent my resistance. An example of how he manifested his resentment was coming into Big Daddy's house, giving Lorie and Lacy ten dollars, and handing me one dollar.

I threw it back and commented, "I don't need your money." I know this was disrespectful, but I felt disrespected also. In addition, we had spent our entire lives moving from place to place, and he and Momma divorced when I was a baby. It was an incredibly challenging period for my father and me. Before this time in my life, my relationship with Daddy was great. We celebrated our birthdays, finding laughter because they were only a day apart. We were very tight, and I loved and trusted him. We were both strong-willed and equally determined to have things our way.

Daddy had begun questioning my virginity, partly because I was spending so much time away from home and partly because I had shared with him (during our more pleasant days more than a year prior) that I liked a boy whom I had met during my piano lessons. He was the grandson of the instructor, and his lesson was right before mine every Saturday morning. We began to talk outside of class and exchanged phone numbers. He even invited me to attend his church, which I did several times. We grew close and even kissed, but I was far from having sex with anyone.

I had to stop taking piano lessons because of Momma's mental state and resulting financial problems. Even though I was no longer taking lessons, the instructor's grandson and I continued to talk by phone almost daily. My boyfriend bought me a large, heart-shaped box decorated with flowers and chocolates on Valentine's Day. I had never received such a gift from a boy. When Daddy visited and saw the large box of chocolates, he accused me of having more than a platonic relationship, insisting that boys do not give girls such a gift without expectations. I assured Daddy that he was just my friend and nothing more was taking place. This friendship became a cause of disagreement with my father and added more strain to our relationship, which ended as we could no longer see each other.

My life seemed so crazy and screwed up at this point. I was overly committed to school activities, working to avoid confrontations with my father. I sought opportunities to escape my reality wherever possible. Thinking about Pete became one of those opportunities. I used my Spanish classes as an excuse and began to practice my new language skills on Pete. He was very appreciative, which made him pay more attention to me. Pete and I began talking more by phone outside school hours. One day, I invited him over. The entire family was out of the house, and Pete and I talked. I cried about my situation, and he held and comforted me. We kissed, and I realized I was on the verge of losing my virginity. Pete did not force the issue—I gave in. My rationale was that since Daddy was accusing me of having sex anyway and I could not get him to believe otherwise, I might as well do it. Pete asked if I was sure, and I simply said, "Yes."

Tensions Increase

One Saturday evening, while practicing dance routines with our group, the doorbell rang and it was Daddy. He said that Big Daddy had not permitted me to stay the night and that I was "running wild and beyond his control." I left with Daddy. The car ride back to Big Daddy's house was miserable. I was wearing lip-gloss and daddy told me to remove it. I explained that girls my age wore much more makeup and lip-gloss was nothing. Daddy asked me if I thought I was cute. I did not respond. He said the lip-gloss was not cute and insisted I take it off. I again replied that it was *only* lip-gloss.

He touched my chest and asked, "Is this the way the little boys touch you?" I shoved his hand away.

Before this, my father had never touched me inappropriately. I believed he was attempting to make a crude point, much as he attempted to make a big deal out of the dollar he had given me, after giving ten dollars to Lorie and Lacy. I rationalized that he wanted to make the point that since I thought I was grown, I must be doing things grown women do. Either way, the point did not go over well. After I shoved Daddy's hand away from my breast, he tried forcibly to wipe off my lip-gloss and we began to fight in the car. We had a good tussle, but he backed off in the interest of returning to Big Daddy's house. We finally made it back to Big Daddy's house. Things quieted for about a couple of weeks, and during this time, I did not stay later than the activity bus for school activities and practicing dance.

My Dance Career Takes Off

Our dance group was a hit; promoters and club owners were now paying us as much as $250 to perform two numbers. We set aside some of our earnings to purchase fabric for new uniforms, and the rest was split amongst ourselves. We all stayed together during nighttime performances at Beverly and Leslie's home. Our routine was primarily practicing and working on new numbers for future performances. The music of the late seventies and early eighties was so upbeat and rhythmic; it was not hard to find great songs that inspired most of our routines.

Things Reach the Boiling Point

Beverly's father owned a gas station, and we girls (the girls in the dance group) occasionally worked there to help on Saturdays. One Saturday morning following a Friday night performance, I opened the store with Beverly, her father and Frida, a woman who was a long-time clerk at the gas station. Frida also happened to live in the spare room of their home. I enjoyed working at the gas station. I learned customer service, running a cash register and overall gas station operations. One Saturday morning, while assisting customers, my father showed up at the station. According to Daddy, Big Daddy "was fed up with my comings and goings," and he had decided to put me out of his house. I told Beverly's father that the last time I was alone with my father in a car, we got into a huge fight, and I feared this would happen again. I did not want to leave. Daddy began to yell, "I am your father!" Daddy told Beverly's dad, "You are trying to steal my daughter!" Beverly's father explained to my father that I did not want to leave with him. Daddy threatened to call the police.

By now, I had reached a breaking point. I was sick and tired of Daddy's abuse and bullying, so I took a chance (from behind the bulletproof glass) and told Daddy that I would call the police for him. I was so thankful for the thick glass that protected us from the public. Daddy could not get to me.

I told him, "You can't make me go. I'm a state ward, and you don't control my life." I had learned about being a ward of the state through years of hearing about Momma's mental status and through the social worker's visits to Big Daddy's house. I knew that Momma was also a state ward as she received a disability check for her mental illness. I continued, "You have no authority over my life, and you can't tell me what to do!" I further explained to my father that under no circumstances would I leave with him. He gave up and eventually left. I returned to my routine of waiting on customers and authorizing gas pumps to dispense the requested amount.

After a couple of hours, and to my amazement, I saw Momma walking across the parking lot. She wore pink boots and several layers of mismatched clothing, including a coat and a rainbow-colored skullcap. We were far from winter or even frigid weather.

In a slow, non-alarming manner, she came inside and called me, "Honeybunch, it's time to go." I breathed a sigh and explained to the others that I needed to go because this directive was coming from my mother; unlike my father, she had the authority to tell me what to do. I was still afraid, but I collected my things and left the store with Momma. Of course, Daddy was waiting in the car, seated on the passenger side of the vehicle. His cousin Ocie was behind the wheel, and Momma and I sat in the back seat. I sat on the passenger side, behind my father. I felt that nothing crazy would happen in the car as both Momma and Ocie were there. Ocie was my favorite older cousin on my father's

"Children, obey your parents in everything, for this pleases the Lord."

COLOSSIANS 3:20

side. He loved us kids and always did nice things for us whenever we visited him. Ocie and I would talk for hours, and he never failed to tell me how proud he was of the grades I brought home from school. I knew that Ocie would not let my father do anything to hurt me.

I sat quietly in the back seat. Daddy began his remarks, denigrating me for embarrassing him in front of others. He reminded me that I was *his* responsibility and that he would show me how much authority he had. I sat quietly. He continued his litany, noting the things that were going to change. First on the list was that there would be no more dancing or spending the night with Beverly's family. I was to go home and to school, period. I was not to speak to the family by phone and participating in the dance group was over.

The list went on and on, seemingly forever. My head began to hurt. I hated him so much right then. I thought, *How can this be happening?* I felt like something, or someone had entered my body. Suddenly I had courage. I was not going to take it anymore. I lost it!

I yelled, "I hate you! You don't own me. You have done nothing for me, and you can't tell me what to do!"

The next thing I knew, Daddy jumped from the front seat into the back seat, reaching around Momma to grab me. He was more pissed off than I had ever seen before. Ocie continued to drive. Daddy proceeded to punch me, and I attempted to fight back. He tried to hit me

"Fathers, do not embitter your children, or they will become discouraged."

COLOSSIANS 3:21

again, and I kicked back as fiercely as possible. He hit me in my mouth, which resulted in a busted lip. He grabbed my legs and pushed my knees to my chest to immobilize me. This worked, and I could not move. Nor could I breathe because my chest was compressed. I became desperate for air. I did everything I could think of to get him off me. I grabbed Momma to pull myself up from the floor. In a shocking move that I could not understand, she pulled my hair, bringing me back to the position on the floor.

I tried to communicate, "I can't breathe; I'm dying!" I then did the only remaining thing I could think of—I spit at Daddy. This made him even angrier.

I stopped fighting, praying that the ordeal would be over soon, and sure enough, we arrived at Big Daddy's house. I went straight to my room, which I shared with Lorie and Lacy, and laid across the bed. I listened to the discussion about how "wild" I had become. Then they called me, and Big Daddy gave me a verbal list of rules, which included not using the phone. I did not respond, thinking it best to stay silent and not escalate the situation further. Daddy left and things quieted down. I wondered where Lorie and Lacy were as they were not home. I fell asleep.

When I woke up a couple of hours later, I heard nothing. It seemed that everyone was asleep. I took the opportunity to sneak in a phone call to Beverly to let her know I was fine. I used the phone in the living room. The house's front door was open and the screen door closed. I could see in front of our house and across the field to the apartments on the next street. I began to tell her what had happened. She expressed concern and said that her parents were apprehensive about me. Her mom picked up the phone and told me they all loved me and for me to call if I needed anything. As I continued my quiet conversation, I looked out the front door and noticed Daddy walking up the driveway. My younger brother Keith was with him. Daddy had changed his clothes and vehicle. He had a big smile fixed on his face. I explained my father was coming but that he seemed okay. He walked into the house, maintaining his smile.

I thought, *Well, maybe he's ready to forgive and forget.*

Daddy walked into the front door, took his finger, pressed the button on the phone to disconnect the conversation, and, without warning, let go of a wad of spit that he had prepared before coming into the house. That gross wad landed right in my face. I could not believe it. I screamed and the chaos began. Momma and Big Daddy woke up, and everyone was yelling at me. I ran to the back of the house as the threats were flying. I ran to Big Daddy's room and called 911—no one realized it. Then, I ran and locked myself in the bathroom. There was banging on the door and yelling for me to come out. I ignored it. I ran to the tub, stepped inside and slid open the window. We kids had come in and out of this window many times when locked out of the house. I looked out the bathroom window and saw the cops drive quickly past. I jumped out of the window and ran down the driveway.

"See, she crazy, lost her mind," yelled Big Daddy.

The police were in front of the house, and I ran across the street to meet them. I jumped into the back of the police car. I frantically attempted to describe the day's events, beginning with my Daddy's visit to the gas station. Daddy came outside and over to the police car and insisted that I get out of the car. The officer told me to stay put. Daddy continued to yell. I was shaking all over. The officer got out of the car to talk to Daddy and told him that he needed to back away. As Daddy became more irate, the officer called for backup and a second squad car arrived. After some time, the officers determined that I should not remain at the house, and I went by police car to the Kinloch Police Station. They took my story and contacted Children's Services to arrange a place for me to stay for the night. After what seemed like hours, they took me to the hospital for a check-up to ensure there were no internal damages, as Daddy had busted my lip during the earlier fight in his car. As we prepared to leave, the officer told me that my Daddy was in a holding cell, that they had arrested him and that he would be spending the night in jail. The police had also found a small amount of marijuana in his possession. I had no idea what had happened to Keith.

Following my visit to the hospital, a caseworker drove me to West County, where I met a White foster family that had agreed to take me in for the weekend. They had a beautiful home and two small children. They gave me clothes to sleep in. I spent Saturday and Sunday there, and on Monday morning, a social worker picked me up and took me to her office for additional processing and interviews. At some point during the day, she took me to Youth Emergency Services (*YES*) near University City, within walking distance of my Aunt Lucille's house. *YES* was a shelter for teens dealing with a host of issues. As I met some of the other teens, I quickly realized I did not belong there. School officials had put these kids out of school. Many of the kids had cases involving drugs or were facing other offenses. All of them seemed toughened by life. Many of them smoked and cursed. They were *troubled* teens. That was not me.

I remained at Youth Emergency Services for just under a month. I had a couple of roommates and we slept in bunk beds. These kids reminded me of the mean kids we encountered while living in the Cabanne Courts Apartments and attending Mitchell School. I tried to avoid them as much as possible because they seemed accustomed to fighting and being in trouble. I needed to get out of the *YES* home as soon as possible.

During my month at *YES*, my caseworker picked me up and drove me to school daily. Her job was to find me an appropriate place to live. My family was the first logical place to start in seeking a permanent solution.

She asked, "Are there any relatives on your mother's side with whom you can live?" As I contemplated this, the option that came to mind was my Aunt Lucille. I never verbalized this option.

Instead, I replied, "No," to having *any* family members. I recalled reaching out to Aunt Lucille more than a year before the problems began. I asked her *then* if I could live with her for a while. She replied that she could not take me in as she had a lot going on in her life, and it was a bad time. Relatives on Daddy's side were not an option for providing me with a safe place to live. In addition, Big Daddy could not manage the problems between Daddy and me; thus, returning to Big Daddy's house was not an option either.

I continued speaking with Beverly's family, who applied as foster parents. They expressed interest in having me live with them and I was thrilled at the thought. Because they lived within a few miles of my high school, I could remain at McCluer North. The caseworker received approval for me to stay with the family for one month, pending approval of their application to serve as permanent foster parents and a decision by the court.

It was a great day when Beverly's family picked me up from Youth Emergency Services. There was a big family dinner, and even members of the extended family attended. I was officially welcomed into their home. I had so few belongings—pretty much the clothes on my back and a few items in a bag. My new foster parents explained that I would have everything their children had. They took me shopping later that week to get essential clothing, accessories and toiletries. The family's signature pair of roller skates and a large, plush burgundy housecoat were two major items on the list for purchase. They worked hard this first month to ensure that I lacked for nothing from shoes to undergarments. I felt fortunate to live in such a beautiful modern home.

Leslie, Beverly and I shared a room. Leslie slept on the top bunk, me on the bottom and Beverly's bed was across from mine. Upon entering their home, our room was on the left side of the house, at the very end of the hallway. Going down that hall, one passed Frida's room on the left. Our parents' room was on the right side of the hallway, just past the bathroom that Frida shared with us, three girls and the two boys whose room was in the basement. The rest of the house included a formal living room connected to a formal dining room and a den off to the right. The kitchen had a door leading downstairs to a finished basement. There was another den with a large television where we often viewed home movies, a laundry room, a large open area with a hi-fi stereo where we practiced our dance routines, and in the back corner was a bedroom that Jared shared with his brother Jason. Jared was the youngest son and older brother to Leslie and Beverly.

Chapter Five

My Years in Foster Care

Day in Court

After a couple of months, I was due in court for a hearing to determine my future residence and custodial arrangements. I knew that my father would likely be there, even though Momma was my official legal guardian, pending a formal decision by the judge. I was so afraid and nervous about potentially confronting Daddy. My case manager told me to wait outside the courtroom until I was called. The judge finally ordered me into the courtroom, and I took the stand to answer his questions. I saw Daddy for the first time in months. I dreaded having to return home. I told the judge about the night my father picked me up from dance practice and about the fight in the car. I then told the judge the unthinkable—that my father touched me inappropriately on my breast and asked me if this is how the boys touched me. I knew that because of this, the judge would do whatever was in his power to find me a place away from Daddy. In the end, Daddy was devastated and humiliated, and the judge placed me in the permanent care of my foster family until my seventeenth birthday. The judge explained that we would continue to have routine visits from the case manager. He explained further that upon my seventeenth birthday, the family's obligation to care for me would end, and any future relationship would be of our making and determination.

Following the court date, I returned home with the foster family. I felt vindicated that I would never have to live with my father or endure his harsh treatment. I was determined to forget him and start a new chapter in my life on my terms. I walked away from it all. I loved my sisters, Lorie and Lacy, but I knew they would be fine as the ongoing fight and core of the chaos in our lives centered on my poor relationship with Daddy. I was the problem, and now, the problem was gone.

A New Family

I was now living with Beverly's family. Things were very different in that they did not attend church. I did not miss going to church. I had gone my whole life and sleeping in on Sunday mornings or working at the gas station was a welcome retreat. School started, and Beverly, Leslie and Jared made it very clear that I was their little sister now. Jared drove us to school each morning, but I walked home in the evenings due to my continued involvement in extracurricular activities. I enjoyed walking home as it allowed me to participate in theater, which I could not do before—the last bus to Kinloch left before theater practice ended.

Lorie was a senior that year and still in high school; attending McCluer North allowed us to see one another during the school day. She and I maintained a close relationship though we no longer lived in the same house. I was not so fortunate to have the opportunity to see my youngest sister, Lacy. We often spoke by phone, but beyond that, our relationship suffered. I believed Lacy felt I had left her behind. She did not like the living situation at Big Daddy's house either; we were very close up to this point in our lives.

I continued to immerse myself in school activities and fell in love with the theater. Acting was right up my alley and allowed me to become someone else for a moment. Even though things were looking up relative to my sense of security, I still needed to satisfy my drive to be involved, take on projects and explore my talents. I heard the theater department at school would cast a large group for *Snow White and the Seven Dwarfs*, and I decided to audition. I was successful and secured my first role as "Doc." I made new friends through the theater and opened a new world of school involvement. My new foster parents did not thwart my desire to participate in theater, nor was it encouraged. They simply allowed me to do it.

As a ninth grader at Florissant Jr. High, I started taking Spanish. I loved Spanish and decided to continue my foreign language requirement with Spanish at McCluer North. In high school, the options were numerous and included Latin, German, French, Japanese and Spanish. I heard Latin would be a great subject to study because of my interest in attending medical school. My science teacher had done an excellent job in illustrating the connections between science nomenclature and Latin word roots—the idea being that if one knows Latin, she could decipher the meaning of almost any word. Although I was intrigued by this thought, I had also heard about the growing need for Spanish language acquisition due to anticipated demographic changes that would come on the heel of population growth anticipated in the Mexican American community in the United States. Thus, my language choice was Spanish. It seemed practical, and I thought I would have the chance to use it. I fell in love with Spanish. I signed up to participate in the school's Annual Foreign Festival, for which I mastered the art of baking "biscochos," or Mexican wedding cookies. I also joined the Mexican dance team and learned the Mexican Hat Dance, which we performed at the festival.

I completed my first entire school semester while living with my foster family. The report cards were distributed, and I was pleased with my grades. We turned the report cards over to Dad, who began his remarks, "Honeybunch has the best grades; she's the smartest." I felt *very* uncomfortable as the others looked on quietly. He continued, "Y'all are dumb; you should be asking Honeybunch for help. What's this? How many flags do you have? You all need to pay Honeybunch to help 'cause she smart." I could not believe he called the others dumb. I felt very bad for them, and I was not at all flattered that he thought I was smart. The others did not hold their dad's rant against me. I was happy about that. I was living in their home, and we kids were very close. I was afraid the report card incident might change that, but it did not.

May of Lorie's senior year came and went. She graduated and enrolled in Southwest Missouri State University in Warrensburg, Missouri. This second vacancy from Big Daddy's house left Lacy alone with Momma to work through the challenges she was experiencing as the family's baby. Lacy had to live with the daily realities of Momma's schizophrenia. I felt bad that Lacy was alone. I could do nothing about the situation. She and I spoke every few weeks though we were losing touch. I heard Big Daddy was tired of Momma's antics and that he put her out again, and Momma moved back into the Boaz Apartments with Lacy. From the secondhand stories, Lacy tried to hang in there with

Momma, though Momma could not adequately care for her. Lacy eventually broke down and decided to move in with my father. Meanwhile, Momma continued down a self-destructive path of walking the streets while failing to recognize the sickness consuming her mind. Momma refused to admit herself to a hospital, as she could not see that she needed help.

A New School Year

I continued to study Spanish in my sophomore year. My Spanish teacher greatly encouraged me, and when the time came for the Department to recommend exchange students to Mexico, I was at the top of her list. My school had never had a Black exchange student to Mexico. My teacher told me I was the perfect candidate, if I applied and could raise a certain amount of funds, they would choose me. I needed about $4,000 total, and the school leaders would find support for as much as half that amount. I was encouraged.

I took my proposal to spend a year of school in Mexico to my foster parents. I did not receive an immediate response. As I pressed further in the following weeks, they told me, "You think we got money for you to travel to Mexico? The world is a dangerous place. Maybe White people got money to send their kids to Mexico, but we don't have that kind of money." That was my answer. I appealed that I would raise the money, but they settled in on the fact that the world was too dangerous a place. I told my teacher I would not be able to apply. I do not know how we would have afforded the trip if I were still with my natural family, but I was certainly sure that the world being a dangerous place would not have been the determining factor.

Back at the foster home, the parents expected us, girls, to keep the home's interior spotless. They assigned us chores, and a different job rotated among the three of us each week. Our weekly duties rotated between making dinner, cleaning the kitchen, doing the laundry, or dusting and vacuuming the house. We also had a schedule for cleaning the bathrooms and making the parents' bed. Keeping the house virtually spotless was mandatory. Whoever was responsible for washing the dishes during any particular week was also required to ensure the stove and sink were clean and clear of items. Not even one cup or spoon should be in the sink at the end of the day. Falling short of the rules was unacceptable and typically led to our father screaming and calling us "lazy bitches." If he discovered a fork in the sink, despite the hour of the night, he forced the one with that week's kitchen duties out of bed and required her to clean it. This usually opened the door for additional scrutiny of the work performed earlier, and he might have even required us to re-wipe counters or vacuum the kitchen carpet.

Dinner was always a full meal and typically included meat (fried chicken, pork chops, cubed steaks in gravy, meatloaf…), starch (rice, mashed potatoes, macaroni and cheese, spaghetti…) and a vegetable (green beans, cabbage, peas, corn and broccoli with cheese sauce…). Making a pot of chili and a side of rice was a welcome change. We never wanted for food. Mom typically prepared the Sunday meal. She was an excellent cook, as were all the girls, including me. I learned to prepare many dishes, watching her and Beverly. Sunday dinners were more elaborate with more courses and were more complex, comprised of roasts or other time-consuming creations. There was the occasional extra meal that we had to prepare for Dad. When required, it was always liver with onions and gravy. I became an expert at this dish but never made it again once I left home.

The Starr-Love Dancers

Now that I was living with Leslie and Beverly, there were no problems with our dance group practices. We practiced several times each week and, whenever possible, entered dance contests throughout the city. We discovered many of our competitors were not that good, but they were popular, and crowd response routinely factored into the judges' scores. We put this reality to work for ourselves. Every morning as we dressed for school, we would listen to the radio, flipping back and forth between Power 108 and WESL, an East St. Louis, Illinois station. Our favorite thing was to call into the stations and dedicate songs to ourselves in the name of our group. As we became more popular, the crowd response at performances and competitions grew in our favor.

We turned our earnings over to Aunt Carla who made our performance uniforms. Aunt Carla was highly creative and helped us to develop a reputation for having a unique presence and uniformity. Where possible, our performance costumes aligned with the theme of our group's new productions, typically performed to the hottest dance songs with the best beats. We relied heavily on beats and rhythms to emphasize certain routine aspects. We had a full Native American style costume, with fringe down the sides of the pants, face painting and feathered headgear. The breakout song for this outfit was "Apache" by The Sugarhill Gang. This performance was incredible, and we could not wait to perform it for large audiences.

It was at a major St. Louis dance competition where we had the opportunity to perform our Apache routine. The crowd went wild as soon as the music started and the lights came up. It just so happened that Power 108 was the sponsor of the competition, and their most famous disc jockey, DJ Gary Starr, was the host. After our performance, Mr. Starr requested our presence in the front office. Feeling great after our crowd-energizing performance, we made our way to the club's front office, where Mr. Starr was relaxing. We were crazy excited to be meeting our radio idol in person.

Mr. Starr introduced himself and complimented us on our performance. He said he was looking for a group to sponsor and thought we were exactly the type of group he had in mind. Mr. Starr said he would facilitate our participation in larger, higher profile shows, utilize the radio to increase our demand and that he wanted our group to take his name. With no more than a handshake, he promised to call in the coming days once he thought of the appropriate name for our group. That call came the next day, and we spoke to Gary, connecting him on three-way phone lines to ensure we were all on the phone together. He gave us our new name; overnight, we became the "Starr-Love Dancers."

We were now quite famous around school, and Starr-Love was in high demand. One of our high-profile performances was a warm-up act for the Little Milton concert at the Kiel Auditorium. The Kiel was a vast arena and home of the St. Louis Blues Hockey Team at the time. Performing at the Kiel Auditorium for a nationally touring blues musician was an opportunity we could not have dreamed of. This is what representation by Gary Starr meant for us. Dancing for such a large crowd was an incredible experience. We even had a green room. The concert's older adult audience appreciated our routines with great applause, and Little Milton signed autographs for us after the show.

It was not long before we realized that there was no *real money* attached to Gary Starr's sponsorship, but the promotion and name recognition were more than sufficient. We continued to devote out-of-school time to practice routines, even when no performance was scheduled. We also continued to work at the gas station on the weekends and manage our chores at home.

All That Glitters

My foster home was lovely. The family seemed to have it all, living in Florissant on a nice street in a three-bedroom, two-bath house, long before the Black population was a blip on the radar in that community. They owned a Cadillac and a Buick LeSabre. The home seemed perfect—clean, well-kept and always filled with plenty to eat. There were family get-togethers, most times at their house. Theirs was the story of a Black family that had overcome the odds. He owned his own business, a profitable gas station and she had a great career. They were supporting their oldest daughter through college, and all was lovely. At least, this was the appearance from the outside. Being inside the confines of the home for a significant period, the fairytale unfolded, and the glitter fell off.

Before I moved into this foster home, Rimp would often describe the father as "nasty." Reportedly, he would make flirtatious gestures and overt passes at her. Deneen affirmed that he was nasty. I had never experienced this nasty side, but I also had not known the family as long as these two. The longer I lived with the family, the more things I noted. There were small hand bells situated about the house. Bells were visible in both the living room and den, and whenever he needed something, he would ring the bell and call out to the person he wanted to beckon. Increasingly, this person was me. It did not matter what part of the house I was in; if he wanted the television channel changed, he summoned me from the basement to do it. If he wanted more Kool-Aid, he would ring the bell and send me to get it. Then came the compliments— "Honeybunch, you make the *best* Kool-Aid." As time passed, he increasingly flirted and crossed father/daughter boundaries. He would take the glass of Kool-Aid from my hand by grabbing my mid-arm and running his hand down it to reach the glass. This creeped me out, and my heart raced whenever he called me when others were not around.

I never believed that what Rimp and Deneen had described would ever happen to me. I was his *daughter*. Then, one day after dark, he was driving me to a meeting at the school.

He asked me, "Are you gonna kiss me goodbye?" I was not sure how to respond. Inherently, I knew what kind of kiss he wanted. It was his tone, a look on his face. I affirmed my position as a daughter. I paused and moved to give him a hug and a kiss on the cheek. He turned his head and tried to put his tongue down my throat. I was disgusted and pushed him away.

I chastised him, "How are you trying to kiss me, and I am supposed to be your daughter?" He responded that he was sorry and insisted that I was to tell no one about what he did. I needed to get away from him, so I agreed and quickly got out of the car. I thought this would be the end of it.

Months passed, and he continued his advances, ringing the bell and calling my name to bring him Kool-Aid or whatever. I hated being called by him as it always led to him making gestures, grabbing my hand, commenting on how nice I looked, caressing my arm when I handed him his drink—it was all quite disgusting, and there was nothing I could do about it. I hated being alone with him but had no choice unless I told someone about the advances. I did not know what to do, so I simply endured. When in the car alone with him, for whatever reason (going to a school practice or something else), he would say, "Ain't you gonna give me a kiss goodbye?" Then I would lecture him, "If I am supposed to be your daughter, you can't be trying to touch and kiss me; it's not right." He simply would laugh and make light of it.

I continued to reach out to my case manager, explaining that the situation in the home was not good and that I needed a different place to live. I did not tell her about the full reasons behind why I needed to be in a different place—I did not want to destroy the family. They had been good to me, outside of his advances. I only told the case manager about the verbal abuse. I also told her that the parents treated us like slaves. The case manager never had good news for me regarding a new place to live. In addition, when she came to visit, all looked perfect. She made excuses about the limited number of families available to foster children and commented that I needed to hang in there until she could find an alternative.

Starr-Love continued to practice and perform. We had several bookings for various clubs and concerts. I needed to tell someone about the father's advances. I began to compare notes with Deneen and Rimp, who shared that he had continually made passes at them. We agreed that we had endured enough and that it was time to end his advances. We agreed that his wife was reasonable and would find a solution that would protect us equally. We thought that our collective stories would affirm his ill intentions. There were children outside of the marriage, and this fact, and the others, comforted us that our reports would not be surprising.

The Truth Hurts

Rimp and Deneen had spent the weekend at the house, and we were preparing to go to school. Mom was preparing for work. We asked if we could speak to her privately, so she invited us into her bedroom and closed the door. We told her the ugly truth about her husband's inappropriate touching and about his blatant propositions to Rimp, which went a step further. She questioned our truthfulness, and we swore we were telling the truth. I could not believe what happened next. She called out to her husband. He came, and she shared with him what we had shared with her. She confronted him in our presence.

He became outraged and responded to his wife, "You believe these little bitches? They

> *"Then you will know the truth, and the truth will set you free."*
>
> JOHN 8:32

lyin', I have never tried to do anything but treat these girls as my daughters." He said, "Honeybunch, after all we have done for you, this is how you treat us?"

At that moment, my life in the home shifted to one of even greater darkness and solitude. If I looked the wrong way or used a questioning tone, they chastised me. I received more than my share of whippings and learned to get along in this miserable state. She resented my presence. There was a great deal of tension in the home, and even my relationships with Leslie and Beverly became strained because I could not share with them what was happening between their father and me. Instead, I put more energy into trying to find a way out. I eventually gave up trying to get my caseworker to relocate me, as this had proven futile.

Amid my inner turmoil, I recalled the judge's instructions regarding my foster care placement, given almost two years earlier. "You are placed in the care of the foster family until your seventeenth birthday when you are considered an adult. This does not mean you must leave on that date; it depends on your relationship. If your relationship is great and you all want to stay together as a family, then that is up to you and the family." I contemplated my upcoming birthday and resigned myself to stick it out; after all, I had asked to be there, and I was not about to call my real father. I kept hearing the words "I told you so" in my mind, and I was unwilling to accept and live with that outcome. I continued throwing myself into school activities and settled to wait out the remaining months.

> "Grace be with all who love our Lord Jesus Christ with love incorruptible."
>
> EPHESIANS 6:24

A Welcome Break

All of my teachers liked me, and most of them had come to know that significant challenges affected my personal and home life. I made good grades, worked hard and participated in class. For years, I made known my desire to go to medical school, and I chose my classes to give me the best foundation for collegiate studies in biology.

I loved science. McCluer North's teachers made the classes fun by incorporating many interactive activities, including animal dissections. In the spring of my junior year, one of my science teachers, Ms. Neta Pope, pulled my friend Nancy and me aside after class to discuss a new summer science program hosted at the University of Missouri at Columbia (Mizzou). Mizzou had received a grant to expose minority high school youth to careers in science, intending to increase their participation in the science fields as a profession. Nancy and I were both good students and had been friends since junior high. The eight-week program was free; all we needed to do was to obtain parental permission and get there. This was the break I needed. If I could separate myself from the drama of living with the foster family, I could make it a few more months.

Nancy was as excited as I was for the chance to spend the summer on a university campus, so she began to work on convincing her mother that this was an excellent opportunity for her future. I began to work on my foster family as well. I did not know how they would receive my proposal, to leave for the summer following my junior year. I recalled the opportunity presented by my Spanish teacher during my sophomore year to be an exchange student in Mexico. After discussing the opportunity with my guardians and explaining that I was "selected" for this opportunity at no cost to them, they agreed that it would be good for me to have the opportunity. Nancy's mother also agreed to let her go, and we were both thrilled to receive such an honor for being good science students. I could not wait for the summer and my countdown to the end of the school year began.

Staff from the minority science program assigned Nancy and me to be roommates. Jared drove me to campus with his mother and Leslie. Once we arrived, they helped me to check in to the residence hall. Mom did not feel great about our residence hall having regular college students. The girls' residence hall faced the boys' residence hall, and she did not like the proximity of the living quarters for girls and boys. We went to the program registration station, and she asked about supervision strategies and visitation policies. Program leaders assured her that there would be supervision at all times and that there were specific curfews for the high school students. There were also designated floor managers who ensured that students followed the rules. Eventually, the family left, and I went to my room to unpack. I was excited to be on my own and ready to experience my independence like never before.

"See, God has come to save me. I will trust in him and not be afraid. The LORD God is my strength and my song; he has given me victory."

ISAIAH 12:2

While unpacking, Nancy arrived. We hugged and screamed in excitement. While unpacking, she pulled out her pajamas—the exact pajamas as mine! As soon as we unpacked, we set out to discover the campus, including the cafeteria where we were to report for our daily meals. As we walked across campus, several collegiate boys drove by and stopped to speak (obviously pleased to see new, young, African American females on campus) and to introduce themselves as "campus experts" should we need assistance. Nancy and I made our way back to the residence hall, and we made sure that we were ready for the next day, our orientation to the minority science project.

Dr. Abraham Eisenstark was the head of the program. He welcomed us and provided the program overview. Each student was required to select a project for the summer, which a faculty member in the human sciences field would supervise. Nancy and I opted to stay together and selected Dr. Esther Thelen, a female professor in the field of psychology. Dr. Thelen was studying the effects of maternal exercise during pregnancy on infant mobility postpartum. The project required us to visit a rat laboratory some distance from the main campus, where we would observe and record the movements of newborn mice across grids. We recorded data for two groups—mice born to mother rats kept in cages where wheels and other elements were available for exercise, and mice born to mother rats without access to exercise. In addition to visits to the rat lab, we visited hospital newborn nurseries to observe and count the leg kicks of newborn babies. We recorded this data, and the professor paired these results with interviews of the mothers where their level of exercise during pregnancy was the primary focus. Other aspects of our summer science included watching videos of infant kicks, recording the height and number, and visiting the computer lab to verify punch cards of data and feed the cards through a giant computer, which filled the room.

We loved our job, and Dr. Thelen was very liberal in how she viewed us. She treated us the same as she did regular college students. She also invited us to join others in her department for cookouts at her home and other departmental celebrations. On one occasion, Dr. Thelen desperately needed something from the drugstore, and she asked if we could drive. Nancy admitted that she drove routinely but had never driven such a big vehicle. Dr. Thelen handed Nancy the keys to her station wagon, and off we ventured to the drugstore. Nancy was shocked, as was I, and we never once thought that this could be a bad thing. Fortunately, Nancy was a good driver and took to the station wagon as if she had routinely driven it. Dr. Thelen grew to be a major contributor to the field of developmental psychology. She introduced new theoretical frameworks for motor development and many cite her pioneering work. Nancy and I did not understand the significance of our assignment to support Dr. Thelen's work during the minority science program until she gave us the ultimate gift of including our name among those she thanked for our role as "observers" for the work we did in the summer of 1981.[7]

Time to Move On.

There were only a few weeks between the end of the summer program and the beginning of my senior year. I was excited. By attending the summer program, I made up my mind that I wanted to attend Mizzou. I decided to major in science as I already knew several professors, and I thought they would comprise a needed support system. I remained focused on attending medical school, and as a result of the science program, I was confident that I could be successful majoring in biology. The break from the family had given me the much-needed time to clear my head.

Once back, the routine continued as if I had never left. There were chores, cooking duties, family get-togethers and the Starr-Love Dancers. We went skating on Wednesdays and weekends and worked as needed at the gas station on Saturdays and Sundays. Other routines continued as well…we girls were back to being the bitches, whores and little sluts that the father wished would get pregnant by the son-of-a-bitches we spent time with at school, the roller rink or wherever. One thing was different; Frida was no longer living with the family. With Frida gone, Beverly had moved into that room.

Things were not any better for me. There was still tension in the house, and I tried to make myself invisible to the extent possible. My guardians encouraged me to open up and participate in family discussions, which I avoided. I thought, *Since when are we having discussions?* During one such discussion, I made

> *"Trust in the LORD with all your heart and lean not on your own understanding: In all your ways acknowledge him, and he will make straight your paths."*
>
> PROVERBS 3:5-6

---

7   Thelen, Fisher, Ridley-Johnson & Griffin, 1982.

the mistake of asking why he called us bitches and whores. That question did not go over well.

He simply responded, "I call you what I want to call you. You all live in my motherf@#king house, and your job is to do what I tell you." At that point, I had nothing else to say, and he took my silence as a sign of disrespect. He later confronted me in my room, where I maintained my silence. He took off his belt and hit me several times. I guess things were back to normal.

I could not wait to get away from him. It was clear that his grudge and anger remained, despite my having been gone for the summer. I just wanted out, and the sooner, the better. My seventeenth birthday was near, and I made up my mind that I would leave on November 4th. With each confrontation I had with Mr. Grove, I gained more strength to leave. I began to arrange clothing items and other personal belongings in a garbage bag in our bedroom closet. I hid the bag under other miscellaneous items so that no one, including Leslie, would detect it. I waited and waited for my birthday.

November 4, 1981: Happy 17th birthday

I woke up that morning and went to school. It was a surreal day that seemed to pass in a haze. At midday, I spoke with my school counselor and told her that I had decided not to return to the foster home. I had spent many days in my counselor's office. She was well aware of my struggles, though, at that moment, she did not know what to do with me and suggested that I give her until the end of the school day to figure things out.

In addition to a counselor, all students had an advisor who was more involved in the selection of their courses and in aiding students in their preparation for life after high school. Assigning students an advisor plus a counselor became a matter of practice in the junior year. My advisor was Dr. Mayetta Williams. She was one of a handful of Black teachers at McCluer North. Dr. Williams taught a Black Studies course, and most of the students in her classes were Black. I had avoided her class as a sophomore. I did not want to be stereotyped — I was generally expected to take Black Studies because I was from Kinloch. Most students from Kinloch enrolled in Dr. Williams' Black Studies class. She was also intimidating. She smoked, wore a wig, and used heavy make-up, accented with her signature red lipstick. Although I managed to avoid her for my first two years, during my junior year, I needed an elective, and "Aging and Dying" was the best option. The only drawback was that Dr. Williams taught that class too.

I grew to love Dr. Williams and admired her teaching ability. I was wrong in my judgment of her as being mean. She did not like to joke and laugh with students and maintained high expectations. Dr. Williams validated students who worked hard by praising them and encouraging intellectual exploration. Those students who wanted to clown around felt the reach of her intolerance for slacking. I guess students assumed that Black Studies would be an easy "A" if you were Black—not the case.

Dr. Williams took great interest in my future, ensuring I was pulled out of class to meet with the admissions representative from Mizzou—Dr. Keener Tippin. Dr. Tippin and Dr. Williams had established a relationship such that by any means necessary, they committed to helping Black students access the opportunities provided through higher education at the University of Missouri at Columbia. Dr. Williams had become one of my favorite teachers and had demonstrated her caring nature in the courses I had taken with her. She also knew, through our conversations, that I lived with a foster family, and she knew my foster siblings who attended McCluer North.

The end of the school day was upon me. After exploring my limited options regarding a place to live for the remainder of the school year, the counselor contacted Dr. Williams, and she immediately came to the counselor's office. Dr. Williams agreed to take me home with her for the evening but insisted on contacting the foster parents to inform them of my whereabouts and that I planned not to return. I was not happy that this call had to take place—after all, I was seventeen years old and legally an adult. In addition, per the judge's own words, I was on my own at seventeen. I sat in the counseling office with Dr. Williams and listened to a one-sided conversation. Dr. Williams explained that she was only trying to help and that she felt it was in the best interest of everyone that I return home with her, at least for the night. After a while, Dr. Williams handed me the phone. I affirmed that I would not be returning and that I would come and pick up my things another day. It was not a fun conversation, and it was not a good day.

Dr. Williams proceeded to share what was said on the phone. Her job would be jeopardized if she proceeded with her plan to take me home as, "Teachers were not supposed to meddle in students' family affairs." They also noted that Dr. Williams had crossed the line by aiding in my plan to leave home. This was not true. Although Dr. Williams was concerned, she remained committed to taking me home for the night until we could devise a better plan. Without the assistance of the foster care system and and me being a legal adult, there were few other options. It was November of my senior year. I had college plans, having already applied to Mizzou. I needed to get through the next six months of high school and find a place to stay until I could graduate and transition to college.

An Unlikely Arrangement

The next day, after spending the night with Dr. Williams, I attended classes as usual. I saw Leslie in the hallway, and she warned me I was in big trouble. She said that her parents were distraught with me. They said I was being ungrateful for all they had done for me. I apologized and assured her I could not go back. Even though I had no idea where I would spend the night, returning to the foster family was not an option.

About midday, Dr. Williams called me to her office and explained that a student overheard her conversation with another teacher about desperately needing to find me somewhere to stay. She continued…the student shared that since her family was originally from Kinloch and her father was a preacher, she was sure her parents would let me stay with them. Dr. Williams asked my thoughts on this possibility. There were no other options, and I knew I could not continue to stay with her and I told her that I was fine with this option, and she set about to verify that the family would welcome me.

That afternoon, I rode the school bus home with this student. She was a freshman. Her mother was home, making dinner, when we arrived. Her mother did not work outside of the home. I introduced myself and thanked her for allowing me to stay. She asked me about my clothing, "Where are your clothes?"

I explained that I only had a few items as most of my belongings were still at the foster home. I told her that Dr. Williams had planned to take me there after school the following day. The mother later showed me a room where I would sleep—shared with the ninth grader. It was a lovely home, also in Florissant. The mother was not a big talker, but we made small talk. She explained that she did not work outside the home because of health issues. She asked about my situation, and I explained. She expressed sorrow in hearing the details. She then explained that her husband was at work and would be home later in the evening.

Later that evening, the father arrived. He introduced himself and explained that he was a pastor for a congregation in Kinloch. I had not heard much about his church though I knew its location. He was charming and talked a lot—he was undoubtedly much more talkative than his wife. Perhaps it was his nature as a preacher. He seemed interested in my life and school experiences and asked many questions. I tried to answer them all. As we continued talking around the kitchen table, his wife occasionally chimed in. Following dinner and conversation, I showered and went to bed. I was glad to have a place to stay, even with strangers. There was no warm and fuzzy feeling, so I convinced myself it was only a matter of time. I would soon graduate and be truly independent.

Dr. Williams had agreed to take me to the foster home to retrieve my belongings now that I had a place to stay. She picked me up and drove to my former home. It felt odd, arriving back under these circumstances. I hoped things would go smoothly. We pulled into the driveway. I stepped out, rang the doorbell, and my sister Leslie came to the door. She announced my arrival. Her parents came to the door. I explained my purpose in being there—to retrieve my personal belongings.

He responded, "You ain't got no belongings here because we bought you everything that you have, and we not gone let you take anything." I tried to reason with him, noting that the clothing items were mine and would fit no one else. They would not allow me to enter the home. Instead, they came out to the driveway, and things escalated. They had strong words for my advisor, who explained that she was simply trying to help me.

As things continued to spiral out of control, the familiar degrading began. "You little bitch! After all, we have done for you; this is the thanks you give us?" I returned the disrespectful epithets. I was at my wit's end and had had enough. Leslie's dad yelled, "go kick her ass," and Leslie came at me. She and I began fighting in the driveway—neither of us knowing why. I am sure she was angry that I referred to her parents using the derogatory names they used with me. Dr. Williams pulled us apart. It was clear I would not be retrieving my belongings. Dr. Williams told me to get in the car and explained that I would need to get a police escort to retrieve my belongings at some future date.

I was upset and embarrassed that I had drawn Dr. Williams into such a horrible situation. I apologized, and I cried. She understood and expressed feelings of discontent that we were not successful and could not reason with the family. She took me to get a few items of clothing and undergarments so I could have another change of clothing. She returned to my new, temporary living arrangement and agreed to work with me to get a police escort, perhaps the following day.

> "*Humble yourselves, therefore, under God's mighty hand, that he may lift you up in due time.*"
>
> 1 PETER 5:6

Having arranged for a police escort, I arrived at the foster home again, with Dr. Williams, to retrieve my belongings. There was little discussion, and they gave me a bag of items. They told me that since I was no longer a family member, they decided to take back those items they had bought because I was in the family. My robe was gone, as were the roller skates. They had also purchased and kept my class ring and my senior yearbook. My yearbook had all of the written notes and special memories from my dearest friends, classmates and teachers. This was so hurtful, but I decided to shrug it off and move on.

A Short-lived Solution

Living with the new family, it did not take long for me to realize that something was wrong. The mother and father slept in different rooms. I understood that her health issues were such that she slept apart from her husband so that his rest would not be disturbed. I noticed how little conversation was between this husband and wife, outside of the necessary—kids, church needs, or other routine areas of importance to maintain the status quo. These two people were together in the same home but could not have been further apart. After only a few weeks, I found myself in the middle of a troublesome family affair. Despite their obvious trouble with communication, there was no discussion about problems in the family.

Once again, an opportunity arose for me to become involved in a major, time-consuming activity. This time it was the "America's Junior Miss" pageant. I submitted an application, completed a series of interviews and photos, and the producers invited me to participate. I was one of only a couple of African Americans in the competition. There were daily practices for dance and other pageant routines. Pageant activities kept me out of the new family's home and out of the family's way for as much time as possible. With no *real* family member active in my life, I did not feel too bad that there was no adult interest in supporting me through the program. I tried not to focus on the fact that all the other girls had family and friends cheering for them. I enjoyed the experience though I did not win. I received a secondary honor akin to a congeniality award and was grateful.

With the Pageant behind me, I began planning to attend the Senior Prom. A friend had asked, and I looked forward to going. The preacher's wife expressed concern about my attending the prom because the ninth grader was not going. I explained that it was my senior year, and this was a crucial time and event for all seniors. I could not believe that the mother measured my allowable activities against what a first-year student could do. After much discussion with her husband, they agreed that I could attend the prom, and they established a midnight curfew. While I was not happy about the curfew, I reluctantly complied.

A Reunion

Now that I was nearing the end of my senior year, Dr. Williams asked if I planned to invite my father to my graduation ceremony. I told her I had not spoken to him since I moved in with the foster family a couple of years prior. Dr. Williams advised that I should reach out to my father and attempt to invite him. She felt this to be an important step in my growth and development. I took her advice and called my father. He was shocked to receive my call. We cautiously approached our small talk, which was not comfortable but undoubtedly safe. Daddy had many questions about my progress in school and how I spent my time, and he asked if I had spoken to my mother and sisters. He also asked about the foster family. Without providing details, I explained that I was no longer there as I was now seventeen. I told him where I was living temporarily until I graduated.

I suggested Daddy and I meet in order for me to give him my graduation announcement. He agreed to a visit. In the interim, I went over and over in my mind what that first meeting would be like. Would Daddy cry and run toward me (I had certainly seen my share of "reunion" movies)? Would he give me a lecture on "The Family"? I could hear his voice in my head, "real families stay together and work things out...." I did not know what might occur; I also had no idea how to prepare for the meeting. All I could think about was he had accused me of having sex years prior when I was not. It stood to reason (based on my last interactions with my father) that he would probably expect that I would be pregnant by now. I concluded that my actions would speak louder than words and that sharing my box of memories would be the best approach for giving Daddy a window into my pastimes. In the box of memories were old school newsletters, articles about my performances in various plays, photos and news clips of the Starr Love Dancers, report cards and other items. I had been a very busy girl over the years and never stopped being overly committed to school activities. The activities, much as in the past, shielded me from the challenging, sometimes painful situations in which I found myself at the foster home. Thank God for after-school activities and the adult sponsors who worked with us to sanction these diversions for students like me.

Days passed, and it was finally time to see my father. I was very nervous. He planned to come to the home where I was staying, and we would spend time together after almost two years of no contact. As Daddy entered the driveway, I flashed back to him spitting in my face. I then saw that there was a woman in the passenger seat. Daddy had a new girlfriend, and she came with him to meet me. I was glad to meet her; her presence was a natural buffer to an otherwise very awkward situation. She was gorgeous and very sophisticated—she seemed quite different from his other wives and past girlfriends. She was very light skinned, had lovely, well-styled short hair and she walked and spoke as a woman of class and means. She was also nice. I knew this from our first interaction.

Daddy decided that we would go for a ride. Again, I recalled our last car ride, pushed the thought to the back of my brain, and worked to hide my hesitation. I sat in the car's back seat, and we began to talk as though there was no issue, only time, between us. I told Daddy about my participation in America's Junior Miss Pageant and my plans to attend Mizzou. He asked me how I had been spending my time for two years. I told him in theater mostly, and I agreed to lend him my box of memories and keepsakes so that he could see for himself. I was very proud of my accomplishments and wanted him to see firsthand that I had little time to think about getting pregnant or falling into another ill fate. I wanted him to see that as much as I was involved in school activities years prior, before leaving the family in Kinloch, school involvement in extracurricular activities remained a focus of my leisure time.

When we arrived back at the ninth grader's home, I provided Daddy with the box of items for his review. He assured me that I would get them back shortly. Before his departure, I invited Daddy to my graduation ceremony. He agreed to come. I was so relieved that our first meeting, a reunion of sorts, was incident free. I thought to myself, now that I have opened the door to our relationship again, surely, he would not do anything to have me close it again.

In the meantime, tensions grew between the preacher and his wife. If there was not enough tension before my arrival, there certainly was afterward. I believe the preacher's wife resented my presence because I provided a listening ear to her husband while at the dinner table. What was I supposed to do? I was living in their home. Was I to walk away and not respond to his questions? I did not know if the wife had heard about the reasons behind my leaving my previous residence—about the father's advances toward me. I wondered if maybe one of the counselors shared some of this information to gain this family's support for my living there. Perhaps the preacher's wife now thought I was part of the problem. Whatever the reason, I was living in their home, and I was not only grateful but respectful as well. Even so, it seemed I could do nothing right.

Homeless Again

Shortly after the prom, the ninth grader's mom sat me down and said the words I will never forget, "I think it is time for you to find another place to live." With that, I assured her that I would and left for school. Who was I to argue? This was her home, and I certainly did not want to stay where I was not wanted. My first stop that morning was the counseling center, considering my need to find another place to live. The imminence of my situation of having no place to go after school, *again*, left me an emotional wreck. My counselor gave me the keys to the pillow room, which had become my special place to cry my eyes out and talk to God. I believed in the power of God and in His ability to make things right. I was not a perfect child, but I <u>was</u> His child and had learned to pray and talk to God from a young age. I locked myself inside the pillow room, cried and prayed. After a while, I pulled myself together and went to my next class choir.

> "I lift up my eyes to the hills. From where does my help come? My help comes from the Lord, who made heaven and earth."
>
> PSALM 121:1-2

As I went into the class, my friend Doni could see that I was not well and that I had been crying. She asked me what was wrong. I tried to hold things inside—it had taken more than an hour to pull myself together enough to leave the pillow room. I could not hold back my emotions and the tears began to fall again. She walked me outside, and we stood in the entryway to the class. I told her that I had no place to stay and that I did not know what I would do to finish the school year. At that moment, two-to-three additional friends arrived and observed Doni and me in an embrace. They asked what was wrong, and Doni told them. Then Doni suggested that we pray. She led a prayer on my behalf right there and then, unashamed and bold. Other classmates joined, and I continued to cry. Doni assured me that things would be okay. We went back into choir class, and she asked the teacher if he would excuse us a few minutes early to visit the principal's office. Our teacher agreed as he could see that we were both upset and understood that the matter was important.

Doni and I went to the principal's office, and she asked to make a phone call to her mother. I had no idea what she was thinking. She told her mom I needed a place to stay, and Doni's mom advised her to bring me home after school. I was so happy and relieved that Doni's mom said I should come home with Doni. I did not know how long I would be able to stay, but Doni had solved my problem, at least for that night. We went back to class and made plans to meet after school to take the bus home to Doni's.

We arrived home after school, and Doni's mom was in the kitchen, cooking broccoli soup. I had never eaten broccoli soup, but it smelled great. Doni took me to her room, where I left my books and other personal items. After a while, Mrs. Driemeier called me into the den to talk. She asked if I was okay and told me that whenever I was ready to talk, she was there and willing to listen. She gave me a warm hug that drove my raw emotions back to the surface. I cried like a baby as she held me. I told Mrs. Driemeier about my Momma's mental illness. I told her about me and my dad fighting in the car, about foster care and my reason for leaving the foster family on my seventeenth birthday. I also told her

> *"Devote yourselves to prayer, being watchful and thankful."*
>
> COLOSSIANS 4:20

about Dr. Williams taking me home and about my stay at the home of the freshman, whose mother suggested I find another place to stay. Mrs. Driemeier was very calming and nurturing and reassured me things would be fine. She encouraged me not to worry.

Later that evening, Mr. Driemeier arrived home from work. The family sat down to dinner. Mr. Driemeier blessed the meal and thanked God for their "special guest." The broccoli soup tasted even better than it smelled, and I ate just enough so as not to be an embarrassment. Tab soda was the drink of choice, and I would have never chosen a low-calorie diet drink, but I was happy to have it. I have learned over the years to be thankful for what I received. I learned to eat various cooking styles from living with many different families growing up. I ate what people cooked, and I was grateful.

There was robust conversation around the dinner table. Mr. Driemeier inquired about our school day, discussed exciting things from his day at work, and made small talk. I thought, *This was how a family should be—eating together around a common table.* Following dinner, Mrs. Driemeier politely excused us, kids, to our rooms. She and Mr. Driemeier spent some time discussing adult matters. Little did I know that despite Mr. Driemeier thanking God for their special guest, he had no idea that the plan was for me to stay for an extended period. Mrs. Driemeier had told Doni earlier in the day to bring me home.

During the conversation after dinner, he learned of my plight and need for a home for the next few months until I left for college.

Mr. Driemeier's response to his wife's inquiry about my staying was simply, "What's another mouth to feed? It is the right thing and the Christian thing to do." Thus, my living arrangements were resolved and I had gained yet another family.

Life with the Driemeier Family

My new family and related experiences proved to be far different from any experience in my life prior. My only exposure to white people was limited to what I saw on television, what I experienced with my friends at school, and what I had seen from afar, recalling the Boaz Apartments and the creek that separated us from the whites who lived in Ferguson. The foster family I stayed with the weekend after the final ordeal with my father also provided a glimpse into the life of a white family. There was also the naked white man from the building next door in Detroit. Finally, there was the white classmate who walked me home from theater practice during the McCluer North musical, "You're a Good Man Charlie Brown." I thought if this family were as they appeared at the dinner table, I would have stability for a while.

"So whoever knows the right thing to do and fails to do it, for him it is sin."

JAMES 4:17

The following days and weeks presented tremendous learning opportunities for all of us. Doni decided that she should give me her room and join her younger sister, Debbie, in Debbie's room. Debbie and Doug (Doni's younger brother) were fascinated that I danced so well. My years as a Starr-Love Dancer paid off in my ability to bond with them through teaching dance moves like the robot. Doni and I spent hours listening to music in her room. The typical lineup was Pat Benetar – "Heartbreaker," Styx – "The Best of Times" (in fact, the entire Styx album), and the soundtracks to "The Rocky Horror Picture Show" and "Grease." On Sundays, we went to church. I felt a million eyes on me the first time I visited. I had never attended a white church and was nervous about the standing and sitting routines. There were more than a hundred in attendance but not one other Black person. I knew none of the songs, but it did not matter. I loved the fact that I was living with the Driemeier family, who, in my opinion, epitomized the "all-American" family.

Like the foster family's weekend routines, the Driemeiers had their routine activities. Instead of roller skating, Doni and her friends liked to attend the midnight ritual showing of "The Rocky Horror Picture Show." I had never heard of the show before Doni's introduction via the soundtrack. Doni instructed me on Rocky Horror protocol to prepare for my first show. We ensured that we had all the elements to make our experience successful, including a cigarette lighter, water guns, newspaper and toast. Outside the theater, I received "time warp" dance lessons, and I was finally ready for what was an unforgettable experience. I loved Rocky Horror, and it only took a few shows before I was a convert, singing and dancing with the crowd and yelling back at the screen.

Going out with friends on the weekend was never a big deal with the Driemeiers. Doug and Doni drove, and we would meet friends at the pizza place, go to the show, or hang out at a friend's house. I had never seen parents so trusting of their kids.

It was simply, "Where are you going? Be careful; be where you are supposed to be" and "when do you think you will be home?" There was no obvious curfew, only simple instructions on being safe and thoughtful. I had never experienced such a seemingly casual conversation regarding going out.

As the weeks passed with my living in the Driemeier household, I met other family members. Grandma Jansen, Mrs. Driemeier's mom and Grandma and Grandpa Driemeier, Mr. Driemeier's parents. We had cookouts and other family get-togethers, and all the grandparents treated me well, as

"Then they also will answer, saying, 'Lord, when did we see you hungry or thirsty or a stranger or naked or sick or in prison, and did not minister to you?' Then he will answer them, saying, 'Truly, I say to you, as you did not do it to one of the least of these, you did not do it to me.'"

MATTHEW 25:44-45

any other grandchild. At Grandpa Driemeier's, I had my first burger, grilled medium well—a bit pink on the inside. Though the thought of eating any meat that was not well done would have previously grossed me out, I had learned to be open to trying new things, and I was thankful for the goodness that had come into my life through my new family.

As we approached the end of the school year, Doni and I made our final plans for college. I would attend Mizzou, and she would attend DePauw in Indiana. Dr. Williams had worked with the minority admissions director at Mizzou, Dr. Keener Tippin, to ensure I had a place to stay in the residence halls. The college required a substantial deposit to secure a room in the residence halls, and I had no resources from which to pay for it. Dr. Tippin made the case to the finance office to waive entering student fees, including the residence hall deposit, in light of my situation and foster care. Once on campus, I could access my grants, scholarships, and other financial aid. With Dr. Tippin's help, my dorm room was reserved, awaiting my arrival on June 13, 1982, one week after graduating high school.

Dr. Williams asked about my attire for the Sunday pre-commencement Baccalaureate ceremony and the Monday commencement exercise. I realized that I did not have sufficient clothing. She asked the Driemeiers if she could take me shopping and buy me two outfits for these occasions as a graduation gift. They agreed, and she and I spent a day in the stores, shopping and having lunch. The outfits were lovely and included a white skirt suit, sailor style with navy bands for the Sunday program, and a green dress for the commencement ceremony. I was very thankful. Dr. Williams was very good to me, and I loved her for her kindness and strength.

Lessons on Black Hair

Having lived with the Driemeiers for some months, my hair had become unmanageable, and I asked their support to purchase a hot comb to straighten it. Thus began their in-depth lesson on the nuances of Black hair. I explained the different methods to straighten hair, including getting a relaxer but noted humbly that the pressing comb was the quickest and easiest way. I did not mention a chemical relaxer. I was so grateful that the Driemeiers had given me a place to live; I did not want to ask for such a costly hair solution. In addition, I was not aware of a Black hair salon in Florissant.

I bought the hot comb and hair grease, washed my hair, dried it and prepared the family for the smoke and smell of pressing hair. We opened the windows, and they watched in awe as I parted my afro in tiny sections, applied the grease and straightened it with the comb and a towel to lock in the heat. I tried to finish as fast as possible, as I could see that the smoke and smell were a bit much in light of their never having smelled nor witnessed such an effort. Being rushed, I did not do as great a job straightening my hair as I could have.

Senior Ditch Day

As we approached the last week of school, the buzz surrounding our last days at McCluer North reminded us of our traditional obligation as seniors—to skip school for "senior ditch day." Ditch day always took place the Monday preceding graduation. Every year, the seniors made elaborate plans on how to spend their ditch day. Ours was a brilliant plan. We obtained permission from the head principal to host our ditch day on the school grounds. We planned to turn the teachers' parking lot into a beach where we would wear our swim gear, play water games, sand volleyball and engage in other beach activities. We had all of Sunday to put the plan in motion to transform the parking lot.

We tasked two students with picking up tons of sand from a donor. The driver had access to a large dump truck that facilitated pick-up and dumping to create our beach. The rest of us set up our beach areas with chairs, umbrellas, volleyball nets, etc. It was a plan like no other ever undertaken by a senior class. As each truckload of sand arrived and dumped its load, we slowly transformed the parking lot into a remarkable beach.

The night progressed, and the weather threatened to rain on our beach party. We did not care; we were in it for the long haul. We received our final couple of truckloads, and celebration time was near. The truck entered the parking lot. The passenger jumped out, went to the back of the truck and jumped onto its side rail to direct the driver during the dump. These two had worked tirelessly as our champions all day to make our dream of a senior beach party in the teachers' parking lot a reality. With the last sand flowing out of the truck, the driver pressed the gas slightly to shake off the excess. With that move, the other student slipped off the side rail, and the truck ran over him. We heard the screams for help. The security guard was on the scene immediately and called emergency services. Word spread quickly that the accident was terrible. It started to rain, and our togetherness turned into an all-night vigil as we prayed, individually and collectively, for our fellow students. It rained all night, and word came before dawn that our friend did not make it. He died of massive injuries from slipping underneath the truck during the final dumping maneuver.

Investigators eventually cleared our beach to return to its original purpose—the teachers' parking lot. We never used the beach for *our* intended purpose, and it rained for days. Our celebrations and graduation plans became somber, and a dark cloud hung over us. The comfort of being with the Driemeier family during this time was greatly needed and valued. They were strong in their Christian faith and had raised praying children. I was thankful that my mother raised me to pray and live my life as a Christian. There was a level of support for us kids that was incredible. Just as we poured sand to fill the parking lot, Mr. and Mrs. Driemeier poured into our hearts words of wisdom and hope for our lives. We were sad but blessed to know that there was more for our lives in loving The Lord.

> "...weeping may endure for a night, but joy cometh in the morning."
>
> PSALM 30:5

Countdown to Graduation

It was the Saturday before graduation, and as Mrs. Driemeier prepared Doni for graduation with a visit to the salon for hair, she inquired as to my hair needs. Mrs. Driemeier noted that they wanted me to have the same opportunity as Doni to visit a salon (thinking back, they probably dreaded having the smell of burning hair!). I explained that having my hair done in a salon would involve a trip to Wellston and, at $45, a bit of an investment. Wellston was the hub for St. Louis' public bus transportation and was about a twenty-five-minute drive from Florissant. There was a hairdresser in Wellston with whom my mother had a long-standing relationship. Her salon was the only place I had ever gone to get my hair done for the holidays. Momma would take us girls there for relaxers and curls. I called and made the appointment for the Saturday before my graduation ceremony. Mr. Driemeier suggested he drive me and insisted that he would pay the cost. This was a great offer as I had no money and no job.

Saturday arrived, and Mr. Driemeier and I left for Wellston. As I gave him turn-by-turn directions, he became increasingly concerned.

He asked, "Are you sure this is the right place?" I assured him that we were almost there. As we arrived, I went inside and gave him the thumbs up, noting all was well. The look on Mr. Driemeier's face said it all—he could not believe he was leaving me in such a bad neighborhood. Even I was surprised.

Over the years, Wellston had become an abandoned shopping district. There were uninhabited buildings, graffiti and very few people. My hairdresser was the same, but she did not know who I was until I mentioned my mother, Doris. After about five hours, I phoned Mr. Driemeier and shared that I was ready for him to pick me up. He was not very far—he had gone to his office at UMSL to wait and catch up on a bit of work. When Mr. Driemeier arrived, he could not believe my transformation. I was a new girl with a new attitude.

Sunday's Baccalaureate finally arrived, signaling our exit from high school. On Monday, we held our Commencement exercises. The Driemeier family planned a graduation party for Doni and me. The entire family came, and they allowed me to invite others. I was shocked when I saw that both Doni and I each had a graduation cake with our names on it. We also each received gifts from the family. This being my first graduation party, I had no idea what to expect and expected nothing. The Driemeier family demonstrated their love of humanity by including me fully in every aspect of their lives.

Chapter Six

COLLEGE YEARS

Off to Mizzou

Over the next seven days, we prepared for my departure to college. Thanks to the efforts of Dr. Williams and Dr. Keener Tippin, I was prepared to start Mizzou's 1982 summer session. My dorm room awaited, and I received several scholarships and grants. University officials waived my housing fees pending my receipt of government aid, including the Pell Grant. Mrs. Driemeier took me shopping to ensure I had all the supplies and other incidentals needed to transition adequately to dorm life and classes from day one. It was a lovely but bittersweet week—I was finally on my own, to sink or swim, to begin my life as an adult, independent and on my terms.

Mr. Driemeier insisted that the family drive me to college. I assumed that I would take the Greyhound bus. They would not hear of it, stating that as sure as they would be taking Doni to school in the fall, they would take me, their newest daughter. I was grateful that they would make the sacrifice to drive me to college. We packed the car with my belongings, including the dorm room items (small ironing board, bedding, etc.) I had purchased it with the graduation money I had received from several sources. We then began our two-hour drive west on Interstate 70 to Columbia.

Once we reached Columbia and found my residence hall, I proceeded to the check-in desk, where staff revealed that I would be in a large, three-person room at the front end of the building. I was not sure how living with two others in a dorm room would play out, but I kept an open mind. Before unloading my things, we found the room and went inside; one roommate, a White girl, had already moved in and selected her preferred area. She seemed surprised to see me and confused that I was with a White family. The room was very large, as described, and I chose my area and left the room. The Driemeiers helped me lug my belongings into the room. My roommate was not friendly and seemed disinterested in my moving in. She left, I assumed to give us space to organize and unload. We cleared the trunk, and the family helped me to set up my room. After a short visit, I escorted the Driemeiers to their car and said goodbye. They gave me $200.00 and told me to use it for anything I needed. It was to tide me over until I received my financial aid. I declined the offer, but they insisted I take it, and I was glad they did. As the Driemeiers drove off, I sighed deeply as reality hit me. I was officially on my own.

I set out for a walk to the Student Union Building to see if I might find familiar faces and explore the bookstore. I returned to my dorm and saw that my third roommate had arrived. She stood and greeted me with a bow and hands together as if to pray. She introduced herself as Naoko from Japan. A limited conversation revealed that she had just arrived from Japan and her English (as described) was "not so good." Naoko was charming, kind, and anxious to get to know me. We immediately hit it off and were in the midst of a great conversation when our White roommate returned. Naoko stood and greeted her the same way she had greeted me. The roommate stared at Naoko, and then she looked at me. She looked at her bed, which was in the middle of ours—she was the first to arrive and had claimed the prime window spot, which overlooked the center of campus. The unhappy roommate then took her things, exited the room and never returned. She did not want to be a part of our mini-United Nations. Naoko and I did not mind. Once it was clear that we two would share a vast room designed for three, we rearranged things and settled in for the semester.

I found my college advisor and registered for two classes, English I and "The History of American Feminism." There was much reading and related work, but I completed the summer with a 4.0, receiving an "A" in each class. After the summer, I moved into an off-campus, independently owned residence hall, Mark Twain Towers. Mark Twain was nice because the rooms were a bit more modern, many of the students were older or upper-level students, and every two rooms of four residents shared a shower and bath. My roommate was Kim. She was from a rural area of Missouri and grew up riding and raising horses. We enjoyed getting to know one another. We could not have been more opposite, but we got along fine and managed to stay out of each other's way, respecting each other's privacy.

By the start of the fall semester, both Nancy and Francine had arrived, and they registered as biology majors. While registering, my advisor recommended that I visit the Languages and Linguistics Department to test out of the Spanish class requirement on my degree plan. Because I had completed four years of Spanish in high school, my advisor felt confident I could save time and money. I went to see the chair of the Department and explained that I wanted to test out of Spanish I.

He asked me how much Spanish I had completed, and I responded, "Four years." He immediately began to speak to me in Spanish, and I froze—it was as if I had never taken Spanish. I was so embarrassed. He asked me if I was sure that I wanted to spend the money to take the test as if I did not pass, I could not get my money back. I was demoralized by my embarrassing attempt to converse in Spanish, and I resigned myself to the fact that I had learned nothing in four years of high school Spanish and, as a result, I should begin again with Spanish I. I registered for Spanish I and other required freshmen-level courses.

Campus Culture

Mizzou was a traditional "land grant" institution. President Abraham Lincoln signed the Morrill Land Grant Act in 1862, allowing the government to grant 30,000 acres of federal land to states to sell and establish educational institutions focused on agriculture, military sciences and mechanics. Even in 1982, Mizzou carried many common segregated traditions among early land grant institutions. Minority and Black student enrollment were low at approximately seven percent, so many Blacks on campus found ways to connect through special interest groups like the Black Student Union or traditionally Black sororities and fraternities. Most memorable was Mizzou's majority freshmen sorority and fraternity rush. Black students observed these practices from afar as White female students lined up in front of their dream sororities to be "sized up," hoping to gain their pass for entry into these elite institutions.

White sororities and fraternities had huge houses like mini mansions. Traditional activities reminiscent of the "old south" queen pageants were the norm with White sororities. The entire pledge process for White students differed significantly from that of Blacks. The Black Panhellenic Council, which governed the activities of Black Greek organizations, did not even allow new students to participate as a pledge before achieving a certain minimum number of credits with a GPA of at least 3.0. Black sororities and fraternities had their traditions as well. As much as the White traditions were foreign to Black students, Black rush and pledge traditions were foreign to White students. Nancy, Francine and I enjoyed watching Black Greek organizations' recruitment events for upper-level students. They often performed step shows in the mall before the bookstore to garner interest.

Step shows have long been associated with Black sororities and fraternities and continue to play a vital role in building camaraderie among fraternity brethren. Some estimate that stepping grew out of a tradition of singing among Black fraternity members in the early 1900s when Black college student leaders founded many of these organizations. Over time, rhythmic moves like clapping and moving in circles and lines enhanced the singing. Stepping is a significant tradition of African American fraternities and sororities, and one can find alums of these organizations stepping even into the elder years. Sororities began taking up the tradition of stepping in the early 1980s when I enrolled and began classes at Mizzou.

My circle of friends continued to grow, and I watched other young women join Black sororities such as Delta Sigma Theta and Alpha Kappa Alpha. On the other hand, my friends and I were not inclined to join a sorority. Still, we took an interest in supporting the activities of Phi Beta Sigma Fraternity, a Black fraternity with a reasonably large membership. They were friendly, smart and did not mind that we were their freshmen fans. We met a few Sigma members during the prior summer while attending the minority science camp, and they took a keen interest in looking out for us as young women on campus. After the Phi Beta Sigma fraternity members realized that as many as ten of us girls were interested in and supporting them during their service projects and campus parties, they agreed to recognize us as "little sisters." Though there was no official little sister group chartered and recognized as an approved student organization, we had t-shirts made to match the fraternity's royal blue and white colors. The Sigmas even allowed us to plan and present our step routines at their parties.

The Sigmas knew a lot about the business of attending college. They told us about the Black Greek tradition. They educated us that their fraternity was the only one with a true founding relationship with a sister organization, Zeta Phi Beta Sorority. The two organizations shared colors and the symbol of the white dove, and their names combined to form "Zeta Phi Beta Sigma." As there were few members of Zeta Phi Beta, the Sigmas had an interest in seeing this group grow, and they called us "I-Zees," short for "Interested in Zeta."

The I-Zees grew to twenty-plus in number, and word spread around campus that Zeta Phi Beta was likely to have an extensive pledge line in the coming semester(s). At Mizzou, only Delta Sigma Theta and Alpha Kappa Alpha had such large pledge classes. The more we followed Phi Beta Sigma, the more other girls joined us. The following spring semester, thirteen members of I-Zee decided to complete the paperwork required to pledge Zeta Phi Beta Sorority. Once accepted into a Black sorority or fraternity pledge class, one was considered "on line" for that organization. Being on line was also visually represented in that pledges were required to line up, usually from shortest to tallest, and walk everywhere together in a line. If two or more pledges were walking together, they must walk in line with synchronized steps. We were also required to greet existing Zetas and Sigmas as Big Sister or Big Brother, preceding their given name. It did not matter where pledges traveled, big brothers and sisters were present on most regional college campuses, and they demanded respect. If ever pledges were caught not walking in line or unison, this was an offense to the big sisters. They never missed the chance to humiliate the pledges publicly or during pledges' training and educational meetings. Since there were no Zetas active on Mizzou's campus, our big sisters attended Columbia College (also in Columbia, MO), and others came from Lincoln University, a historically Black college in nearby Jefferson City, the capital of Missouri.

In addition to studying biology and working part-time as a work-study student, I pledged Zeta Phi Beta Sorority along with Nancy, Francine and a host of new sisters. The pledge experience built character and strong will. Zeta Phi Beta pledges were officially called "*Archonians*." Archonians could not look directly in their big sisters' eyes, could not laugh unless a big sister directed us to do so, and, in most cases, big sisters relegated us to serve their needs. This "service" might involve cleaning their rooms, washing their cars, doing laundry, or doing other chores. Pledge meetings found us in the dorm rooms of our big sisters, and we were required to arrive together dressed in traditional pledge gear, either a black dress or jeans and a pledge t-shirt. Big sisters gave each of us a nickname, consistent with what the big sisters had gleaned from our personalities and quirks. Mine was "Non-observant." It took me some time to get it. Still, the more they called me Archonian Non-observant at key moments during our sessions, the more I realized that I was somewhere else in my mind, certainly not observing or engaging in whatever they felt was most important.

Even though our White sorority counterparts did not understand the traditions of the Black fraternal experience, we were proud to demonstrate our unity by walking in a line. Apart from individual classes and work responsibilities, big sisters expected us to be "one"—one line with one goal, "to cross the burning sands." The entire pledge experience was to prepare pledges for this ultimate goal. Crossing the burning sand meant undergoing the final, formal pledge experience and induction into the sorority. Big sisters only inducted those pledges who completed all requirements, though some of the requirements were arbitrary. For example, we earned points for doing well and lost points for doing bad—the big sister, according to her mood that day, determined all this. For the pledge to be inducted, she was required to earn so many points. If we needed 250 points to finish but were 3000 points in the negative, we might earn 10,000 points on the last day.

A night of activities designed to push the limits of pledges' stamina preceded crossing the burning sands. On this "hell night," big sisters blindfolded pledges for periods during which they transported us to and from various locations. They asked us to drink blood, which turned out to not be blood, and meandered through a mini obstacle course. Once hell night activities were completed and all rituals recited, we removed our blindfolds and our sisters welcomed us as full-fledged sorority members.

Many years have passed, but I realize that even today, I am non-observant in many ways. For example, I generally do not notice specific clothing items or shoes people wear, or I can be so focused on an intense project in my mind that I do not see a friend who may have approached me. I often miss cool opportunities that might happen in a fleeting moment, like catching a glimpse of a famous person walking through an airport or not zeroing in on a "free offer" of something or another. Once while enjoying a family trip to Disney World, comedian Chris Rock and a small entourage walked past my family. When I realized what was going on, my son had captured a great photo of the back of Chris Rock's head—an image that my son will never live down. Although I miss some things, I have noticed a positive side of being non-observant. I have an uncanny ability to focus and knock out huge projects. While others view me as non-observant, I am usually thinking intensely about and working through an issue during these periods. Because of my non-observance, I can focus more on bigger things that have a greater life impact.

Year One Ends

May of my first year came, and I was saddened to learn that Nancy would not continue her studies at Mizzou. She decided to return to St. Louis and attend Southern Illinois University at Edwardsville. Nancy, like most students, had finalized her summer plans, which for the most part, entailed returning home. Others chose to remain on campus and work. I assumed that would also be my plan—staying on campus and working. Being an independent student, I needed to earn as much as I could to ensure my ability to cover all costs related to attending college. I was stunned (and cautious) when my father suggested I return to St. Louis and live with him for the summer. Daddy and I had slowly reestablished our relationship. He suggested that I take some time to think about it. I struggled with this decision partly because it was as though my years of avoiding living with him had now come full circle and, alas, I was destined to live with him anyway. As I contemplated this major step, I reconciled that since my brother, Sam Junior and my sisters, Lacy and Lorie, were now living there, perhaps it would be a good opportunity for me to reconnect with my siblings. I packed my bags, and Daddy drove to pick me up. I was apprehensive about the trip, and I wondered (and hoped) if he might once again bring his girlfriend along for the two-hour drive. He was still dating the woman I had met while living with the ninth grader. I now knew that she was a court stenographer and lived in Chicago.

To my surprise, Daddy came alone. This time, it would be just him and me for the first time since that fateful day forever changed our lives and relationship. We loaded the car and began our drive. It was mostly small talk at first, catching up on who was where and things going on around the family. Then the conversation changed. I do not recall which of us took the courageous step to move the conversation to the next level. We began discussing why I did not want to live with him when I was fifteen. As I contemplated my response, my reason was simple. It stemmed from the fact that I had spent *many years* fighting while growing up. As much as I had to fight growing up in Kinloch, nothing was worse than the brief period when my sisters and I lived with Momma in the Cabanne Courts. The constant threats and bullying from other girls and even their mothers, and the seemingly never-ending neighborhood turmoil was always at the forefront of my mind when I thought about life in the City of St. Louis. I shared with Daddy that I had made up my mind at age thirteen that I would not fight anymore and was afraid that I would have to fight every day if I moved in with him. I recalled the act of simply walking down the street in front of a house with children and teens and having rocks thrown at me by strangers. I did not want to experience that again.

"*Call to me and I will answer you, and will tell you great and hidden things that you have not known.*"

JEREMIAH 33:3

I then asked Daddy why he treated me so badly relative to my sisters during the years leading up to my entering foster care. I will never forget his response…, "I always saw you as my strongest child. You are a leader; even though you are not the oldest, others look to you for advice and guidance. When I saw you resisting and not wanting to live with me, I knew that your sisters would not want to go either. I know it was not the best thing to do, but I tried to force you to live with me so I could have all you kids together." With that, I saw the entire situation differently. He acknowledged my strength and leadership ability. He saw me as the *strongest* child. It made so much sense. I did not ask any more questions. This was a breakthrough. The remainder of the trip was pleasant, and the discussion was light.

Arriving at Daddy's house and seeing my sisters and brother was the best homecoming I could imagine. It felt like a family reunion. We were loud. We laughed and reminisced and we made dinner plans. As always, there were only two options—we all said it together, "White Castle or chop suey." White Castle won the decision that day, but I knew we would have chop suey on the next day. Chop suey in St. Louis differs from the typical Chinese food in other cities. It was like soul food chop suey. Chop suey joints were on many of the neighborhood corners, with the typical neighborhood having two or three.

We never missed an opportunity to debate whose chop suey was the *best.* Almost all of these establishments were "hole-in-the-wall" places where one would simply walk in and up to a window, place the order and wait for them to yell out their name with the order about five-ten minutes later. One could also call the order in by phone. Typical orders were either half or full-sized. There was pork, rice, beef, shrimp, ham, duck, chicken, or special fried rice. Special fried rice was a box of rice with all the meats, green peppers, more onions and bean sprouts. The best way to top it off is with egg fu yung gravy. The fried rice was very dark and highly seasoned, and the meat included onions and a bit of fried egg. Never would one find vegetables like peas and carrots in their rice, as is the case with most other Chinese food restaurants in the country. Another chop suey joint favorite is the St. Paul sandwich. The Shrimp St. Paul is what I preferred, and they added the same meats available for fried rice to St. Paul. The sandwich was similar to the typical egg fu yung patty that one might find at a Chinese restaurant but fried the way Black people in St. Louis liked it. As White Castle won out the first night home, chop suey would have to wait until the following day.

My first order of business after arriving and settling in was to find work. I could not imagine the summer without a job. A new Kentucky Fried Chicken (KFC) was to open on the corner of Grand and West Florissant Avenues. This was only about a mile from daddy's house. I applied and earned a position. My primary duties consisted of cashiering and filling orders. I worked the entire summer and enjoyed being able to bring leftover chicken etc., home after closing. Daddy continued on the graveyard shift at McDonnell Douglas. Hence, we kids enjoyed sitting around late into the evening, eating KFC and listening to the sounds of the streets from the upstairs balcony. It was a pleasant situation.

As the weeks wore on, I began to feel the distance and disconnect that had taken place over the years, especially between Lacy and me. Lacy felt and voiced her view that I was receiving special treatment from Daddy. She and Daddy's relationship was strained for any number of reasons for which I was not privy, and she made a point of noting that I was out of touch with the way things were with my father. After all, I was "just visiting," which Lacy also pointed out to remind me. Daddy and I had missed so much time together that we spent hours reconnecting. I enjoyed hanging out with him. He had purchased several apartment buildings, which he renovated and rented as an added source of income. I enjoyed going with him to collect rent or do the apartment's maintenance. He seemed very proud to take me along (much as he did in my early years), and we enjoyed ourselves, laughing often and trading bad jokes we had picked up from friends and strangers. Though I was put off by my sister's sentiments of special treatment, I tried not to take it personally. I recognized that our lives had all taken different paths.

The more time I spent with the family, the more I learned various pieces of the puzzle, pieces that were missing in my understanding of what had taken place since my removal from Big Daddy's house years prior. Momma had tired of walking the streets, and Lacy's housing situation became precarious. As much as Lacy wanted to be with Momma, the declining situation with Momma's mental illness forced Lacy to accept the offer of a home with Daddy. Shortly after Lacy moved in with Daddy, Momma admitted herself to the hospital for treatment. This occurred sometime early during my first year of college. By now, Momma had spent significant time in the hospital. Lacy had been dealing with her unique problems, and she was now working through the challenges of living with Daddy. Momma remained in the hospital, and we visited as we were able. I felt Lacy was hurt by my leaving her alone when I went to live with the foster family. I accepted this to be the case as she and I were very close, doing most things together up to that point in our lives. Rather than defend my position or try to explain how things were different for me back then, I recognized this home with Daddy was *her* space. I was merely visiting for the summer. I decided to work on not taking things personally—we each had our burden.

That summer, I began reconnecting with other family members whom I had not seen in years, which forced me to deal with the hurt my separation had caused others. One of Daddy's brothers did not give me the warm and fuzzy welcome I had anticipated. We had a great relationship before I left the family. I do not know how much my father shared about the day in court years prior, but I convinced myself that my uncle knew all the details. This was my rationalization as to why my uncle was so angry with me (or so it seemed for many years).

I also reconnected with Cousin Ocie. That day, he was the car's driver when Daddy came to the gas station with Momma to take me back to Big Daddy's house. I wondered how this meeting would go, as I had not seen Ocie since that fateful day in the car several years prior. On this particular day, Ocie rang the doorbell early in the morning. He was there to confer with Daddy as Ocie had been helping him refurbish his apartments, so they were ready to rent. I opened the door, and he gave me a huge smile and a hug. It was as though nothing ever happened. I was glad to know he was not harboring anger as I felt others were. I offered him breakfast, and he was happy to join us. We did not revisit that day from the past—we simply moved forward from that point on, being cousins and enjoying laughter and bad jokes, just like old times.

Finally, I made peace with and forgave my foster family. My foster sister Leslie called me and wanted to visit. I agreed and she arrived with my yearbook and class ring. We talked for hours. It would be many years later before she learned why I left, but we left the past in the past, effectively picking up our relationship as sisters again. Her love and sincere heart made forgiveness easy, and since the death of her father, I have maintained a close, loving relationship with my foster mom and all of my foster siblings. I am a better person because of the good things that came from these relationships.

As the summer neared its end, I prepared to return to school. I was glad that the summer had gone so well. The past was behind me, and all I needed to do was stay on the path to finish college. I thought about Nancy and her decision to return to St. Louis for college. Going back to St. Louis and changing my college were not on my list of things to do. I loved my life as a student at Mizzou, and I was ready to have my independence again.

My sophomore year brought new and exciting opportunities. I had a job as a "work-study" student in the Physical Therapy Department of the University Hospital. This was an amazing learning opportunity. University Hospital was the major medical facility in the region and as such, the trauma center routinely airlifted critically wounded persons from accidents that occurred in the outlying, rural areas. After doctors released patients from the intensive care unit, many of these patients moved to the physical therapy ward, where staff could address rehabilitation for head injuries, strokes and other life-altering medical conditions. Working in the hospital environment provided many opportunities for me to see and experience the medical environment up close and personal.

Later that fall, doctors in St. Louis released Momma from the hospital into the care of the State. She had a room in a transitional housing center for men and women who all suffered various mental ailments. During my trips home, I had the opportunity to visit her. Visiting those places was not pleasant—they were always dingy, creepy and smelly, and everyone looked at you strangely. Furnishings included mismatched, old furniture nicely placed to welcome visitors and offer a comfortable seat. Momma was always glad to see her daughters, and the feelings were reciprocal. We girls were delighted to see her adequately cared for and off the street.

Show Me the Way

Completing my academic coursework was a non-stop but necessary chore. By my junior year, I no longer wanted to attend medical school. I was exhausted from the constant competition amongst my classmates, and sick of the way they tried to intimidate their fellows with lies about how easy tests were for them and other stories. I couldn't wait to get away from them–and the thought of another four to six years of folks hoping I'd fail so they could succeed on a curve was unacceptable.

Though I was certainly capable of better grades than the "C" average I maintained in my core science classes, I was happy with the many other extracurricular activities that made college life a great experience. I resigned myself to the fact that even though I no longer wanted to become a physician, I'd invested too much time into achieving a bachelor's in biology to change my major. So, I decided to stay the course and convinced myself that I would figure out my new career path later.

My extracurricular activities included pledging and actively supporting Zeta Phi Beta Sorority, *Just Singers* (a choral group of some forty-five members in which I was the only African American), and Black Theater Workshop. The workshop was a university course that met one of my elective credits. Having dedicated so much time to acting in high school, I thought it would be a great diversion and a way of connecting to Mizzou's performing arts community. My dream had always been to be a famous actor, but the reality of my life and the need to secure a "real" job was constantly before me.

Just Singers became one of my favorite affiliations. It reminded me of my time in high school choir and theater. We practiced several times per week in preparation for any number of performance requests received. We annually delivered singing telegrams on Valentine's Day. This was a major fundraiser for the group. Teams of four delivered the telegrams, with each team assigned ten to twelve stops. It was during this process that I became acquainted with Kevin. Kevin was a very talented undergraduate music major. He lived in the residence hall, and since I was now living in an apartment with Francine, more than eight miles from campus, Kevin's dorm room became my hangout place when there was downtime. We found ourselves laughing, sharing secrets, dreams and music. He introduced me to the Rolling Stones and one of my favorite songs, "Beast of Burden." He also loved to play "Brown Sugar" for me. We sang as loud as we could. We became inseparable, and many folks thought we were dating.

Dating was undoubtedly something that Kevin had a high interest in pursuing, though not with me. One of the secrets he shared was the fact that he was gay. He had been "in the closet" his entire life and explained that his parents, with their strong Catholic faith, would disown him if they knew. The more we shared, the more he opened up about his crushes and love interests. As the fall semester of 1985 neared completion, Kevin shared that during the holiday break, he would go home to see his parents and tell them the truth about his sexuality. He said he wanted to live his life as he felt and that he was prepared to lose his relationship with his parents if it came down to that. We completed the semester and went our separate ways, looking forward to the spring semester and our ability to resume our shenanigans.

Spring semester came, and the Black Theater Workshop held auditions for the Langston Hughes play, "Tambourines to Glory." I decided to audition and landed the starring role of Laura Wright Reed, a woman who had experienced the worst of what life had to offer, only to find herself leading and pastoring a storefront church. The devil transformed himself into the character of "Buddy," made himself attractive to Laura, wooed her, and she fell for his charm. Having sold her soul to the devil, Laura's church grew, and she became pastor of the most popular church in New York. Laura was now living in a penthouse apartment, conducting all manner of foul business while using the church as the backdrop. Laura's only escape was to murder Buddy. Along her journey, Laura discovers the true love of Jesus Christ.

The music score, script, set design, and overall presentation required significant preparation, time and effort. As I began to devote my time to mandatory practices with "Tambourines to Glory," I had less time to hang out with Kevin. We continued to speak by phone and saw each other when we could. Several weeks had passed, but we had not found the opportunity to connect and debrief about his meeting with his parents.

It was January 28, 1986. I was in the Student Union and noticed a large group of students focused intensely on the television. I decided to approach and see what was going on. The Space Shuttle Challenger had just blown apart, and the nation was in shock and mourning. I tried to reach Kevin but could not get him on the phone. I spoke with a mutual friend in whom Kevin had begun to confide. This friend shared that Kevin was in the hospital, in a psych ward. I was confused and requested details for a visit. I went to the hospital and Kevin's room without wasting any time. He explained that his parents would not accept his homosexuality and that it was such a bad visit; he was depressed and wanted to kill himself. He had overdosed on pills and had to have his stomach pumped. I was so angry with him. How could he try to take his life when he had so much for which to live? He was so talented and handsome. He had great friends. Why had it come to this? Doctors released Kevin from the hospital with his assurance that he would not attempt suicide and his promise to attend counseling sessions as scheduled. Once Kevin left the hospital, I tried to spend all my uncommitted time with him and attend evening practices for "Tambourines to Glory." I was burning both ends of the candle.

On January 30th, I tried to call Kevin after practice, but he did not answer. I was so tired, and since Kevin was not in, I made my way home on the city bus. I settled in for the night, and not even an hour passed before Kevin called me and asked me to come over. He seemed to be having a party. There was a lot of noise, music and laughter in the background. I was glad he was having a good time and returning to normal. I declined the offer to come back to campus as it involved calling a taxi and spending money I did not have. In addition, I was exhausted. Kevin understood, and we agreed to speak the next day.

Daylight came quickly, and I went about my schedule as usual. I tried to call Kevin, but there was no answer. I decided at the end of the day to return home. I called him again. This time, someone answered the phone. The voice was unfamiliar, and they asked who was calling. I replied this is his friend Sandra. There was a strange silence for a moment that seemed like an eternity, and then the man who answered the phone explained that he was a police officer. The resident assistant asked to enter the room after receiving a concerned call from another of Kevin's friends. The officer explained that Kevin was not available. Kevin had reportedly hosted a late party until 2 am. The officer shared that when they entered Kevin's room, they found that he had hanged himself. I could not believe that this was how they broke the news to me. I was hysterical. They told me an officer would come to see me because Kevin had left me a note.

The next two hours of waiting for the officer to arrive were the worst and longest two hours of my life. In the meantime, my doorbell rang. It was a person selling cookbooks door to door. I needed a cookbook like a hole in my head, but I did not want to be alone, so I entertained the sales representative and even bought a few books I could not afford. Finally, the officer arrived with the letter. I could

"For everything there is a season, and a time for every matter under heaven: a time to be born, and a time to die: a time to plant, and a time to pluck up what is planted: a time to kill, and a time to heal: a time to break down, and a time to build up: a time to weep, and a time to laugh: a time to mourn, and a time to dance: a time to cast away stones, and a time to gather stones together: a time to embrace, and a time to refrain from embracing: a time to seek, and a time to lose: a time to keep, and a time to cast away: a time to tear, and a time to sew: a time to keep silence, and a time to speak: a time to love, and a time to hate: a time for war, and a time for peace."

ECCLESIASTES 3:1-8

not believe that Kevin was gone. He was so happy the night before—or so it seemed. How could I have missed the signs that he was in trouble? I felt that if I had only gone to the party, perhaps he might still be alive. The note was beautiful, yet very sad. Kevin urged me to *live* my life, emphasizing the word "live" by underlining it. I realized that our good times had ended. I agonized over Kevin's death, wondering what might have happened if I had just taken the taxi to his dorm the night before. I wondered if I might have been able to help him. To move forward, I had to forgive myself and reconcile in my mind that I could not have helped—he had attempted suicide days prior and was determined to end his life on his terms.

A group of *Just Singers* made plans to attend the funeral. We met his parents. I didn't quite know what to say—I did not say anything other than to introduce myself as a friend of Kevin's. We returned to Columbia, and I had little time to grieve as the play, and the people in the play were consuming all my time. Friends who knew of my relationship with Kevin commented on how well I could maintain my composure. I guess his death never sank in. That is, until about a month after we completed a week of sold-out performances. "Tambourines to Glory " made history because it was the first play to sell out all performances before opening night. There were standing ovations every night. Laura Wright Reed was a hit. She cried on cue and put forth exceptional monologues. The crying came very naturally to me because all I needed was to reflect upon any aspect of my life. God knows there was plenty about which to cry.

A Shot at Stardom

The year passed slowly after the play ended, and I moved on to the next project, "A Soldier's Play." I played the only female role cast, that of a club singer. I met Reginald "Reggie" Ballard during this play, the director cast him as "C.J. Memphis." Reggie was a Mizzou football player. After completing this play, all Reggie could think about was acting. One cold winter day in Missouri, he made a split-second decision to pack his bags and relocate to California. He landed a role on "The Martin Show" as "Brotherman... from the Fifth Floor."

I read about a national competition entitled "The Great American Screen Test." Budding actors from around the nation completed and submitted written profiles as step one of the competition. I thought that I had as good a chance as any, and I thought that perhaps this could be my big break. From the profiles submitted, judges selected some 10,000 people to participate. I was one of them. Though I was still skeptical about the contest, I thought I had nothing to lose and decided to move forward to the next stage. Judges narrowed the field to 5,000 contestants who entered stage two, which was a personal interview. From this level, they chose 1,000 persons to proceed to stage three. I could not believe that I was still in the running. Since the creators of the competition had not asked for any money, I continued to compete, hoping this would be the opportunity of a lifetime. During this stage, each contestant received an appointment time and a certain number of minutes to present their best dramatic acting monologue to a recorded line. My first instinct was to perform Laura Wright Reed's monologue about her mother. I presented the same powerful emotions performed during the play with the Black Theater Workshop.

After giving stage three my all, I waited and waited. About a month passed. Then, I received a letter that I had made it to the semi-final round. Only 100 people in the nation received this opportunity. All in the final 100 would convene in Dallas, Texas, at the Studios at Las Colinas to perform a screen test. Included in the letter was a check for $1,000 to help defray my travel costs. Competition organizers allowed me to bring one person, so I invited the head of Mizzou's Black Theater Workshop, Professor Clyde Ruffin. The media got wind of the story and interviewed me on a major prime-time news show. In addition, a major story appeared in the local newspaper. I began to practice my speech: "It is great to make it to the final 100."

The experience at the Studios was amazing! I was to perform a scene from "His Girl Friday." At that time, I had never seen the movie. There was no easily accessible internet, and even movie rentals were a cumbersome task during those days. With only a script and my imagination regarding the scene, I gave it my best 1980s spin. I did not make the final ten. Those individuals received invitations to Hollywood and an agent to assist in moving their acting careers forward. I concluded that God had different plans for my future and returned to my regular daily grind of being a senior in college.

A New Interest

I was thrilled to enter the 1987 Spring Semester. This would be my final semester. A credit review by the registrar the prior semester showed that my grade point average in my core science classes was just below 2.0, the minimum required for my degree in biology. My only option was to take an independent study under a professor of choice and make an "A." This would bring the minimum above 2.0, and I could graduate with the spring class. Such a predicament left me with one option—I would approach Dr. Eisenstark, the professor who oversaw the minority science scholars' program I participated in the summer following my junior year in high school. If anyone wanted to see me achieve my goal of graduating with a biology degree, he was that person. Dr. Eisenstark agreed to take me under his wing to work in his lab, assisting him and other graduate students in their research. I dedicated the time necessary to fulfill my course obligation.

While walking the hall in the Biology Building, back and forth to the centrifuge room, I noticed a man who had also clearly noticed me. We must have passed each other for a month when he finally asked about my project. I explained, and we continued to speak and smile as we passed in the hall. He was about my height and had incredibly blue eyes that were large and round, making it difficult not to stare as he passed. He introduced himself as Robert Webb, a new post-doc working in the department chair's laboratory. He studied at Temple University and claimed Philadelphia as his home. Dr. Webb was a microbiologist. He routinely took breaks to smoke. We had a connection, though it was going nowhere. The semester was ending, and I needed to make plans for my life beyond the bachelor's degree.

The time had come for me to finalize my independent study. I completed the required final paper on the experience and learning outcomes. I received my final paper back, days before final grades were due, and I was to receive a "B." How could this be? I knew I did not give the study 100% of my mind, but I still thought it would be an easy "A." I guess I was more than a little distracted by Dr. Webb. My final paper did not demonstrate the growth Dr. Eisenstark thought I needed to attain the highest mark. I immediately requested an appointment and explained that without an "A," I would not graduate. I told him I would work for him through the summer to make up the grade and learn additional information if he changed the grade. I honestly needed the time to decide exactly what I would do. Was research the career for me? Dr. Eisenstark agreed to change the grade and allow me to continue supporting research in his laboratory.

Robert was excited to hear that I was continuing to explore the field of science and agreed to offer me support and encouragement. We began to spend time together, going to restaurants and getting to know each other. I took him to my favorite Italian restaurant for happy hour. Robert explained that he was half-Italian and half-Irish. His mother was Italian, and his father had left home when Robert was younger. He described his father as an alcoholic whom he hated and had no interest in ever seeing again. He "became the man of the house after that," and his mother depended on him to manage the household, which he resented. As a result, he and his mother were not very close. She moved from New Jersey to Philadelphia and then Florida, where she worked with a telephone company. Our conversation ended at his place. The drinking continued well into the night, one shot after another of Jim Beam.

Robert never officially asked me to be his girlfriend; we simply entered a dating relationship. I was included in gatherings and parties at the Chair's home, and Robert and I were almost inseparable. As the summer passed, I decided research was not how I wanted to spend the rest of my life. What was one to do with a biology degree? The pharmaceutical industry was beginning to boom, with representatives making more than $80,000 a year. People told me that the most challenging aspect of selling pharmaceuticals was learning the drug names and related chemical compositions. With a degree in biology, I figured this would come easier for me—tie that degree with a Master's in Business, an MBA, and perhaps I would be the most eligible candidate for a pharmaceutical sales opening in the future. With this path in mind, I completed the Graduate Management Admissions Test and applied for enrollment in Mizzou's MBA program. Business School officers granted me a Ponder Scholarship, awarded to low-income minority graduate students studying business. With the start of the fall semester, my future was well on its way.

I loved being in the MBA program, which complemented my new position as an assistant manager at a retail store in the mall. I was once again very busy, working thirty hours per week, going to graduate school and dating Robert. I was happy and spent all my extra time at his place. Occasionally, his mom would call, or he would call her. The conversations seemed short and trite for the most part, consisting primarily of small talk. I had the opportunity to say a few words to her once or twice, but the conversations never went past the surface. Robert drank every day, shots of Jim Beam followed by Rolling Rock beer chasers or water if there was no beer in the apartment. I tried to keep up with him for social purposes mainly. I also thought it would make us closer as a couple, to share in everything.

I thought our relationship was doing great until the day he told me his girlfriend, whom he dated while at Temple University, would be coming to Columbia for a visit. What? I knew I had heard wrong. I thought, *Your ex-girlfriend is coming to Columbia to stay with you at your apartment, where I have been spending all my free time for months?* It seemed that they never *really* broke up, and she was coming so that they could see if they would try to maintain a long-distance relationship or end things. I must have had a "fool" tattooed on my forehead, as this caught me completely off guard. I decided to play the bigger person and give him the space he requested. *Really?* He described her as Asian, and I imagined her as every Asian woman I saw for a while. She would be staying for an entire week. I was so upset but acted as though I understood. Where had she been all this time? They were still dating in both their minds. I wondered what other secrets Robert might be holding.

His girlfriend came and left, claiming that nothing occurred of a sexual nature. When he left me at the apartment one day, I decided to snoop and see what I could learn. In addition to finding her little sexy panties, I discovered boxes of porno magazines in his closet, which he had moved with him as he relocated from place to place. There were so many, most dating years back. It appeared to be a collection. As I looked at the titles of these magazines and the covers, they all seemed to have an "exotic women" theme. I began to see a pattern. They were all women of color, and I figured I was yet another intrigue.

Now that I knew the secrets in the closet, I had to figure out what to do with this information. I decided I would not mention the magazines; however, I would confront him about the sexy panties and his claim that he and his girlfriend did not have sex. He returned to the apartment, and I questioned him again about his time with her. He started on his daily shots of booze, but I did not join him. I was armed and ready to take on the argument. I showed him the panties and asked him to explain. He was furious that I would go through his things. I apologized and commented that if there was nothing to hide, why was he so angry? He swore nothing happened and that she wanted something to happen, but he couldn't because of me. After a while, I let it go and gave him the panties, thinking he would throw them away. He didn't. Instead, he put them back in a drawer and set his sights on convincing me that he loved me, telling me he told her about us, and it was over between them. I was satisfied and decided to drop the matter.

Things were going okay with school, and my job was also reasonably well. My relationship with Robert was rocky at best, but I was committed to making it work. Why? I had zeroed in on recent news reports and magazine articles about Black professional women and their inability to find eligible Black men who were both professionally secure and available for relationships. This shortage of available Black men had forced Black women into interracial relationships, and there was a growing trend. Hearing such reports repeatedly, I thought for sure that I would be one of those Black women who would end up alone, lest I made an effort to attract an eligible, professionally secure man of any race. Though Robert was far from secure, I thought his career would eventually take off once he completed his post-doctoral assignment and secured a permanent position.

He kept telling me, "Things will get better once I finish my post-doc." I believed him and surmised that we would someday make a decent living because he had achieved a Ph.D. in Microbiology. I thought things would improve, and I committed myself to stay with him through the tough times.

Later that fall, word spread that Robert's boss, the chair of the Biology Department at Mizzou, had accepted the position of chair of biology at Purdue University—the entire lab and all post-docs and research assistants would relocate with the Chair. Naturally, I was immediately concerned. Robert would relocate the following summer of 1989, and I assumed I would be going with him. This would require that I quit my course of study. Robert was not willing to discuss this. He provided me with no sense of security relative to our relationship. I was surprisingly stupid for thinking we were secure. I continued to work at the mall and registered for spring classes.

Signs, Signs and More Signs, Everywhere

Before Christmas that year, I received a call from an old friend. He wanted to meet as he needed to share something important. I agreed to meet him. He was there with his cousin. We had some wine and caught up on old times. Then he shared with me that his cousin was dating the mother of one of the former employees at my job. My job had worsened as the regional manager hired a new, local, store manager, Margie, and Margie hated me. She also resented anyone who liked me and cut the working hours of this high school student such that she resigned from her position. My friend's cousin had heard a rumor that Margie was out to get me and that it had something to do with a credit card and the store discount. I never abused my employee discount and did not own a credit card. He warned me to keep a watchful eye. I thought nothing more about it and continued, as usual, with my daily routine and business.

I reflected on the countless issues I had experienced with Margie. Before Margie, I fulfilled the role of interim director, following the departure of a previous store manager. I applied for the manager's position. I thought retail managers could make a good living, which would be another fallback position should things not work out with Robert. I was still pursuing the MBA. They hired Margie instead, and she proved to be a calculating witch. I was responsible for introducing her to the data management system used by the company, which I did. She was not appreciative. She reduced the hours of the high school salesclerks who worked with us. She forced them to look for more working hours elsewhere. This eventually led to the salesclerks quitting as Margie scheduled them for as few as five hours per week. Margie hired salesclerks from the store she previously managed down the hall. She surrounded herself with these imps and systematically let go or forced out most everyone else.

My presence and position as assistant manager were nuisances. I challenged Margie's approach to management on several occasions. Margie struggled with properly using the payment system and resented that I had proven correct in asserting that she was not performing proper reconciliations. Margie left denigrating notes for me in the public workspace all employees shared.

Notes generally ended with exclamation points and questions such as, "Can't you do anything right?"

It was time for my evaluation. Margie phoned me and explained that she was taking the day off, that my evaluation was there for me to review, and that since it was due in the mail that day, I was to review it, sign it and put it in the mail. When I arrived at the store, I found the evaluation was where she said it would be. I looked it over and could not believe it. Margie had given me a poor to average performance rating. She gave me the lowest score possible in an area she did not understand. If she had understood it, she would have had no option but to give me the highest rating possible on that measure.

I decided to call the manager and challenge the evaluation overall and the measure being questioned in particular. She was so upset. "How dare you call me on my day off with this bullshit." I apologized and explained that I would neither sign the evaluation nor mail it in its current form. She challenged my premise, so I gave her my glaring example that the evaluation was not a fair measure of my performance and that she would need to review it with me. I told Margie that I wanted her to make edits, and only then would I sign it. She yelled and cursed but agreed to come in. She was mad as hell, but I did not care. I would not be her next victim.

The holidays came and went, and I began to pressure Robert to let me know if he intended to include me in his relocation plans. He was very frustrated. He had avoided the question for months, and I could not wait any longer. I needed to put plans in motion as much as anyone else did if I was going to move to Indiana. Because of my continued pressing for answers, Robert finally explained that he could not take care of me and noted that I did not have a job in Indiana. I explained it was not my intention for him to take care of me, that I was and have always been independent and able to care for myself. I did not doubt that I would get a job. He needed to affirm the relationship by inviting me to relocate with him. After discussing the possibilities, Robert agreed he wanted me to move with him.

I made known my plans to relocate. Margie seemed indifferent. I did not care; I was moving forward with my life. As the relocation date neared, Robert took a trip with others in the lab to find a place to live. All was falling into place, and I was prepared to say goodbye to the place I had called home for almost seven years. Two weeks before I was to move to Indiana, a White man entered the store where I worked and asked if he could speak with me. I thought he was a previous customer. I asked if everything was okay with his purchase, and he asked to speak privately. I suggested we step outside the store. He suggested that we meet in the store's office. I thought this was strange as I realized I had never seen this man before, but he seemingly had the authority to ask me to the backroom. One glance at Margie, seeing her sneer, I knew she was up to something.

I followed the man to the store's backroom. He asked me several questions about the assistant director and her credit card. Sue and I had worked together for almost two years and had a great, professional relationship. He mentioned buying clothes. I thought he was trying to persuade me to implicate Sue for improperly using her discount. I was confused. I assured him that if Sue had bought a large quantity of clothing, she had parental support to assist her in paying the bill if needed. Then, he clarified he was not speaking of *her* and her credit card, but *her credit card and me*. Now that I was more confused, I assured him I neither understood his line of questions nor the point. He then shared with me that he was a corporate investigator. He proceeded with a demeaning line of questions. "Sandra, I am trying to understand if you are like the 'little kid from the ghetto' who stole an apple and is sorry and therefore able to be helped, or if you are the 'hardened criminal' who would steal from someone and look them in the face without blinking. Now you can help the little kid from the ghetto." He continued, "So which one are you, Sandra? I am here to help you, but you must help me."

I continued to deny his accusations and assured him that I was clueless relative to the discussion. "I do not own a credit card and know nothing about Sue's card." He became furious and yelled at me, stating, "If you don't know anything, then *why* is this company investigating you?" He then showed me a fourteen-page document with my name throughout. I was under investigation for fraud, reportedly for charging more than $400 in clothing with a lost/stolen credit card, which belonged to the assistant manager. I was shocked and horrified—how did my name wind up in this document? I became angrier, wondering what was going on. He flipped through the pages and asked, "Isn't this your signature?"

I looked at the so-called proof—an obvious forgery of the assistant manager's signature and replied, "no, that is not my signature." He would not give up, "Well, if it is not your signature, then I think it's one of your friends. Weren't you in St. Louis on that weekend?" Who knows? I may have been there. Being a native of St. Louis, as were half of the students at Mizzou, I made regular trips home. It was less than a two-hour drive. Whatever the case, it was neither my signature, nor had I ever shopped at the retail establishment. I told him that I could not help as this was all news to me.

The man asked me to resign, and I responded that under no circumstances would I resign, as I had done nothing wrong. He tried to coax me with the promise of receiving my vacation pay. They would only pay me the several weeks of vacation hours I had earned if I resigned. I refused, and he told me they would fire me that day if I did not resign.

I responded, "You have no grounds to terminate me as I have done nothing wrong."

"Well, Sandra," he responded, "you have left me no reason other than to fire you."

I asked, "On what grounds?" He then told me that I should think about the loss of my vacation pay and that they would give me the night to decide if I wanted to resign or have them fire me and forfeit my earnings. He then asked for my keys, and I explained that they were in my purse, under the store counter out front. He gave me the option of saving myself the embarrassment by going out to retrieve them and returning them to him in the back room. I would be neither ashamed nor embarrassed. I told him to come and get them if he wanted them.

I politely left the backroom, looked at Margie with her sneering, malicious smile and Sue looked sorrowful and confused. I grabbed my purse and tossed him the keys.

Sue approached me as I walked out and said quietly, "Sandra, I am so sorry; I don't know what happened. I know that you did not take my credit card."

The man told me to come in the next day, and they would give me an answer about the grounds for my termination. Just as I was walking out the door, a friend I had not seen in a while just happened to be passing. She took one look and asked what was wrong. I broke down in tears. I had kept it together until that point, and the emotional release was overwhelming. She said that I should come home with her so that we could talk about it. I had never been to her house, though I had known her for years. Ironically, there she was. We got to her place and talked for half the night. I explained the whole day's events and my confusion about how it could happen. It was as though I had escaped a bad dream. She went to bed, but I could not sleep. I knew there had to be an answer as to

> "Even though I walk through the darkest valley, I will fear no evil, for you are with me: your rod and your staff, they comfort me."
>
> PSALM 23:4

how this came about and how the investigator attached my name to this case. I prayed for God to give me insight and answers. I prayed, silently, most of the night. All I wanted to do was finish my job on good terms and move to Indiana. Now, I had to deal with this mess.

As I prayed about the situation, I remembered pieces of my conversation with my other friend before Christmas. I recalled his warning that "they" were trying to get something on me. That morning, I called him to learn more about the history of that story. Then I tracked down the source of the story—one of the store's former employees whose mother dated my friend's cousin. I placed a call to the former employee. What this teen shared with me was incredible! Accordingly, my colleague Sue had lost her credit card (or it was stolen), and someone charged clothing at a department store in St. Louis. She continued, detailing that Sue casually discussed her loss in Margie's presence. Margie insisted that I was likely responsible for stealing Sue's credit card. Sue assured her that I would never do such a thing, that we had worked together for almost two years, and that I was not that person. The former employee told me that after Sue left the store that day, Margie called the department store where the clothes were charged, gave them my name, and told them that I was likely guilty of this. She then went so far as to send the company copies of my signature from my employment application. *That* is how the investigators linked my name to the case. I had never met such a hateful person. Why me? Why did she hate me so? Was it because I was Black and smart? I never carried the *Black power* sign. I never blamed White America for my life's predicaments. Margie had tried to destroy my life.

Armed with this new information, I made calls to see if any attorney would agree that this company had grossly violated my rights. I tried to find anyone willing to assist me in challenging the store. After a few calls, it was clear that no one locally was interested in taking on such a cause. I went back to the store to pick up my final check.

Margie gave me the check, and when I asked about my vacation, she asked if I was resigning, to which I replied, "No. You can fire me, but I will not resign." She affirmed that I would lose my earned vacation pay.

"So, I'm being fired," I asked.

"That's right," she said. I asked for a reason. Margie then phoned the investigator on standby to assist her with this process. "She is asking me for the reason she is being terminated." I could not believe what came out of her mouth next, "For unauthorized use of the telephone." I once had a minor car accident driving from St. Louis to Columbia and had to open the store that morning. When I arrived at the store, I made a short call to my father to explain that I had an accident in the car he had bought for me. This was an unauthorized call.

In the middle of preparing to move and trying to get justice for the wrong I had suffered, I stumbled upon the Missouri Commission on Human Rights. Its purpose was to ensure that companies doing business in the state were fair with their employees and followed workplace hiring and nondiscrimination rules. I made a call to the Commission and was able to share my story with one of their associates. I received a packet with many pages of questions that I was required to answer and return. I would already be in Indiana by the time I could complete and return the paperwork. I visited with Robert about the matter and my need to respond to consider the matter resolved. Robert advised me not to waste time and to ask the store to clear my name, and receive a letter of apology, my vacation pay and define my reason for leaving as resigned. He was concerned this could drag on forever if I requested more than that. Robert then said something I will never forget, which has stuck with me my whole life.

Robert said, "He who laughs last laughs best." This inspired me to move forward with the process, despite the large amount of paperwork—I kept replaying in my mind the scene of Margie's arrogant smirk as I handed over my keys and left the building. She was so satisfied that she had won. I was determined to have the last laugh. I filed my official complaint against the company and set my sights on the move to Indiana.

Chapter Seven

Indiana, Here I Come

Breaking the News to Daddy

Our drive to Indiana took us through St. Louis. I had told Daddy that I would be moving to Indiana with Robert, and Daddy was unhappy.

"How could you move across the country with a man that hasn't even put a ring on your finger," he asked. I told him that we planned to marry eventually; however, I knew that this was, at best, my biggest hope. Daddy was right. I was relocating with a guarantee of nothing. Though he never brought up the issue of race, he had issues with this as well. He could not understand how *this* was the man with whom I chose to live my life under uncertain terms. I told Daddy that with or without his support, I was moving to Indiana with Robert and if he could not see welcoming him into his home in St. Louis, we would simply keep driving and pass on through. Daddy calmed down and asked me not to do that. I felt he must have thought about the last time I walked out of his life—it took years to mend our relationship.

He then said, "Baby, don't do that. Please come home. You and Robert are welcome to stay here." That settled it. Daddy would have the opportunity to get to know Robert better, as we were now definitely together as a couple.

When we arrived in St. Louis, Daddy was over the top with exaggeration. He had bought champagne to toast our move to Indiana. His actions were so fake—he was not the least happy, but I accepted his "kind" gesture and enjoyed the drink.

We completed our drive to Lafayette the next day and pulled up to our new apartment. The owner had divided a turn-of-the-century home into about four apartments. I was not sure I liked this place, but I had to go with the flow and accept that moving to Indiana was my choice. Our apartment was on the first floor. One entered the living room with a small bathroom off to the right. The living room connected to what was previously a large formal dining room but now served as the bedroom in this small apartment. There was no door to separate the living room from the bedroom, and the bedroom led to the kitchen. There was no door there either. It would take some time, but I was determined to make it work. We settled into our tiny place, and Robert immediately started to work. My first order of business was to find employment.

I figured any job was better than no job, especially since this was Robert's biggest concern. I made my way to Manpower to become a temporary service worker. I had heard that many times temporary assignments led to permanent employment. They gave me a typing test and took my application. They told me then, upon seeing that I had worked as a student employee at The University of Missouri, they might have a month-long assignment for me at a two-year college. College officials sought someone to assist with data entry

> "But he gives us more grace. That is why Scripture says: 'God opposes the proud but shows favor to the humble.'"
>
> JAMES 4:6

for prospective student inquiries. A Manpower representative called me later that afternoon and asked if I could report to the administrative offices for Ivy Tech. I accepted and was thrilled to be going to work, even though it was for minimum wage. I was seventeen credits short of an MBA, new to town and unemployed, therefore, there was no room to complain.

After about a week of entering data, my supervisor allowed me to answer the phone and take basic admissions questions. I learned to work the switchboard and covered for lunch breaks. At the end of my four weeks, the special assistant to the college dean invited me to his office. He explained that they had noticed I was not the average temporary service worker and asked if I would be interested in a longer-term placement of six months. They planned to expand my responsibilities and increase my hourly pay rate. I agreed and was thrilled I wouldn't have to find another assignment.

Hoosier Life

About five months passed, and the college's Recruitment Coordinator accepted a position with another company. I immersed myself in the admissions processes and learned about the school's academic programs and related requirements. The recruiter suggested I apply, and after little thought, I did just that. By this point, the matter with my prior employer in Missouri was still pending. I was very conscious of how potentially damaging it could be for the interviewers to know that I had filed charges against my former employer. I was afraid of others getting a false impression of me—that of being likely to sue for the sport of it, if I weren't happy for any reason. This wasn't the case, but I was not willing to take the risk of exposure. I decided to leave that position off my resume, which created a two-year gap in my work history. Instead, I listed my time as attending school (which I did) and selling Mary Kay Cosmetics (which I did for a period) during these years.

Officials granted me an interview, and the panel comprised some eight people. I had never interviewed with a large group. I considered this my first "real job" interview. Other interviews were for jobs I needed only to make money while preparing to do something else. The interview was proceeding great, and I was doing great.

That was until the special assistant to the Dean stated, "Sandra, you have an impressive history of work throughout your time in college. I'm a bit confused as to if selling Mary Kay part-time is all you did for the past two years." That did it! The cat was out of the bag. Not being a liar and unable to continue the charade, I explained what happened in Columbia with the retail establishment. I further explained that I do not make waves at a company; however, in this case, the manager's actions were so egregious and mean-spirited that they left me no choice but to take action and file a report. Then I could not hold back the tears. I was *done* for sure. Who cries in a job interview?

Though the session ended well, I did not expect positive news; thus, when the special assistant to the Dean summoned me to his office to discuss the position again, I was shocked. I went to the meeting, and he was alone. He explained more details about the position, including some of the counties I would visit covering the school's eight-county region. He told me about the history of White County and its history with the Ku Klux Klan. It was White County because Blacks were not welcomed there at one point. He asked how I felt about visiting a place like that.

My response was, "Well, sir, if I behave as a professional, I expect to be treated as a professional. I have lived and been educated alongside White people for years, and I am not afraid to travel to White County or any other county." He asked if I was ready to start work, and my journey began as the college's recruitment coordinator.

Back on the home front, Robert continued daily drinking…shots of Jim Beam and Rolling Rock chasers. We met more people and began to socialize regularly. Most of the folks we socialized with were Robert's colleagues or folks he met along the way at other friends' get-togethers. My credit was good enough to purchase my first new car now that I was working. We went to the dealer, and I bought a Pontiac Grand Am. It was a good car and gave me greater independence.

Robert's job was stressful, and he was rarely in a good mood unless he drank. He received an invitation to attend a wedding back in Missouri for one of his former colleagues. I could not attend because my job was too new. He decided to travel by Greyhound Bus because his car was not likely to make the trip. After a few days, I went downtown to pick him up at the station. He was so excited to tell me about his trip. He had a lot of time to think while away. Robert told me he loved me and wanted to spend the rest of his life with me.

He said, "This is kind of goofy, but I thought since I decided on this trip, I want to give you something to commemorate the occasion." He reached into his satchel and handed me a miniature Greyhound bus. I accepted that this would serve as my engagement "gift." Yes, it was goofy, but at least he had experienced a breakthrough.

A couple of months passed, and Robert received word that his sister was getting married. He was very excited to take me with him to Philadelphia. I had learned that Robert was from New Jersey, very near Philadelphia. However, he claimed all things Philadelphian or Pennsylvanian—the NFL Eagles, cheese steaks and Rolling Rock. There was Hershey and the famous Hershey Hotel. This is where he decided we would stay when we visited for his sister's wedding. We arrived at the hotel and settled in. He could not wait to connect with his two sisters and his mom, who was also in town for the wedding. I was anxious to meet his family, especially in light of our marriage plans. He asked me to stay behind while he went to "assess" the situation with the family. I was not sure what this meant, but I knew he had concerns about his mother's discomfort with our relationship—this was not a secret, but we chose to ignore it and move forward in our relationship. Now that we were all in the same town and had traveled such a distance, I knew we would finally meet.

Robert returned later that evening. I was in the bar listening to a local band and enjoying a bottle of wine. I met an incredible woman named Domino. Her spirit was infectious, and we had a blast, hanging out in the lobby bar for almost three hours. I introduced Robert as my fiancé. He joined the two of us, and she shared stories of her life. Domino lived in Domino Apartments on Domino Lane. I asked her to prove it, and she showed me her driver's license. Domino and I vowed to stay in touch, and she asked for an invitation to our wedding, which I promised to send.

Robert and I retreated to our hotel room, where he broke the news that his sister did not invite me to her wedding. I thought I must have heard something wrong. Did Robert say I could not attend the wedding? I was pissed off. How have I come this far, and I'm not invited to the wedding? Robert said that his mother shared that she "…did not care to meet the n***" and his sister was concerned that her brother and his Black fiancée would get more attention at her wedding than she and her husband. I could not believe this. All I could think was, what kind of a man is this? Where are his guts to stand up and do the right thing? The right thing for him was to allow his sister the benefit of no drama on her wedding day. Therefore, I spent my entire time in Philadelphia at the Hershey Hotel. I did not meet his sisters and, more importantly, his mother.

I was glad to return to Indiana. A letter had arrived from the Missouri Commission on Human Rights, and it noted that they had settled. They gave me exactly what I asked for and doubled my vacation pay. The investigation uncovered a host of issues. I later heard my former employer fired the store manager for perpetrating fraud involving prom dresses. There was a regional competition, and the store director that sold the most dresses would win a significant gift, like a cruise or something. This woman had all her young employees tell their friends to come and buy their dresses at her store. When the store was out of a design, she ordered it shipped from a sister store. She sold so many dresses that they declared her the winner until the dresses started returning after prom. What a story! This was poetic justice, and I figured this must be the last laugh.

Wedding Preparations

The time had come for us to set a wedding date. Robert decided that he wanted to get married on his birthday, December 15th. I looked at the calendar and discovered that the 15th was a weekday. Thus, we would need to get married on the 17th if we were going to have the wedding in St. Louis so my family could attend. His family was his two sisters and his mother. I was not going to hold my breath that any of them would attend, so we agreed to the 17th.

I spent months planning our wedding. My colleagues at Ivy Tech had become great friends, and they offered to assist. One friend was a tailor. When she overheard me discussing my concerns regarding the gaudy styles and prices of bridesmaids' dresses, she volunteered to make them if I could pay for the fabric. Seemingly, out of nowhere, one of my cousins connected me with a fabric store, and I was able to purchase velvet for less than half price. My Maid of Honor would be Dana, my best friend in Lafayette and the other bridesmaids would be my sisters, Lorie and Lacy, Doni and Nancy, my closest friend from high school. They each sent their measurements, and the gowns were beautifully made, fitting them perfectly.

My father's sister, Aunt Etta, served as my wedding planner and recommended her pastor conduct the wedding ceremony. This worked well because I had no church connection in St. Louis and no idea who might officiate the ceremony. Robert and I were required to meet with the pastor a few times before the wedding for pre-marital counseling. After the final session, the pastor concluded that we had successfully met the requirements.

We had a lovely church wedding and attended a short post-marriage counseling session with the pastor, a requirement of all couples he married. There was a great turnout of relatives on both sides of my family. I was surprised that Robert's sister Mary and her husband Dan attended. He had another sister who did not attend, and neither did his mother, and I honestly never expected she would. Even Domino from the Domino Apartments in Philadelphia attended our wedding, just as she promised. We honeymooned in New Orleans. It was a great week, and I felt more secure than I had in a long time.

Another Wedding Surprise

With our wedding behind us, we returned to Indiana and work. Robert joined a colleague and began assistant coaching the Purdue ice hockey team. I attended games when possible, having never been a hockey fan and knowing nothing of the sport. Many games went late into the evening and the time spent waiting on the team after games was more than I expected. There were many team cookouts, and hockey became near and dear to Robert, giving him a greater sense of purpose and appreciation.

I received a call that my mother was going to be married to James, a man she met while living in the group home. My Aunt Lucille planned to host the wedding at her home, and Robert and I made plans to attend. The wedding was on a Saturday following a Friday night playoff game for the hockey team. Since the game was just outside of Indianapolis, about an hour's drive from Lafayette, Robert and I agreed to follow the team bus and drive to St. Louis that night after the game. This plan also put us about an hour closer to St. Louis than leaving from Lafayette. Meteorologists predicted snow, but we figured we would have sufficient time to get ahead of the weather.

As the game progressed, it began to flurry. I was so happy when the game ended because we needed to get on the road. It was almost 10:30 pm. We headed down the freeway, and the weather became noticeably worse. The snow was coming down hard, and Robert was driving. Large eighteen-wheelers zoomed past us, and we experienced whiteout conditions. At one point, Robert hit a patch of ice, and the car began skidding and turning. There were so many trucks! I called on God for help, and the car stopped spinning, just short of hitting the guardrail.

We now faced oncoming traffic. All we could do was wait for the oncoming traffic to pass. Once the traffic passed, Robert turned the vehicle around, and I insisted that we get off the freeway, find a hotel and see what the morning would bring. It was so late that I feared for our lives had we proceeded under the snowy conditions. Robert agreed; we exited the freeway and found a place to stay. That morning, we decided to return to Lafayette.

Lacy told me that Momma's wedding was beautiful. I was sorry to have missed it, but I did not regret our decision. Since Momma and James were both state wards and could live independently with case management services, their case management team relocated them to an apartment near

"God is our refuge and strength, a very present help in trouble. Therefore we will not fear though the earth gives way, though the mountains be moved into the heart of the sea."

PSALM 46:1-2

downtown St. Louis. James had several children, and Momma was his second wife. Other than that, we knew very little about him, except that he also had a mental condition with an unknown diagnosis.

We Gain a Roommate

During subsequent visits to St. Louis, Robert and I spent a lot of time with my brother Sam, Junior. He was about twenty-three years old and had trouble with St. Louis' law enforcement system. Sam was a very smart young man, and Robert and I talked about his life, figuring that if he could get away from St. Louis's urban street life, he might have a chance for a better future. Having become an expert on college admissions and financial aid because of my work at Ivy Tech, I knew that even without a high school diploma, Sam could test for the "Ability to Benefit" provision, which would allow him to receive financial assistance for classes while working on his General Equivalency Diploma (GED). He would sleep on our living room couch, which would impede our privacy. The matter of privacy did not seem to matter that much—our sexual relations were not regular, not even monthly, by that time in our marriage. Robert resented any attempts to discuss the matter of intercourse, so I avoided the subject altogether. We agreed to move my brother to Lafayette and explained to him, he had limited time to obtain his GED, enroll in school, find a job and a place of his own.

Having another adult male in our small apartment was awkward. Robert took it in stride, and I used Sam's presence to rationalize Robert's lack of intimate relations with me. My brother slept on our couch for about four months. With Sam's move out of our efficiency, I hoped that Robert and I would reconnect. I felt our marriage was one of convenience, like roommates—sharing bills and sharing a bed. Perhaps, we were more like siblings.

Robert continued to binge drink. On Sunday, he realized that we were out of Jim Beam, and he wanted a drink. He left home and returned with a plastic vial. He mixed the contents in the vial with coke. I asked him what it was, and he explained that it was pure alcohol from the lab—grain alcohol or whatever it was they used when conducting experiments. He was so desperate for a drink; he resorted to drinking what amounted to poison.

Robert visited the lab every day of the week and worked long hours. He was nearing the end of his post-doctoral research assignment, and it was time for him to seek a permanent position. He had published several papers and established himself as a talented young scientist. Robert achieved this despite his alcohol use and abuse, and I convinced myself that he was not an alcoholic.

Alcoholics could not achieve what he had achieved. I also had the misguided notion that alcoholics did not go to work every day. I had a couple of uncles, who were *true* alcoholics, and I never saw Robert in the state that I had seen men who were stumbling drunks and could not keep a job.

Finally, A Permanent Position (Things Will be Getting Better...)

By now, we were financially strapped. Robert had accumulated student loans, as had I, but he avoided arranging to pay them. I was repaying mine, and between my car note and entertaining others, we did not have excess money to cover unplanned expenses or emergency purchases. Robert told me things would improve once he obtained a permanent position. I could not wait for that time, as life was not good. Robert became increasingly hotheaded and aggressive with his colleagues. He found joy in bringing up polarizing issues to instigate debates. Politics and religion were his favorite buttons to push. The discussions typically ended with him cursing out one of our guests, which usually ended the evening's get-together.

Robert's colleagues began applying for jobs, and each received multiple offers. Robert started his application process about eight months behind the others. He applied at several universities and interviewed at three or four. Unlike his colleagues, Robert received *one* offer. He was so smart. What happened? I figured the interview committee must have sensed that he was a difficult person. Robert was a heavy smoker, which I was sure he would neither hide nor temper. I wondered if the interviewers sensed his affinity for consuming alcohol. Whatever the case, he received one offer. As a result, we would relocate to El Paso, Texas, where Robert earned the position of assistant professor at the University of Texas at El Paso (UTEP). The position came complete with a laboratory, an equipment budget and student assistants. I thought my career was going fairly well after a few years in Indiana, and I could not imagine what I would do in El Paso.

In the early summer of 1992, I began to look for jobs in El Paso. I made a few cold calls to the UTEP Admissions Office, hoping that I could transfer seamlessly to a similar position as Ivy Tech's recruitment coordinator. The admissions director informed me that there were no openings. The more I learned about El Paso, the more I heard that one needed to speak Spanish to get a job. All I could think about was the slim chance of my being hired with my less-than-perfect Spanish while competing with residents, most of whom were fully bilingual in English and Spanish. I was very concerned about my job prospects in El Paso.

I was a member of the Exchange Club in Lafayette and discovered that there were three clubs in El Paso. In 1911, a Detroit businessperson founded the Exchange Club as he wanted to exchange ideas for making his community better. Today, the National Exchange Club has, as its major goal, to eliminate child abuse. I became a member of the Downtown club in Lafayette shortly after presenting to its members about Ivy Tech's academic programs. The Lafayette club had no African American members, and the average age was over fifty. There were also no women in the club, but that did not deter me. I graciously accepted their nomination for membership and became a very active, engaged member.

I was hopeful that with three Exchange Club chapters in El Paso, I might be able to make a local connection. I sent letters of introduction to the three, explained my plans to relocate in the coming months, and noted my interest in learning more about their projects and opportunities to transfer my membership. Two months passed, and I heard back from none of the clubs. About a month before the move, I received a call from a woman who said she worked with one of the local clubs. She was excited to speak with me and said her club would welcome my membership. She asked where I would be living, and I explained that Robert and I had not made that determination. She was good friends with a realtor and promised to reach out to him to enlist his support in finding options for us.

I shared this conversation with Robert, and he told me that the UTEP Biology Department Chair had agreed to pay for a trip for either Robert or me to look for a place to live. The search team had previously arranged a tour of homes for Robert when he interviewed for the job. We were not in a position to purchase a home. We agreed that I would make the trip. I made the travel and lodging arrangements and planned to connect with the El Paso Exchange Club representative. When I landed in El Paso, she picked me up at the airport and took great care to make me feel welcome and comfortable. I met the realtor the next day. After considering a couple of options, I decided on a duplex on the west side of town, where most University faculty and staff lived.

With housing now squared away, it was time to complete our packing and move. We rented a Ryder truck, hitched the Grand Am to the back, and started our long drive to the southwest. I used my final paycheck to cover the relocation expenses. We left on a wing and a prayer. It was a very long drive, and we decided it was best to stay on the major freeways. Thus, after leaving Indiana, we connected to I-40 West which dumped into I-30 West, proceeded to I-20 West and finally to I-10 West. Somewhere between Interstates 20 and 10, the muffler fell off the truck and we waited hours for a repair. Once repaired, we were back on the road. There was nothing between I-20 and I-10 and the green trees gave way to desert foliage, big skies, and mountains in the distance. We arrived safely in El Paso and made our way to the duplex.

El Paso's mountains, sunrises and sunsets were most beautiful from the west side. Life seemed to improve overnight. Those first few mornings, drinking coffee on the back porch and smelling the fresh desert air up high on Belvidere Street was exhilarating. Although I did not have a job, I had plenty of work to do for the first few weeks, organizing the duplex. I was comforted knowing that Robert finally had his job with all the benefits that came with it, and I looked forward to our improved relationship. Robert had reminded me, year after year, that things would get better once he completed the post-doc and obtained a faculty appointment.

A New Job: The Lord Works in Mysterious Ways

Once the unpacking and organizing was complete, I began to seek employment. Robert told me that he ran into a Vice President who had a copy of my resume. He had no idea how the Vice President got it, but someone had passed it on and shared it with folks in the Biology Department. Robert suggested that I take the opportunity to send the Vice President an updated resume with our new, local address and thank him for any assistance he might provide. I followed up as suggested.

My job search continued, and I went to El Paso Community College and applied for a position in their "Women in Technology" program. I visited the YWCA to apply for a vacancy in their Teen Leadership Department, and I traveled to New Mexico State University (NMSU) to apply for a counseling position in their Upward Bound Program. Having had success with temporary service agencies in Indiana, I also visited a local placement agency and left an application and resume. I received a call back from NMSU and was invited to interview for their Upward Bound vacancy. I decided to visit the UTEP Upward Bound Office to gather materials on the program in preparation for the NMSU interview.

Upward Bound was one of five "TRIO" programs that resulted from the "War on Poverty," declared by President Lyndon B. Johnson in his January 8, 1964, State of the Union Address. At that time, the United States had a national poverty rate of nineteen percent[8] , and President Johnson pledged to create a

---

8   Retrieved December 10, 2014, from http://en.wikipedia.org/wiki/War_on_Poverty

"Great Society." The goals of Great Society programs included addressing historical and pervasive racial injustices and ensuring educational opportunities for all Americans. All TRIO Programs supported the development of skills and access to resources necessary to ensure college enrollment and completion among low-income students whose parents had not attained a bachelor's degree. In addition to Upward Bound, other programs included Educational Talent Search, Educational Opportunity Centers, Student Support Services and the Ronald E. McNair Post-Baccalaureate Achievement Program, which assisted eligible students in preparing for and enrolling in doctoral studies. TRIO received its name based on its original three programs (Upward Bound, Talent Search and Student Support Services). Since that time, the legislative mandate added other programs. Head Start and Job Corps were also War on Poverty initiatives and continue today.

Even though NMSU was a thirty-plus-mile commute to Las Cruces, New Mexico, I was committed to obtaining work in my field. On the day of my interview, I arrived and made my way to the Upward Bound Office, where I interviewed with four people. I could not wrap my head around the awkward sense I felt, but it never left. It was as though the team was merely going through the motions. After the hiring committee assessed my background, the focus shifted from my qualifications as an academic counselor to my ability to spend the night on campus (Monday – Friday during the summer months) in a residence hall with high school students who annually participated in their Upward Bound summer, on-campus, residential experience. I explained my marriage of only two years, and my willingness to get up very early and leave late. I would not spend the night. I knew I was not a favored candidate, but I was confident I had given it my best shot.

About six weeks passed, and I received a phone call from the same UTEP admissions officer I had contacted while making cold calls in Indiana. He explained that several positions were open and that his supervisor, the Vice President, asked him to be sure that I was aware of the opportunities and encouraged me to apply. This was a remarkable turn of events! I applied for two positions: Director of Upward Bound and Director of the High School Equivalency Program (HEP). I thought, *What an interesting coincidence that I was turned down for an Upward Bound counselor position at NMSU, but I am applying to be the director at UTEP.* I certainly felt more prepared for the Upward Bound position due to the need for Spanish language fluency in HEP, which focused on helping migrant and seasonal farmworkers to obtain a GED. Even though I spoke Spanish, I previously had little opportunity to use this skill in Indiana. Spanish was also required for Upward Bound. Still, unlike HEP students, most Upward Bound students were bilingual in English and Spanish, and I figured I could manage basic conversations with parents, as needed.

Following interviews, required writing samples and reference checks, UTEP hired me in October 1992 to direct Upward Bound. I phoned my colleagues in Indiana to let them know they may be receiving calls from UTEP hiring officials.

The administrative assistant for the Student Services Division proclaimed, "Yeah, they already called! There was a gentleman named 'Javier,' and I talked to him too."

I gasped, and my thoughts spiraled. "*You* talked to him? What did you say?"

She continued, "I told him you did all the recruiting and that you did a great job helping to increase enrollment and that the students liked you. I'm sure you're going to get the job." I did not understand how the assistant took the call. She was not on my application and not someone I would have considered for a reference. I thanked God that I had never had ill words with her. It was definitely in God's hands, and I believed it would be so if I were destined to be the Upward Bound Director.

I was relieved when the UTEP Vice President offered me the position of Upward Bound Director. My staff included a coordinator, counselor and secretary. In addition to the three full-time employees, six part-time instructors led the Upward Bound Saturday and summer academies. My first order of business was to understand the program's operations and status relative to meeting federal performance standards. I immersed myself in reviewing the approved application and Federal Regulations that governed program implementation. I also reviewed financial records and spent significant time reviewing participants' files, which were incomplete in most instances. There was no database of electronic records; I purchased a program to build electronic files, to run a report of required but missing documents.

I immediately discovered my next project as the main office computer was too old to accept the software. Purchasing a new computer required federal approval. In the interim, I reviewed our provision of services to assess if they aligned with those proposed in the grant, and if they were allowable, per program regulations. I held weekly meetings and staff put forth a united resistance to my inquiries—I challenged their assumptions regarding our best approach to addressing participants' academic challenges during the limited time they were with us. These discussions were difficult, and staff resisted the changes needed.

When my new computer arrived, I built a student records database and spent a lot of time reviewing records in the secretary's office. She was frustrated with my level of involvement and scrutiny of records. Still, because this was a federal program and I was ultimately responsible, I had to be certain we were serving eligible students, and I discovered more than a few who did not meet the required criteria. She quit, forcing me to enter all records into the new database, myself. I could not delay the process by waiting for another secretary.

After entering records, I ran a report, met with staff, and shared findings and next steps. I developed a series of form letters, noting missing items required to remain in the program. After the third attempt with no response, those students with incomplete files were exited from the program—they had already stopped attending. It was a difficult, first six months in my new job. Still, I found comfort in knowing that I had improved the program's technology, written communications and our capacity to track and report services. Accepting eligible students and knowing we were compliant brought me satisfaction.

Chapter Eight

LIFE IN WEST TEXAS

The Art of Entertaining

Robert had settled into teaching and was enjoying the process of ordering lab equipment. His colleagues invited us to their homes, and we joined department functions at the Chair's home. Robert also invited folks over to our place, several times per week. He was an excellent cook and prepared meals three to four times per week. Our guests were mostly students who worked in Robert's lab and did not judge his excessive drinking. As was typical, after many drinks and a great meal, combative Robert arrived with his bag of explosives. Indiana Robert, who promised things would get better when he got a job, was now manifesting himself in Texas. It was like replaying a lousy movie—it would not be long before the fun ended, and our guests realized the party was over.

Work did not improve Robert; it only emboldened him to be more of an ass, yelling "f@#k you" to our guests as he disagreed with their positions on hot-button issues. Our guests never seemed to take it personally. I accepted his embarrassing behavior and went along with this weekly routine, as Robert seemed more ready for intimacy after the drunken dinner parties. Though I hoped for *any* level of intimacy with my husband, nothing happened in the bedroom (nor any other room) ninety-five percent of the time.

An Unlikely Solution

Our intimate relations became even more distant and far between, averaging once every four months. Arguing about it widened the wedge between us, and rather than set the stage for "the sex talk" nightly, we resorted to sleeping in separate rooms. Though disconnected I was committed to trying to make it work. I thought, perhaps I would feel more fulfilled if I could have a baby… (*I know, don't scream*). Robert avoided baby conversations, noting he might not be a good father. He bemoaned his lack of relationship with his father, which became a mirror of himself. Then, in a manner akin to the awakening he must have experienced when he decided to ask me to marry him, he had an epiphany. Out of the blue he said he had been thinking about my desire for a child.

"I think a child between us will be wonderful, and I would love to have a little girl," he said. What? Just like that, he wanted to have a little girl. I did not worry about the consequence of not having a girl; I went with his vision and imagined a little girl for us.

Robert was serious about the baby. We began to have regular discussions about children, perhaps more for me than for him. I stopped taking the birth control pill and began to track my ovulation cycle. Of course, one cannot make a baby if you are not doing it, so I tried to focus the few times we met sexually, annually, on the times when there was a greater likelihood that I might become pregnant. He was drinking often and heavily, and he would pass out following the laughing, joking and debates during our weekly dinners.

After so many missed opportunities to have sex because of Robert's drinking and passing out, I began to question whether he was avoiding me, and faking his desire for a child. He was clearly avoiding intercourse. I worried that he no longer found me attractive or desirable. My self-esteem tanked, and I threw myself into work as a matter of productivity and to better use the space that had grown in my brain where Robert was concerned. Our routine conversations, discussions that I thought were rational and necessary, turned to screaming, cursing and ugly words on his part. I needed to understand how he proposed we might make a baby when he made neither the time nor effort for sexual relations.

"What, you wanna f@#k? Fine, let's go f@#k!" he screamed. As one might imagine, this did wonders for setting the romantic mood, so I walked away, crawled into the bed in my room, and cried inside the silent sadness.

Another Promise to Save the Marriage

I was miserable. Even though my job was great, I increasingly disconnected from my life at home. I told Robert we should seek marital counseling because I felt we were losing our marriage. Then came the next promise—he promised that things would get better when he achieved tenure. What? I was sick of promises—first, it was the post-doc, then the job, and now, tenure. So, now I must pray and hope he gets tenure, *someday*? I resigned myself to the fact that things would never get better without counseling, which he was unwilling to consider; thus, I decided to focus on myself and what *I* wanted. I realized how much I had sacrificed and given up having a relationship with this man. I had grown apart from my family, friends, God…all the things that mattered most in my life. I began to accept invitations from almost anyone, to do *anything*. I needed exposure to living outside of 1520-B Belvidere. I needed Robert to experience me, increasingly disconnecting from the marriage. I hoped he would wake up to the reality that we needed help.

I became more involved with the El Paso Exchange Club and became President. The Club's membership grew. We hosted an awesome annual golf tournament featuring players from several National Football League (NFL) teams. The golf event raised money to support our local Exchange Club Child Abuse Prevention Center. In my quest to take advantage of every opportunity to be out of the house, I started hanging out with one of the new members, who recognized that Robert had major issues. She insisted that we seek counseling. If I stayed, she painted a picture of gloom and doom for my life, so I pressed Robert that counseling was the only way forward. I threatened to leave the marriage if he refused. I was spending so much time away from him, he saw and felt my disinterest in his needs and wants. He agreed to counseling but insisted on a male because he did not want "two women to double-team" him.

A Marriage Counselor to the Rescue

During our first few counseling sessions, Robert struggled to discuss his past. He only wanted to discuss the here and now, and our mutual baggage relative to making the marriage work. As the counselor slowly forced him to open up, I saw how Robert's repressed feelings affected his approach to the world. He hated the sessions and resented the male therapist. Robert could not rationalize why we were in this situation. On the other hand, I held nothing back. I shared all my thoughts and concerns about him and our marriage. I had nothing to lose and much to gain if Robert and I could become better, together.

Robert showed himself to be a real victim of *something*. I realized that I was far stronger. Robert blamed everyone closest to him for all of his problems; he never once reflected on his shortcomings. Either the alcoholic father or the mother forced him to be the man of the house. It was his selfish sisters or me, the pushy wife, who lacked an understanding of the pressures of his work. Then, something amazing happened. As I sat quietly, listening to Robert's excuses for the miserable life he had created, the counselor figured it out. He said that he needed to work one on one, with Robert. I was not surprised. I felt vindicated, as I knew Robert had real problems, and now, so did a psychologist. The doctor thanked me for participating, suggested he may need to bring me back at some future point, and wished me well. He invited Robert to make an individual appointment.

Robert was furious after that last counseling session. He mocked the doctor, asserting that he did not need any counseling. Robert drank the rest of the day and eventually passed out on the couch. I sat there, listening to him snore—a drunken, weak and sorry man. That is whom I married. I could never fall asleep angry, so I woke him and told him that we needed to talk. He cursed and yelled. Unwilling to talk, he jumped up angrily from the couch as I proceeded to press him. He continued toward his bedroom and noticed my picture on the wall in the hallway. He punched a hole in the wall next to my picture. That was it—the final straw. I was no fool and certainly would no longer be his victim. His violence might not be against a wall next time, it might be against me. I had no choice but to leave.

> "For I know the plans I have for you," declares the LORD, "plans to prosper you and not to harm you, plans to give you hope and a future. Then you will call on me and come and pray to me, and I will listen to you. You will seek me and find me when you seek me with all your heart."
>
> JEREMIAH 29:11-13

I knew I was not the problem, and I knew I would get through what was bound to be a major life event. I called my friend from the Exchange Club, and she invited me to stay in her guest room. If I did not have a place to go, I do not know that I would have ever gotten the courage to leave Robert. Thankfully, the door opened on the opportunity, and I walked through it. Robert entered his room after punching the wall and passed out, again. I gathered as much clothing as possible and any very personal items and left. I would not return. Within the week, I filed for divorce, and he received notice. It was April of 1994. I didn't know it at the time, but God's plan was already unfolding for my future. As I was losing my husband, a man I had not met was losing his mother to death, and his wife due to lies and deceit.

When Robert received the divorce papers, he called me, screaming at the top of his lungs. He didn't know where my friend lived, he threatened to kill her, knowing she gave me the confidence to leave. He refused to sign the divorce papers. He called constantly for the first couple of days. I wondered about his mental stability. I thanked God that Robert did not bring our fight to the University. His concern that someone might know his business helped ensure this would never happen.

We All Make Bad Decisions After Traumatic Events... Don't We?

Shortly after I left Robert, I began to work on my independence. Robert and I had always filed separate tax returns, despite being married. A major factor was Robert's refusal to pay for his student loans. As this became more problematic, the IRS started to withhold any potential returns due to him. Robert did not want my return and his combined. As weeks and months passed, I continued to work on myself, rebuilding my self-esteem and discovering what mattered to me as an individual.

I recalled one of Robert's statements on our financial position, "We'll never have or afford a Cadillac." I never understood his fascination with the Cadillac, except that in his mind, it represented status. Though the discussions about the Cadillac seemed so pitiful to me then, they inspired me to prove I could have anything I wanted on my own.

I could care less about a Cadillac, but owning one became my driving desire. I visited the dealer and set my sights on the most beautiful, expensive Cadillac I could find. Its color was money green, and it had a cream-colored leather interior. Chromed wheels, a sunroof and a 32-V NorthStar engine. It was eye-catching, and it was mine for the price of a monthly home mortgage. No matter. I had no kids, no major expenses aside from my student loan, and I was an independent woman who could do whatever I set my mind to do. With a new car, Robert could not easily spot me.

With a new car and my mind set on new adventures, I began traveling with the club and even took a trip to St. Louis to attend my family reunion. I was beginning to find myself. I bought new clothes and changed my style. I learned about a talented psychic who was *the real deal* and began seeing her monthly. She offered great insights into Robert's life, and she told me that he would be dead by fifty years of age if he did not stop drinking. She also asked me about a man in the military and explained that she saw me with a man who was in or connected to the military. Even though I knew no one who fit that category, the thought of dating again became a reality, and I was, once again, very hopeful for my future. I attended events in El Paso's African American community and met new people, including artists and musicians who would become lifelong friends and colleagues. The stronger and more confident I became, the less I concerned myself with Robert's wrath. The longer I stayed away and avoided him altogether, the more he seemed to settle into his life without me. Life was good, and I began to realize the need to find an apartment of my own.

Time to Focus

After directing Upward Bound for two years, it was time to write the competitive grant for future funding. My need for a place of my own became more urgent. Upward Bound's future was contingent upon the University's successful performance during a national competitive proposal process. UTEP's performance was contingent on my efforts. I had never written a grant, and the average length of the grant applications was one hundred fifty pages! Many directors simply dusted off their old applications, added up-to-date statistics and turned them in. I prepared for the grant-writing process by attending training sessions hosted by the U.S. Department of Education and The Council for Opportunity in Education, a professional TRIO training and advocacy group.

Grant trainers warned program directors of possible new requirements and a rewrite of the program's regulations. They urged us to be certain of having the latest information. I paid close attention to the discussions surrounding potential regulatory changes. The Department of Education released the new TRIO Federal Regulations, with significant changes. Whereas in the past, a college or eligible program entity could submit only one Upward Bound grant per institution, the new Regulations allowed eligible entities to host more than one Upward Bound Program if they were serving "different populations." This had huge implications, so I set out to understand what defined different populations.

The UTEP Upward Bound program served about sixty-five kids throughout El Paso County for many years. At most, perhaps two kids were participating from each school. Per the new rules, the U.S. Department of Education wanted a greater impact in each of the partner schools. As I learned more, I was convinced that one could consider different school districts as different populations. I visited with our program officer in Washington, DC, and he cautioned that my premise could be correct; however, he did not want to guarantee that interpretation.

One of my biggest gripes in managing the Upward Bound program was that in cities where there were many colleges and other eligible institutions (e.g., Dallas, Austin, Houston), there were many Upward Bound programs serving thousands of eligible high school students. In El Paso, there was UTEP and El Paso Community College. Each institution had a program, and each served about sixty-five kids. With each three-year grant competition, if we were successful, we might add another five kids to the number served by each program.

Another new and welcome rule was institutions that successfully met the goals and outcomes of their current funded grant would be eligible for up to fifteen prior experience points. Because new programs were not eligible to receive prior experience, this bonus provided continuity for existing, successful programs. I convinced UTEP administrators that we had a great opportunity to expand our service from sixty-five kids to more than 115 by separating the districts in our current service area and submitting two applications. With this plan came a significant risk—we had to decide which of the two programs would receive prior experience and which would be a new application and, therefore, not eligible for prior experience. New applications would have to be very strong, and my second proposal would need to stand on its merit for the Department to fund both. Despite the risk of losing a portion of the community should the new application not receive funding, there was a greater risk of submitting the grant application in its current form to serve the entire county. Grant trainers had also warned Directors that the interest of the Department of Education officials was on smaller target areas whereby they could achieve a greater impact. The days of having one or two students from an entire school were over.

TRIO Program grants were notoriously competitive, with new programs typically scoring ninety-six to ninety-eight of a possible 100 points. I needed to develop and write two grant applications. I stressed over the application because of the added risk of losing the program for half the area we were currently serving. Success was my only option. To focus my energies, I sought an affordable place where I could live quietly and alone. Most of my check was going to the mortgage I drove. I went to the Warren Inn in Mesa. It was close to work, affordable, payable by the week or month, and no long-term contract was required. I continued to rely on my instincts and became increasingly grounded that I was on the right track with writing two applications.

By this time in my life, I increasingly trusted my instincts. Older adults in my family and the community described me as having a gift of discernment. Discernment is a Christian virtue whereby people known to possess it are able to make wise, nuanced decisions, sometimes with limited information. I trusted my plans and decisions, and I spent a lot of time reflecting and praying for God's guidance. I paid attention to the details and signs surrounding my decision-making to ensure I was not missing something God might be trying to tell me.

I arrived at the Warren Inn and went to the office to sign the rental agreement. A nice woman greeted me and told me I could move in immediately. Even more surprising was what she said next.

"You are being assigned apartment 123."

Wow, 123? What an amazing number! There was a message in that for me, a message of order. Not only did I see the order in my apartment number, but I also saw and

> "We have different gifts, according to the grace given to each of us. If your gift is prophesying, then prophesy in accordance with your faith: if it is serving, then serve: if it is teaching, then teach: if it is to encourage, then give encouragement: if it is giving, then give generously: if it is to lead, do it diligently: if it is to show mercy, do it cheerfully."
>
> ROMANS 12:6–8

understood the meaning of a new beginning. I felt great about my new little efficiency apartment and realized that I had never lived alone except for a few months in college. My life was about to begin. Things were falling into their proper place, both figuratively and literally. It was almost August of 1994. Now, I just needed Robert to sign the divorce papers.

Robert told me after I left him, "No one will ever love you the way I do, and I'm not going to sign divorce papers, and have you end up with someone who doesn't love you." I was at a loss—I did not want anyone to "love me the way he did." More than anything, I just wanted someone to admire and respect me and to make me feel like a beautiful woman—a queen, and above all, *safe*. I also wanted someone who knew and honored God, which was certainly not the case with Robert. I always believed that a husband and wife should attend church together. Moving forward, a man who loved God and desired to practice Christianity with me was an important factor in my life.

I thought back to the news reports I had heard years prior regarding there being little to no Black men available for educated, progressive Black women. I realized that I no longer cared about news reports. I just wanted a strong, confident and *good* man. I wanted to feel secure. I wanted the comfort of knowing that my man protected me. I hated feeling that I was the stronger person, feeling *I* needed to protect *him*. It was clear that I was stronger than Robert, which played into every aspect of my leaving him. I left him everything in our home because I did not want to upset his world further. I believed he would fall apart if anyone disrupted his "stuff." I knew that I could rebuild and recapture those things in time—I was a survivor who had been on my own before, with no answers and no particular place to go. I knew that I would be okay.

Since Robert would not sign the divorce papers, I decided to open myself to a future relationship. I still desperately wanted kids, and I was now pushing thirty years of age. I made up my mind that I had no time to waste trying to change a man who did not want to change—Robert proved how fruitless that process could be. I would go forward, seeking what I wanted. I would not settle again for a man who gave me the wrong answer when asked about life's important subjects. No matter how smart, successful, handsome, or a suitor's superficial characteristics, in discovering the new man for me, I would not second-guess it if I didn't like his answer. I would deem him an inappropriate match for me and quickly move on. I gave up the notion that a woman can make a man change. No more "things will get better when…" for me. I wanted a man who was the *truth* and one who would appreciate my straightforward and candid approach to life.

Dreams, Dreams, I Can't Shake the Dreams

The more I spent time in apartment 123, the more I began to dream while sleeping. Since childhood, I experienced vivid dreams, some scary and others quite silly, but I never thought the dreams had a point or connection. That changed when I married Robert. After our marriage, I began to experience a recurring dream. The storyline surrounding the dream would change, but the outcome was the same—me looking into the face of a storm and running like mad down a basement staircase to find shelter. Many times, the stairs took the form of the stairs at Big Daddy's house. His basement could only be accessed from the outside; thus, one needed to get there quickly in the event of a tornado warning. My dreams of violent storms and running to the basement for safe shelter were routine during my years with Robert.

I had a new storm dream. My sisters and other family members were scattered about a hotel, and a major storm was on the horizon. In the dream, I was running all over the place to gather them together. There was an entire wall made of glass on the ground floor, and I led them up the stairs away from the glassed area, even though the lower floor seemed to be the logical place during a tornado. In the dream, I knew we had to go up the stairs, so we did that. I awoke before the storm hit. The more I dreamed, the more I tried to make sense of my dreams and find meaning. What hit me between the eyes was the fact that never in my life of dreaming storms had I dreamed of running *up* a staircase to safety. I was not only shocked but also inspired to purchase a dream dictionary.

As I researched the significance of the stairs I had dreamed of for many years, I learned that running down a staircase was symbolic of losing oneself. Running up a staircase meant that one was finding herself or gaining control of their life or circumstances. Wow, what a breakthrough! It made so much sense. I had dreamed of storms throughout my marriage with Robert. The more time I spent with him, the more I lost myself to those things that mattered most. Now, I was finding myself, both figuratively and literally, for the first time. Being alone in apartment 123 allowed so much time for reflection and soul searching. I knew I was on the right track, and nothing was more empowering. I was finding myself again.

I continued to spend time with my Exchange Club friends and the rest of my time was devoted to research and grant writing. Dolores, my administrative assistant, told me she dreamed she was holding a baby, bouncing a beautiful little girl on her knees.

The child had lovely, curly hair and she asked the baby, "Whose little girl are you?" Dolores then told me that it was *my* little girl. I could not imagine where this little girl would come from, especially since there was no man to think of relative to my having a relationship that would lead to a baby. Dolores had proven herself a woman of God, humble, prayerful and always giving herself to others, and I trusted her wisdom and counsel. I prayed that she was right. I prayed that God would answer my prayers and bless me with a child.

I completed my grant applications and successfully submitted them both. Christmas 1994 came and went. Shortly after the New Year, I was spending time at the home of a very active couple in the Exchange Club.

Their daughter interrupted, "Sandra, you're not much older than we are, you should go out with me and my friends tomorrow." Their daughter, Valerie, explained that they would go dancing at the club on Biggs Field, the home of the Army Sergeants Major Academy. On Saturday nights, El Paso's African American community frequented the club. Soldiers danced and mixed with the civilian community. I was not comfortable with the thought of going to a club.

I asked, "What time do you leave?"

Valerie responded, "Around 10 o'clock."

"In the evening?" I questioned. I told her that 10:00 pm is usually my bedtime. She insisted that 10:00 pm was not late and that I would have lots of fun.

I thought about Valerie's comment that I was not that much older. I usually spent my time with folks as much as twice my age. I liked older people and learned a great deal from their experiences. I agreed to join Valerie and her friends for their night out the following day. We agreed to meet at Valerie's (her parents' and my friend's) house for a card game with everyone. After cards, we planned to go dancing at the nightclub on Biggs Army Airfield. Valerie constantly bragged about her friend, Eric, who was in the Army. He was "so cool" and "had a little boy." He drove a "tricked out" blue Thunderbird, and many girls wanted to date him. Eric would be joining us with a few of his friends. Valerie also invited another female friend.

Chapter Nine

A NEW LOVE

The Young Soldier

I arrived at Valerie's the next day at about 6:00 pm for the card game. It was January 7, 1995. I pulled up in my Cadillac. I was completing a phone call when a young man (I assumed to be Eric) walked outside to check his car. I went inside where a group of soldiers, still in their military fatigues, and Valerie's parents played spades. As is typical in an African American home with a card game going on, it was loud, and there was a lot of trash-talking.

The card game was in full swing, and I jumped in when a spot opened. The beers flowed as soldiers told stories, traded jabs and talked trash. I noticed that Eric was neither drinking nor smoking, like the others. When offered a drink, he declined.

I looked at Eric and commented, "A young Black soldier who doesn't smoke or drink?" Eric explained that he never got into drinking and hated smoking. I thought this was very refreshing, even though I was smoking then. I made small talk with everyone. I was not accustomed to hanging out with soldiers and felt somewhat out of place, though I enjoyed the game very much.

The time came to change clothes and get ready for the club. I did not need to change. Eric went to his Thunderbird to retrieve a freshly laundered, heavily starched, multi-colored suit. He put it on, and I noticed *him*. He looked damn good. It was time to go. As we walked outside, Eric came over to admire my Cadillac.

He handed me a CD. "Check this out on the way over. This is my boy, Gerald Levert." I loaded the CD into my player.

Eric said, "Be sure to listen to track four." We agreed to trail each other to the home of another female, a friend of Valerie, who would be riding with Eric. I started the CD at track one. When we arrived at the girlfriend's house, she was not ready. Valerie expressed concern that we would not find sufficient seating for our group if we did not make our way to the club. Thus, Eric agreed to wait, and others rode with me. We made our way to the soldiers' club on Biggs Field. I had never been on base and felt like a fish out of water. Other than Valerie, I only saw strangers, wall to wall.

I was relieved when at that moment, "Urkel" walked in. His name was not Urkel, but he looked exactly like Steve Urkel, the nerd from the popular television sitcom, Family Matters. I met him at a community event. He worked on base as a civilian government employee. I was thrilled to see a familiar face, and he was pretty surprised to see me there. We decided to dance to an upbeat song. Eric finally arrived with Valerie's girlfriend. Urkel joined our group, and we talked and laughed. Urkel and I danced the entire night. Eric made fun of us because we both wore glasses, and while we were dancing, Eric took our eyeglasses and put them together, facing each other to make a statement that we were the perfect couple. Eric and I had very little to say to each other that evening as I was happily occupied with my familiar dance partner.

At the end of the evening, everyone went their separate ways, and I returned to my efficiency. I completely forgot what track I was supposed to listen to and simply let the CD play. Monday morning, Valerie phoned me at my office. She was working temporarily in the UTEP Registrar's Office. Valerie told me I had hurt her friend Eric's feelings because I would not talk to him at the club.

I responded that she must be kidding, "That guy didn't even notice me." Valerie said that he was hoping to get to know me better. What? This young soldier is interested in getting to know *me* better?

I thought she must have been dreaming until she said, "He's coming by your office because you still have his CD. He thought I had it, but I told him it was left in your car, which is at your office, so he is on the way." I asked her what track he told me to listen to, and she recalled track four. I went to my car and listened to the song "I'd Give Anything."

As I listened, I thought, "Why would he want me to listen to *this* song?" The lyrics were:

"I'm waiting for someone who can turn my life around, someone who can make me feel the way I used to feel, but she never comes…all the lovers in the world don't amount to much and what I really want is just one true love. And I'd give anything and everything to fall in love; just this one time, I'd like to find what I've been dreaming of. Well, I can find someone to hold me, but that wouldn't be enough; I give anything to fall in love."

I brought the CD into my office and suddenly felt like a teenager, waiting for a new crush to walk past in the school hallway. Eric was coming to my office, and he had my attention. I told my assistant Dolores to expect him.

About twenty minutes later, Eric showed up with one of the soldiers at the card game. I invited them into my office and shut the door, as privacy was necessary. They were both in their green battle dress uniforms (BDUs), and I looked at Eric for the *first* time. He was very handsome, well built, had a great smile and smelled good. We both blushed and engaged in small talk while his friend looked on and jumped in the conversation awkwardly from time to time.

Eric mentioned they were going to see "Brotha Man" on Friday night. Brotha Man was a character who appeared on the "Martin Show." He always entered through Martin's window and held up four fingers, introducing himself as "Brotha Man from the 5th floor."

I said, "Oh, you mean Reggie Ballard? He's coming to town this weekend?"

Eric responded, "Yes, he will be performing at The Cadillac Bar."

I continued, "I know him. We did theater together in college."

Eric said, "You don't know Brotha Man," and I replied again, "Of course I do. We went to Mizzou together where he played football, and we met in a play. He played a major character in 'A Soldier's Story.'" I suggested we all go together. Eric agreed though he still questioned my knowing Brotha Man. We agreed to meet at Valerie's house and carpool from there. With that, he asked for my business card. I wrote a note on the back of it, saying, "Call me anytime," and included my cell phone number. His friend asked for a card also, which I gave him.

Friday came, and as planned, our group met at Valerie's and carpooled, early, over to the bar where Reggie was to appear. He was already inside, and one of his promoters walked up. I gave him a card with a note that said "Honeybunch from Mizzou" was there.

Minutes later, the promoter returned and said, "He can't wait to see you and would like to hook up after the show." Eric was impressed. This professional woman was driving his favorite car, a Cadillac, and I was Brotha Man's friend. Now that Eric knew I was telling the truth, we began to chat. We pulled away from the group and found a nice corner in the front entryway of the bar, still outside, as the doors were not yet open to the public.

With each conversation topic, I liked Eric more. I recalled my vow to never settle for any man again, and I vowed I would never try to make a man become something he is not. I decided to dive further, to explore Eric more deeply. I often heard that one should not come on too strong with first dates lest she scares the man away. I had nothing to lose and no time to waste. If a person could not have a serious conversation, he certainly was not in the market for what I was looking for—a true, committed relationship. I guess our conversation was risky by most dating standards.

Eric asked me why I smoked. I told him I could quit anytime, as it was primarily social. I was never a hard-core smoker, which I picked up while acting on stage in various plays while in college, and I had continued to smoke because Robert was a heavy smoker.

I clarified to Eric, "I would quit instantly for the *right* man." He laughed and said, "Yeah, right." I expressed my sincerity and reiterated that I had no addictions and could quit whenever I decided.

Eric responded, "Well, maybe I can be that man." I took that as a positive sign that he was interested in me as much as I was interested in him. We continued to talk about our lives. Eric explained his divorce was pending and that he had custody of his two-year-old son, Jesse. Jesse was in Colorado with his grandmother, and Eric's soon-to-be ex-wife was planning to leave El Paso. I explained I also had filed for divorce eight months earlier. I failed to mention that Robert had refused to sign the papers up to this point.

Being True to Myself

Knowing that Eric already had a son and a stepdaughter from his marriage, I continued with deeper questioning. "How do you feel about more children?" I anxiously waited for his answer. At that moment, I knew the wrong answer would end things with Eric before they started. I knew that if Eric was not interested in having more children, he was not the man for me, as the opportunity to have a baby was non-negotiable. I was prepared to turn away.

Then came his answer, "I used to think I would not want more children. But, with the right woman, I guess I could have more children."

I thought, *Well, maybe I will be that right woman, and he will be my right man.* The rest of the group began to notice that we were no longer with them, but in our private space, in the front of the bar. Being in this space with Eric felt very good.

The doors to the club opened, and we found tables up front and center. Eric sat next to me, close enough for our knees to touch. We laughed, and he held my hand. I was unsure where this warmth and excitement would lead, but I was certainly taking it all in. The show was tremendous, and Brotha Man acknowledged me as his home girl from Missouri in the middle of his commentary. That was cool! Undoubtedly, I scored more points with Eric as a result.

After the show, Reggie met us as he had promised, and Eric had the opportunity to get to know him. Eric asked Reggie how he ended up in California on the Martin Show.

Reggie replied, "I was in Missouri in my apartment watching the news. It was snowing and cold, and I saw on the news it was sunny and warm in California. So, I decided at that moment that I would go there." We stood outside Reggie's limo, laughing and joking for about forty-five minutes. He autographed our posters, and we took pictures. We had a great time.

Eric rode back with me to Valerie's place, as his car was one of those we left. Valerie exited the car, and Eric played me a song. We talked in the car for another thirty minutes while sitting in front of the house. Eric asked me if he could kiss me. I was very hesitant as I knew he *hated* cigarettes. I did not want to mess things up by kissing him with cigarette breath. He leaned forward, and we kissed gently. This was my ploy to avoid an all-out kiss that might turn him off if I had cigarette breath. We said our goodbyes and agreed to speak to each other during the week. The Army had scheduled Eric to attend field training exercises with his unit that week.

Days passed, and I could not wait to hear from Eric. He called as I was taping a program at the cable company on Airport Road. Eric agreed to meet me there as he was on base only a few minutes away. I had already stopped smoking for close to a week. Eric offered to drive, and we rode together to the northeast side of Transmountain Drive. We parked in an area next to picnic and shade shelters and looked around the city. Eric looked at me and came closer. He put his hands around my waist and asked me to kiss him again. I agreed. It was explosive! That was it. I was falling fast for Eric, and I had no idea where this budding relationship was going. I only knew that Eric was strong, and when he wrapped me in his arms, I experienced a feeling I had long awaited for many years. Eric told me he spent the entire time in training thinking about me and could not wait to see me. After a bit, we headed back down the mountain. We said goodbye and agreed to see each other in a couple of days. We made plans to join a different group of my friends on Friday evening at a bar behind Clicks Billiards on El Paso's west side, on Mesa. My friends, Ethel and Michael, were older than the group Eric was accustomed to hanging with, and they thought it would be fun to hear a live band scheduled to play at Clicks on Friday.

We all agreed to meet at the bar. I was alone with my friends and other married couples. Every time I thought about Eric, my stomach fluttered with anticipation. I simply could not wait to see him. As soon as Eric walked in, I melted. He pulled a chair behind mine and wrapped his arms around my shoulders. I felt very secure as he held me for an hour, talking with my friends, laughing, and getting to know them as they got to know him. Everyone thought he was great, and so did I.

What Happens in the Hospitality Room Stays in the Hospitality Room

I was now president of the local Exchange Club, and El Paso served as the host site for its Annual Regional Conference. As club president and host committee chair, I secured lodging and conference rooms at the Marriott. During the conference, I would complete my last official duties as president. Regional leaders also voted me into a new role as president-elect of the regional association, and officials planned to induct me during the conference. As host, I had the key to the conference hospitality suite, where we held receptions and happy hours. Eric wanted to see me during one of these conference nights, so I invited him to meet me in the presidential conference suite. He came, and we talked for what seemed like an eternity. The hours passed, and even though we were both tired, we continued to talk, not wanting the night to end. About two o'clock in the morning, we pulled out the cot and laid across it, fully dressed. The hours flew by as we shared our life stories and mutual marital nightmares.

Eric's story shocked me, and I shared my story about the night Robert punched a hole in the wall next to my picture. We finally dozed off at about four and were awakened by hallway noises at about six o'clock. I began to freak out as there was another key to the hospitality suite, and I was afraid that someone might walk in on the two of us, even though we were clothed. I was concerned about the impression one might have of me as regional president-elect. We ended our night and planned to see each other again.

Eric and I became inseparable after that. We talked daily, making plans for every moment we could find to see one another, if only for an hour. I knew after his stories that his marriage was as over as mine and there was no turning back for either of us. I decided to cook dinner for him at my place, and he spent the night. I knew I would never be the same. I loved him and felt strongly he loved me too.

Our dates continued. We drove to Las Cruces on another evening to have dinner at an Italian restaurant. By now, I knew that Italian was Eric's favorite food. Our trip to Las Cruces would be like a mini getaway, an opportunity to not run into friends or have other distractions. Eric told me he needed to talk seriously with me, and the drive and dinner in Las Cruces afforded us the quiet, alone time we needed. As we quietly dined, he handed me a card, including a handwritten note saying he loved me. Eric's note filled my spirit, knowing how he felt. I shared my love for him as well. We were now about four weeks into what was proving to be a whirlwind romance. Meanwhile, Eric's divorce seemed to be racing toward a conclusion, and Eric spent much of his time away from her and gave her the space she needed to gather her belongings in the home on base. Meanwhile, I had all but given up that Robert would ever sign our divorce papers.

God Works in Mysterious Ways

About a week passed. I needed to fly to Cleveland for an Exchange Club meeting of regional presidents. Rather than leave my car at the airport, I decided to leave it with Eric. I knew he loved it and thought he would enjoy driving it during my absence. His estranged wife also left El Paso that same day. That night, Eric and I were talking by phone. He told me that he still could not relax and could not believe she was gone. After about thirty minutes, a phone call interrupted us. Eric clicked over, and I waited.

Moments later, he clicked back to me, "Shit, shit, shit!" I asked what was wrong. He said it was the Border Patrol on the other end, and they told him they had stumbled upon his wife's wreckage outside Sierra Blanca.

"My wife's wreckage? Is she dead?"

The agent responded that she was fine, but they were airlifting her back to William Beaumont Army Medical Center for evaluation. Eric would need to meet them there because she was technically his dependent until the divorce was final.

"She won't go away," he lamented. I tried to calm him down. We agreed to talk later because he had to get to the hospital. Sierra Blanca was about eighty miles east of El Paso, but the trip by air would be quick.

Eric called me a while later and explained that he would have to bring her back home and aid in her recovery for a few days. She had flipped the car several times but managed to walk away with only a few bruises and a scratched big toe. Eric explained that he did not want her back in the house. He was still angry because she had taken all of his electronics. I reminded Eric that he was a good man who always did the right thing. The right thing was to accept her back into the home as required and to do what he needed for her to get on her feet. Eric took her home and even had to bathe her because she was sore and dirtied from the accident. As Eric bathed her, he asked her about the stereo equipment. She told him that she had sold it.

The next day, Eric drove her to Sierra Blanca to get any personal belongings from the wreckage before the tow truck hauled it away. Eric expressed his shock upon seeing the wreckage—it was amazing that she survived. They recovered her belongings, and Eric hoped to find his stereo equipment. What he found made him even angrier…pawnshop tickets! She sold his equipment to a pawnshop for pennies on the dollar. Later that evening, Eric phoned and we discussed more of his ex-wife's troubled history. The car she wrecked was in Eric's name, and he received word from the insurance company that they would classify the vehicle as a total wreck and cut him a check to pay the balance in full.

I had a revelation I decided to share with Eric at that moment. Based on his wife's bad history with money, she would never financially manage a car note. So, what was the point of the accident? The more I thought about our future together and that we were well on our way to a genuine, long-term commitment, the purpose of the accident became clear to me. I shared my thoughts with Eric:

> "Eric, you have made major sacrifices in this marriage and continue to do the right thing. God knew that based on her history, she would never be able to carry a car note and the bank would likely repossess the car as a result. If that happens, then you are ultimately responsible because the car is in your name. I believe that God wanted you to be fully clear of her. It was not his intent that she would die, so it must simply be that the purpose of the accident was to allow you to sever the remaining financial ties."

"The righteous person may have many troubles, but the LORD delivers him from them all: he protects all his bones, not one of them will be broken."

PSALM 34:19-20

Eric agreed and decided to buy her the bus ticket to Dallas. After a few days, she was well on her way, and I was on my way back to El Paso. The more time Eric and I spent together, the more we wanted to spend together.

I began to think that Eric's divorce was racing to a conclusion, with a court date in March. It was now late February and Eric and I had been seeing each other for about six weeks. I had not spoken to Robert in months regarding his refusal to sign the divorce papers he was served in April. I decided to call Robert and tell him about Eric.

"Robert, I have met a wonderful man, and I want to be with him. I need you to sign those divorce papers so I can be with him properly."

He paused and responded, "Okay, meet me at Jaxon's in an hour." Just like that, he said, meet me in an hour. Since Jaxon's was right across the street from my efficiency, Eric rode with me and waited at my place. I told Eric to look for me if I was not back in thirty minutes.

I took the brown envelope containing my copy of the papers and crossed the street to meet Robert. As I crossed the street, I recalled the angel from Detroit who helped Lorie and me get home that night, many years ago, when we went to get cigarettes for Momma. We crossed the street, and the man was simply there. I had grown in my faith, sufficient to understand that the man who walked us home had to be an angel—he never went into the building. Any normal human would have wanted to see that we indeed lived there and would have wanted to

"After this manner therefore pray ye: Our Father which art in heaven, Hallowed be thy name. Thy kingdom come. Thy will be done in earth, as it is in heaven. Give us this day our daily bread. And forgive us our debts, as we forgive our debtors. And lead us not into temptation, but deliver us from evil: For thine is the kingdom, and the power, and the glory, forever. Amen."

MATTHEW 6:9-13

meet our mother. I prayed that God would be with me as I took this step to meet with Robert, after so many months of him resisting.

Robert asked me to tell him about "this man" I had met. I told him that Eric was a soldier, a sergeant in the Army. He asked if he was Black, and I told him yes. Years before our separation, Robert had told me that if something ever happened to him, he envisioned me with a Black man. Hearing that Eric was African American gave him some level of comfort. Robert said he wanted nothing more than for me to be happy and would only sign the papers if he knew I would be happy. I told him I was thrilled, and Eric and I were happy together. He took out a pen and signed the papers. Robert then asked if he could meet Eric, and I told him that he was at my place across the street and he was welcome to come and meet him. We left the restaurant, crossed the street, and entered my tiny efficiency. When I opened the door, we saw Eric seated at the table by the window.

I introduced the two of them, "Eric, this is Robert, Robert, this is Eric." They shook hands, and Robert told Eric he had a great woman. After a few minutes of small talk, Robert left and Eric and I embraced. It was finally over.

The following day I delivered the papers to my attorney, who told me that he was sure we could obtain a court date and have the divorce finalized in a relatively short period. Robert and I had no children and no joint-owned property. We stated that we would each keep our respective debt obligations and retain the personal property we brought into the marriage. On March 10, 1995, Eric received his final divorce decree. Ironically, mine came seven days later, on March 17, 1995. I thought it interesting that we met on January 7th, and our divorces were finalized seven days apart. I believed that for his divorce to be in the works for months and mine stalled for months, only God could have shown such grace as to allow my divorce to have a speedy resolution. I thought it had to be God because seven is God's number. I understood the significance of seven as a sign of completion. In the Bible, God created the heavens and earth in six days and rested on the seventh. The Lord's Prayer has seven petitions.[9] I read between the lines again and took from the number seven that there must be a level of destiny to our connection.

With our divorces final, Eric and I spent every night together at his place on base. I would only go to my place to retrieve clothes and to check on things. As we neared the end of March, I realized I was no longer staying at my place. Money was tight, and I did not want to pay another month's rent if Eric and I would continue to "live together" for all practical purposes.

---

9   Retrieved September 27, 2022, from https://www.christianity.com/wiki/bible/
     what-is-the-biblical-significance-of-the-number-7.html

I asked a challenging question, "Eric, what are we doing?"

He responded, "What do you mean?" I explained my dilemma, wondering if I should pay for another month's rent.

Eric paused briefly and responded, "Come home, baby, let's go and get your things." Just like that, we decided to become a couple under one roof. Neither of us knew where we were going. We only knew for now, we wanted to be together, all the time, sharing our lives in the same household. We wasted no time, immediately going to get my things. I informed the front desk clerk at the Warren Inn that I would not be renewing another month. That night felt different because I knew I would wake up to this man every morning and come home to him every day after work. I did not tell anyone of my change in residence as it was still not permanent in my mind.

I Gain a Son

Eric had gained custody of Jesse during the divorce. With the custody decision having ended as planned, Eric was anxious to have Jesse home and to have me meet him. Eric's planned trip to Colorado Springs was on the heel of my work-related trip to Washington, DC. We agreed that I would make my return flight into Denver, and we would drive back to El Paso together. I landed in Denver and while waiting for Eric, I bought a teddy bear for Jesse. Eric and Jesse arrived, and I gave Jesse his gift.

Jesse asked me in a raspy voice, "What is his name?" I thought fast and named him Denver since that was where we first met. Jesse liked Denver, and I passed the first challenge. We drove back to Colorado Springs, where I faced my next challenge, meeting the ex-wife's mother. The ex-wife had only been away from El Paso for a few weeks. My friends commented on the fast pace of my relationship with Eric.

We arrived at Jesse's Grandmother's house, and she welcomed me and invited me to come in.

She insisted, "Make yourself at home because Eric has already told me all about you, and if you are going to be in my grandson's life, I want us to have a good relationship." This helped to break the ice, and I was immediately comfortable. She and I enjoyed a couple of glasses of wine and discovered that we genuinely liked one another. We spent the night there and had plans to return to El Paso the next day.

Weather forecasters had predicted a winter storm for Pueblo, Colorado, and northern New Mexico. The Raton Mountain pass that we would travel through on our way back to El Paso was notoriously dangerous during snow and bad weather. We planned to have lunch at a local pizza restaurant. I rode with the grandmother and Jesse, and Eric drove his car. During our drive, I observed Jesse as he unbuckled his car seat and climbed into the front seat while interfering with his grandmother's driving (it was a standard gear shift). His Grandmother explained that when she received Jesse in her home, he was an angry and frustrated little boy who needed to learn to accept love. She further explained that a major reason for his frustration was that he could not hear and had recently received ear tubes.

Finally, she acknowledged, "I have not attempted to discipline him, only to show him love, so now, he is ready to show love but rough around the edges where discipline was concerned." At the restaurant, we sat in a high-back booth. Jesse stood on the bench, terrorizing the couple in the adjoining booth. I observed Grandmother did not attempt, beyond a gentle nudge, to ask Jesse to sit, eat and not bother the other couple.

I thought, *This kid is out of control and needs serious training.*

After lunch, we packed the car, said our goodbyes, buckled Jesse into his car seat, and started our road trip. We made it through Raton Pass without incident. Eric exited the freeway into a rest stop as we came out of the Raton Pass on I-25. I asked what was wrong, and he said he was seeing something odd ahead that he did not like and wanted to look ahead from the rest stop before proceeding. I did not see anything. While at the rest stop, Eric noted the maneuvers of cars and trucks headed into the next stretch of land. Eric re-entered the freeway and drove at a much slower pace. We drove on hail pellets that had piled deep on the freeway in a matter of minutes. Large trucks kicked stuff up onto the windshield of our car. This hail phenomenon had just occurred and ended as abruptly as it began. Had we continued driving at the rate of speed we were traveling, we would have entered this treacherous area unprepared. I felt so safe with Eric. I thanked God when we finally reached the warmer towns of New Mexico. Jesse was a surprisingly great passenger, never removing his seatbelt.

Decisions, Decisions…

I had already started to assume the role of a mother figure for Jesse, and I jumped right into doing those things a mother would do. I found a quality home-based daycare center and began driving him there daily. I loved my time on the road with Jesse. Because his daycare was located in El Paso's Upper Valley, each way was a twenty-plus minute drive from Ft. Bliss, passing UTEP on the way. I played children's rhymes and songs during our trips, and Jesse never gave me trouble in the car. He seemed content, and once I secured and buckled him into his car seat, he remained there until I took him out.

April 15th was Jesse's 3rd birthday, so we planned a party at the Ft. Bliss Bowling Alley and invited our closest friends. I was happy to play an important role in Jesse's birthday celebration. I ordered a cake, and we bought a small bike with training wheels. My assistant, Dolores, came with her family and young children, as did several of Eric's military friends with their children. Eric helped Jesse to aim and roll the ball, and I mingled with Dolores and other moms. We sang happy birthday, cut the cake and opened gifts that friends brought him. Presenting Jesse his new bike was the icing on the cake, as Eric exited the bowling alley, he brought the bicycle in from the car, and I covered his eyes for a big surprise. Jesse wasted no time, asking to ride it as Eric placed him on the seat, pushed him around the table, and explained he would have to wait until we were outside to ride the bike.

> "Ask and it will be given to you: seek and you will find: knock and the door will be opened to you."
>
> MATTHEW 7:7

With Jesse's birthday behind us, we settled into our routines. Being an avid sports enthusiast, Eric had an interest in most sports. He played softball on the weekends and, sometimes after work. I attended some of his games with Jesse. By late April, I had missed my period. I shared this concern with Eric. He asked if I thought I might be pregnant. I assured him I did not believe so but suggested we do a home pregnancy test. Eric had a softball game that evening, so he agreed to purchase the test on the way home following the game.

Before Eric left the house, he told me, "I think you are pregnant."

While waiting for Eric, a million thoughts went through my mind, *What if I am pregnant and Eric does not want me to keep the baby?* I resigned if I were pregnant, I would keep the baby as I had been asking God for this blessing and would not tempt fate. I felt I had a good job and could manage to care for a child, even if it had to be on my own.

Eric finally returned from his softball game, and before I could say a word, he said, "I know that you are pregnant because you have not been late before. I have been thinking of names for our son."

Our son? I responded, "What makes you so certain it will be a boy?"

Eric confidently responded, "Because Braham men only make boy babies." He went down the list of all the Braham family's male offspring who had fathered children—from his list, all the babies born were boys. I decided to put very little stock into his male-child theory. We proceeded with the pregnancy test and discovered I was pregnant! The timing was uncanny. All these years of trying to get pregnant, I was with a child. I thought Eric would not be happy that I was pregnant early into our relationship, but he was excited. He told me he loved me and was excited I was carrying his child.

The following week, I shared the news with Dolores. I could not forget her dream about holding a little girl who was mine. Dolores was certain I would give birth to this little girl she saw in her dream months before I met Eric. April turned out to be quite a month as we also celebrated Eric's birthday on the 28th. I was delighted and fulfilled.

Our fairytale romance abruptly stopped when Eric received orders to serve overseas. This became a focus of our discussions. A major factor in his location choice was access to care for Jesse's medical needs. At the time, Eric was concerned that Jesse would require more medical attention. Eric needed to choose a place that afforded the best possible care for Jesse's hearing and speech development. We also discussed a one-year assignment, but the family was required to stay behind in such an instance. We discussed whether Eric should leave Jesse with me. We had so many questions. We explored options, including me quitting my job, marrying Eric, and traveling overseas with him.

Meanwhile, I was anxiously waiting to learn the status of my two grant applications. This outcome would also play a role in considering whether to quit my job and become a military wife or stay behind as a single mom and manage two programs. An expanded role would mean an increase in my salary. Weeks passed, and our conversations became even more urgent. I finally received word that both grants received funding, adding pressure to the decisions we needed to make. I had already decided I would be raising this baby with or without Eric, though I preferred we do it together. I had no desire to force Eric to decide on life for us together as husband and wife.

Eric's rotation for CQ duty came up, and I took that opportunity alone to put our options on paper by developing a major pros and cons list about our situation. I felt we had to be honest with ourselves and look at real-life scenarios. We needed to move beyond the "what ifs" and study our options based on the hardcore facts. I developed pros and cons for both good and bad options. It was quite comprehensive. We had made no plans to marry despite the pregnancy, so there was no legal provision that would allow me to take care of Jesse in Eric's absence and no provision that would allow me to keep Jesse if Eric died overseas. Thus, the reality check regarding our future was timely and much needed. I had pros and cons, including our long-distance relationship, breaking up and going our separate ways, and many other scenarios. I could not wait to sit down with Eric and review it. One of the options was he could get out of the military—a most controversial option, but an option, nonetheless.

When Eric came home, we had dinner and began to talk. I told him what I had done with the pros and cons list and asked if he wanted to see it. He wanted to see it, so I gave it to him. I sat quietly as he looked it over. In several areas, it was clear that the cons far outweighed the pros. Eric was surprised to see the option that we part ways and do our best to remain friends, with my raising our child alone. He challenged me on that one, and I encouraged him to expand on this list with pros and cons of his own. He began to add some things but agreed that I generally did a great job of capturing all of the angles. He was stunned when he saw the option to get out of the military. He did not know what to do with that and did not see how this could happen. We talked that night, though we did not make any decisions. He clarified he did not want me to raise our baby alone. I felt very good because I did not want that either.

After a few days, Eric returned and said he had run into the neighbor down the street. She was getting out of the Army on a chapter akin to a "no care plan." As a single parent, she had no one to leave her children with if deployed to war or on an overseas assignment that prohibited children. At that moment, Eric was shocked that he had run into her just a few days after discussing that getting out of the Army was not simply something that one did. He realized that women had been using the "no care plan" as a chapter under which to leave the military for years, but he had never heard of a man using it. He thought about his life and that his mother, father and maternal grandmother had all died in the past four years. Jesse's mother was not an option for filling the care plan requirement for Jesse. Once Eric started that conversation, I determined I would not be an option either. Though serious, we were not married, and our relationship was still very young. Eric

> "Now then, stand still and see this great thing the LORD is about to do before your eyes!"
>
> 1 SAMUEL 12:16

shared his situation with the supervisor, who counseled him on the need for a plan. After a series of counseling sessions and Eric's continued focus on what was best for Jesse, it became clear that Eric would have no viable, safe plan. This gap led to Eric becoming among the first men to receive an honorable discharge from the military for the reason of being a single parent with no childcare plan. Eric's supervisor told him to expect a letter.

With notice of discharge date, Eric and I began to make plans for his transition out of the military. We agreed to work together through his transition out of the military. A big factor was ensuring that we could financially cover our collective bills on my salary, his severance and unemployment benefits while he searched for employment outside of the military. As we laid out our obligations, I intentionally neglected to disclose my car note on the Cadillac, hoping he would not notice. I did not want to tell him about my monthly car note because the size of it was outrageous. I was not in the right frame of mind when I bought it; now, it was mine. Once we finished compiling our collective expenses, Eric noted that the Cadillac was missing from the list. He asked me if I had paid it off. I thought, of course not, but I knew he would freak out about the details.

"So how much is the car note?" he asked.

I replied, "$857/month."

Eric continued, "Are you kidding?"

"No," I replied. He made it very clear that we could not afford the car and agreed to use his credit to find me a smaller, used car with a manageable note.

He asked me to meet him at the dealer to see my new car. It was a used Ford Escort. When the salesperson demonstrated the "features" of this car, I cried. It was not that I longed for the Cadillac; it was just a dramatic difference. I was experiencing a high level of emotion around all the changes; perhaps, the pregnancy also contributed to this. We did not have a choice. The Cadillac had served its purpose in helping me assert my independence and that I could do whatever I wanted following my separation from Robert. The way I saw it, I was losing a car and gaining a family. We took the Escort and returned the Cadillac to the bank the next day. We knew that they would auction it, making us liable for any shortage in the note due and the actual sales price. We acknowledged the clause written into the bank's return agreement. We had no idea what that amount would be, but we had no other clear choice. We agreed to cross that bridge when we reached it.

Eric and I began looking for a place to live, and the issue of obtaining an affordable car was resolved. We found a duplex on El Paso's West Side and moved in. Eric received his severance check. We would have to make this money last. Other than an unemployment check, Eric's timing and future income from obtaining a steady job were uncertain. It was August of 1995 when he transitioned to civilian life. After about two weeks in our new apartment, Eric received a call from his relatives in New Haven, CT—his only brother, Kevin, and the one remaining living member of Eric's immediate family had been murdered. Kevin was only twenty years old. News of his death was devastating, and we immediately made plans for Eric to travel to New Haven to make funeral arrangements. Eric recalled his mother had made him promise to continue making payments on Kevin's life insurance policy, and Eric thanked God he had kept that promise. Though the policy allowed Eric to plan a nice funeral, we did not have money to pay the cost of the last-minute airline ticket for me to travel with Eric to New Haven. I could not bear the thought of Eric enduring the process of burying his younger brother alone. A plane ticket on such short notice was very expensive. I suggested to Eric that I call Robert and see if Robert could loan us the money for me to make the trip. With no other options and Eric's desire for me to join him, Eric reluctantly agreed. I called Robert and explained the situation, and he agreed, without hesitation, to loan us the money. By now, I was well into my pregnancy and could not hide it. We went to Robert's apartment to pick up the money, and Robert congratulated us on the pregnancy and wished us a safe trip. We made provisions for Jesse to travel with us.

Mrs. Edge invited us to stay in her home. The Edge family had known the Braham family for many years, as they migrated from South Carolina around the same time as Eric's late father. Eric had been best friends with the Edge's son, Michael, since Kindergarten. Mrs. Edge, being a devout Christian, made provisions for us to sleep in separate rooms because we were not married. Mrs. Edge politely explained that I would sleep in the pink guest room (which was pink), and Eric and Jesse would stay in the blue room that was, yes, blue. I thought that the "damage" of our having relations outside of marriage was already done; what more could we possibly do? Mrs. Edge maintained her home in a manner that would be pleasing to God, and unmarried couples would not share a bed in her home. Being a Christian also (though admittedly far from perfect), I had to respect this even though I was not happy about it.

Among Eric's first tasks was the need to identify his brother's body as the surviving relative. He visited the police department to obtain a report on the incident that led to Kevin's death. During what appeared to be a robbery, someone had stabbed Kevin to death in the basement of an apartment. Eric noted Kevin's affinity for street life, and the local New Haven gang crowd knew Kevin well. In addition to making funeral arrangements, Eric calmed many of Kevin's gang associates, who vowed to get even and avenge his death. Eric pleaded with them to let it go and to allow the law enforcement to do their job. Eric was appropriately concerned that had a gang retaliatory event occurred, things could spill over to the funeral ceremony, and he simply wanted things to proceed peacefully. Police wasted no time finding and arresting the man responsible for Kevin's murder, and this brought Eric some comfort in knowing the murderer was off the streets and behind bars. Eric knew having the murderer off the streets would calm the emotions surrounding the funeral.

Meanwhile, at the Edge home, Eric and I had settled into our respective pink and blue rooms and searched for moments to snuggle and comfort one another. Mrs. Edge and I spent much time in the kitchen together as she was an excellent cook. She always prepared a home-cooked meal for her husband and guests. During our time in the kitchen, Mrs. Edge observed a conversation between Jesse and me. Jesse was prone to throwing temper tantrums and to arguing about what he was not going to eat. Jesse was also learning, after about four months under my care, that he would eat what was prepared. I explained to Jesse that he could not have more juice. To share his displeasure with my answer, he hit me. Before I could catch myself, I popped his backside and he fell to the floor.

I explained, "Jesse, you will not hit me or anyone else." Eric frowned and looked at me with disgust but said nothing. Mrs. Edge said nothing but noted the chasm between Eric and me when parenting Jesse and doling out discipline.

Later that evening, after I went to my room, Mrs. Edge and Eric talked. According to Eric, she noted the look on his face when I popped Jesse.

Mrs. Edge explained, "Eric, you seem to have found a nice young lady in Sandra. She is smart, hardworking and loves you and Jesse. I saw how you looked at her when she hit Jesse; it was not right. Jesse had no business hitting her, and she did exactly what she should have done." Eric sat quietly as Mrs. Edge continued, "If it had been me, he wouldn't have gotten up from that floor for quite some time. Jesse needed his butt whipped, and if you don't allow Sandra to discipline Jesse, he will destroy your relationship, and you will lose her." Mrs. Edge clarified her views, noting Eric's responsibility to ensure we jointly parented and disciplined Jesse.

We continued spending time with Eric's close friends and family and Kevin's girlfriend, Sandra. Sandra was the mother of Kevin's eight-month-old son and namesake. Eric learned as much as he could from Sandra concerning Kevin's last days. Eric vowed always to be there for her and little Kevin, knowing that he was the only member of the Braham family to give Kevin a connection to his father. Eric noted how much Little Kevin looked like his father and considered the toddler a special gift left by his brother. Despite Eric losing the last member of his immediate family, he was remarkably strong.

Kevin's Funeral

Thanks to the insurance policy, Eric could cover all the funeral and burial expenses. Numerous family members, including Eric's paternal grandmother, Armatha Braham, traveled from South Carolina to support Eric. All eyes were on Eric during Kevin's funeral. Many who attended the funeral expected Eric to break down, but he kept his emotions in check. I sat next to Eric on the first-row pew during the funeral. Kevin's friends offered remarks during the service, as did several family members. Once the funeral director opened the casket for the final viewing, ushers released attendees, row by row, to view Kevin's body. As these individuals passed the first pew, many stared and whispered. Family members whispered loudly and debated if I was the "same wife." It seemed my unfamiliar face and obvious pregnancy brought as much shock as Kevin's death. I remained seated next to Eric in the front row and supported him as a wife. Following the funeral, Eric clarified the mystery surrounding my identity. It was nice to end the stares and whispers. Eric's grandmother told me that I was "much nicer than Eric's first wife." I found this weirdly comforting. Even though I was with child and unmarried, Grandma also reassured Eric that he had a nice girl.

We returned to El Paso and spent significant time talking. We recognized the importance of our being on the same page relative to child rearing. Repaying Robert immediately was high on our priority list, so we did. Also, on our priority list was to attend our doctor's visit, during which the ultrasound would show us the gender of our baby. Eric maintained his ground that I was carrying a boy because it was "destined per the Braham family's genes." After putting the gel on my stomach, the doctor began to rub the tip of the wand over my stomach. The results were conclusive and immediate—Eric's eyes popped as he saw his little girl, legs wide open as if to rub his theory in his face. Eric could not believe it—he had broken the family chain. I could not be happier to have seen his outrageous theory proven wrong. Later that evening, Eric and I decided to get married. Whether it was the experience of sleeping in pink and blue rooms or Mrs. Edge's discussion that pushed us toward this decision, whatever the reason, we agreed the baby (Eric's little *girl*) would be born a Braham. We discussed the nature of a marriage ceremony and agreed that since we had both been married, we did not care to put on a major show with friends and family. It was a different time in our lives; both recently divorced, Eric with a child and me carrying another. Instead, we decided to fly to Las Vegas and have a simple ceremony, just the two of us.

Chapter Ten

MY PERFECT MARRIAGE

I Now Pronounce You Husband and Wife

I researched options for a Las Vegas wedding and made arrangements online. We were to be married at the Little Chapel of the West, a lovely and historic chapel located on Las Vegas Blvd., just in front of the Hacienda Hotel. Jesse attended private, home-based daycare, and his daycare provider agreed to keep Jesse for the three days we planned to spend in Las Vegas. We left El Paso on Southwest Airlines, changed planes in Phoenix, and were excited to join the Vegas crowd for our final leg of the trip. We shared our plans to be married in Las Vegas with the flight attendant. To our surprise, the attendant announced our wedding plans over the intercom, and she brought us a full-size bottle of champagne. Everyone on the plane cheered, and our wedding celebration began.

We checked in to the Hacienda Hotel and called my dad to inform him of our marriage plans. Daddy had never met Eric, and I figured he might be skeptical. He congratulated us both and wished us well. Eric and I enjoyed our first night in Las Vegas by attending the Lance Burton Magic Show, the house show for the Hacienda Hotel. The show was mesmerizing as Lance made doves turn into beautiful models, made models appear and disappear and then cut them in half. Eric and I joked that perhaps Lance Burton had sold his soul to the devil—the magic was scarily real.

We took the bus downtown the following morning to apply for our marriage license. We arrived at the county building and could not believe the line of couples waiting to do the same thing, we were definitely in the right place. After about thirty minutes, a clerk named Victoria called us to her window. Victoria was an older white woman who wore her hair in a bun. She was the total opposite representation of the loud, jovial mood of the office, with all the couples laughing, some of them having had a few drinks. Eric tried to engage Victoria in small talk, but she remained focused on her task.

As she worked with us to complete the required paperwork, a determined Eric bent on charming her leaned in and asked, "So Victoria, do you have any secrets?" Victoria peered over her glasses. Not making a smirk, she paused a moment, responded, "no," and continued to process our marriage application.

Eric glanced at me, and I whispered to him, "You're crazy."

We received the required paperwork and decided to stop at one of the downtown casinos to play nickel slot machines. I selected a Double Diamond machine against the back wall. I put in five dollars, made a few spins, and hit the jackpot, just over $250. With these funds, we purchased matching Fila sneakers from one of the downtown stores. After a bit of sightseeing in the downtown area, we returned to our hotel. Being more than six months pregnant, I was exhausted and needed to rest. To my surprise, we walked into our room and there was a lovely arrangement of a dozen roses sent by my father. He congratulated me on my pending wedding to Eric and said he loved me. Eric too was surprised. Our wedding week was progressing perfectly, and I was happy and satisfied.

Our wedding was 4:00 pm the following day. We spent the morning finalizing our dinner plans, ironing our outfits and simply resting in preparation for the evening ahead. We arrived at the chapel at 3:00 pm to meet the minister and review the purchased wedding package. Also present was a florist who presented me with my bouquet. She also served as the official witness for the marriage ceremony. An organist was also present, and he played the traditional wedding march song for my walk down the aisle. The minister was a former military chaplain. Our planning paid off, and within no time, we were ready and proceeded through a lovely wedding ceremony, just the two of us and our officiating party from the Little Chapel of the West. Our vows were traditional, and we promised to love, cherish and obey, forsaking all others and remaining together in sickness and health until death. With an exchange of rings and a kiss, we sealed our future as husband and wife. Following signing papers with the minister, we took a taxi and had a lovely dinner at the Rio buffet, which was highly recommended. We spent one additional day in Las Vegas before returning to Jesse and our home in El Paso.

Reality Sets In

When we returned, a letter from the bank greeted us, informing us that they had auctioned the Cadillac and we owed the bank $12,000, the difference between the balance of the note and the sales price. This reality took the wind out of our sails, as we had no idea how we would come up with the money to pay the bank. Not paying the balance would ruin our credit and future desire to buy a home. We needed a true miracle.

Eric had been receiving unemployment, which was about to run out. He was so desperate to find work that he was willing to do just about anything. He noted that 7-Eleven was hiring. I expressed my concern that if he applied to work at 7-Eleven and they hired him, he would have a hard time moving forward in other careers, as other potential employers would view him as a 7-Eleven clerk. I reminded Eric that he had managed hundreds of soldiers in his Army unit and millions of dollars in inventory. I was afraid it would be tough for him to make his way back if he accepted anything less than a management position. Eric continued to apply for jobs and took the El Paso Police Department test. The Christmas season came and went, as did the New Year holiday. I was due to deliver "Erica Monët" any day now.

It was two o'clock in the morning on January 7, 1996. Eric and I had been sleeping, but I woke up because of shooting pains up my butt. I woke Eric and expressed concern that I might be in labor. After a bit of discussion and describing my feelings, Eric concluded that I was not in labor and that we could go back to sleep. Having never been in labor, I decided to take Eric's advice and try to get some more rest. After about thirty minutes, I woke him again, and he agreed to set his watch, "Wake me when you feel the next pain." Three minutes passed, and I shook Eric and told him I had the pain again. Eric decided to call the nurse. She suggested that he get me to the hospital.

By now, I was feeling stronger contractions, so I started to breathe accordingly and do my Kegel exercises. I needed to go to the bathroom. While there, I had a strong desire to push. I was in deep labor and knew I was in trouble. I had to force myself out of the bathroom and to the car. I continued my breathing and Kegels.

Meanwhile, Eric woke up Jesse, called the babysitter, and found me in the Thunderbird. We took off from Alto Rey to the Upper Valley and dropped Jesse off with his daycare provider.

"Bye, bye, mommy," Jesse said in his cute raspy voice, and I turned to him as in the movie The Exorcist and responded with an elongated, "Get out!" I begged Eric to hurry as he raced to the freeway. It was getting harder and harder for me to keep from pushing. I wanted to push but remembered that I needed to do Kegels and breathe until it was time.

We exited Schuster Avenue at seventy miles per hour, and I said to Eric, "I think my water just broke."

Eric responded, "In my car!" I was about to have the baby. It was just after 4:00 am when we pulled up to the emergency room, and he ran inside to let them know my status. A nurse greeted me and urged me to get into the wheelchair.

I struggled, and she kindly said, "Mrs. Braham, you don't want to have this baby in the driveway, so please help us get you inside." Eric still did not grasp the gravity of the situation, asking the nurse where he should park the car. She told him that if he did not leave it exactly where it was, he would miss the birth of his child. A short break in the contractions allowed me to get into the wheelchair, and the nurse wheeled me into the emergency room.

Things happened quickly, there was not even a sheet on the gurney they placed me on. The on-call doctor ran into the emergency room with one arm in her white coat. The baby was coming. To everyone's surprise, I squeezed the handles above my head, and the gurney fell flat. A large nurse with a German accent lifted the top of the bed, pushed it back to its original position, and with that bit of help, Erica came sliding into the world. It was Sunday, January 7, 1996, at 4:20 am. Exactly one year prior, on that date, I met Eric. What a coincidence! I felt like Erica's birth was yet another sign of our destiny, adding another seven to the dates in our list of significant events.

Erica suffered a bit of jaundice, so they put her under a lamp on a counter to my right. I looked at her as she looked at me with wide eyes. She kicked her perfectly formed thick legs, and I thought, *She's going to be a track star.* Erica never made a sound, she simply observed everything around her and seemed happy to be in the open. Because she had jaundice, the doctor moved her to the nursery floor for treatment, and Eric went with them. After about forty-five minutes, Eric returned to the emergency room as he wondered why I had not made it to the hospital suite in the childbirth ward. They would not release me due to our need to pay the $50 emergency room copay.

Eric was distraught. "Where do you think we are going to go?" He paid the fee, and they released me to my room. Eric notified all the family and friends from a prepared list, and it was not long before visitors began arriving.

There was Dolores and the entire crew from Upward Bound. Even Robert showed up and held the baby. I stayed one more night, and the doctor released us to return home on Monday.

I began Leadership El Paso the Friday following Erica's birth. During this program, current community and emerging leaders meet monthly for a full day to learn about and engage with various entities and topics of importance to the community and region. Participants network and discuss ways to improve the community through future growth and development. Our first session was a weekend retreat in Las Cruces, New Mexico. The retreat required an overnight stay. Because of being a new nursing mother, organizers authorized me to have a single room, and Eric agreed to join me and keep the baby since he was not working. Throughout the two days, I took routine breaks to nurse Erica. My classmates were impressed to learn that I had given birth earlier that week.

We returned to El Paso, and our outlook continued to improve. A new sporting goods store was opening, and Eric decided to apply for a position. After a couple of meetings, they recognized his vast knowledge of many sports and offered him the manager position of their Team Sports Department. Eric began working within the week, assisting with inventory and merchandising. He was able to interview, hire and train his team. Eric was happy. As he settled into his job, I tried to settle into the role of mother to a newborn.

> "For from His fullness we have all received, grace upon grace."
>
> JOHN 1:16

Erica was a challenging infant. She cried all the time and seemed happy only when with her dad. As I was out of work for a period and Eric worked weekends, I visited Dolores, who helped me learn some of motherhood's tricks and calming newborns. Dolores lived on El Paso's east side - about a thirty-five-minute drive from where we lived on the west side. One day, while driving home from Dolores' house, Erica cried, screaming at the top of her lungs during the entire drive. I tried talking to her; I put on music and pleaded with her to no avail. I prayed that God would help me to understand Erica's needs. When Eric came home, I immediately passed Erica to him. I was testy, sensitive and sad because I felt like a bad mother. I could not make my child happy.

One day, Eric returned home and asked me what I had done all day. Though he was simply asking me how my day went and what I had done, I immediately went into defense mode and responded, "What do you mean? I have been taking care of your baby all day. She won't stop crying. I'm exhausted, and NO, the house is not clean, and I have not made dinner."

Eric then shot back, "What is wrong with you? Why are you going off?" I decided it was time to get everything off my chest. I felt as though I had been holding things in for weeks, and Eric was not sensitive to what I was dealing with.

"I'm sick of your coming home every day, questioning what I have been doing. Don't say anything if you don't have something nice to say!" Eric was beyond shocked that I was so on edge. Eric calmly apologized, realizing I was interpreting his questions all wrong. He reassured me that I was doing an excellent job and that the least of his concerns was the household chores. After additional discussion, I realized that I was experiencing a type of hypersensitivity. In time, I recognized that while I was prepared for natural childbirth and was confident in my ability to deliver a baby, I was not prepared and had never considered matters of postpartum emotions. With Eric's awareness of my fragile emotions, support and attention, I was able to deal with my emotions and eventually overcame my new mommy blues.

One of my Leadership El Paso classmates, Reverend James L. Williams, was a Baptist preacher and Pastor of Mt. Zion Baptist Church of El Paso, Texas. Eric told me that he had attended Mt. Zion for a period and that Reverend Williams had performed Jesse's baby dedication ceremony when Jesse was only about three months old. I liked the Pastor. Since Eric and I were determined to raise our children in the church, we agreed that Mt. Zion would be a church to visit. The next day, after the close of the Leadership El Paso retreat, Eric and I went to Mt. Zion Church.

Eric and I sat near the back of the church to have an easy exit should the kids begin to act out. There was a small church daycare but not knowing anyone, we were uncomfortable sending Jesse there, and Erica was far too young to turn over to a stranger. After service, everyone asked about Erica's age, and when I shared that she was one week, most were impressed that I was out with her. An older woman scolded me for having her out in public. They said I should not have her out before a month because her immune system was not developed. I shrugged it off as an old wives' tale.

Eric and I attended services the next week and weekly thereafter until we decided to become members. Sundays were big days for baseball, and even though we were committed to attending church weekly, Eric was equally committed to playing baseball. Eric continued to play baseball, and most of his games started at 1:00 pm. Every Sunday, it was church and then immediately off to baseball. Now that Eric was no longer on active duty, he played with a team and some of the members he knew from his days in the Army.

Church members routinely joked because Eric would wear his jersey to church and only needed to change pants to be ready for play. The more we attended church with Eric dressed to play baseball, the more jokes and embellishments grew. Our friend Marco was one of the best storytellers. Marco's version of Sunday was, "There was the Braham family, sitting on the back row, and Eric on the edge of his seat, tossing the ball in the glove, fully dressed in his baseball uniform." Marco continued, "Eric was on the edge of his seat not because of the Pastor's message but waiting for the message to end so that he could be on time for the first pitch." Eric and baseball were the go-to subjects to get the jokes and laughter started.

Those early days at Mt. Zion were great. I had longed to return to my Christian roots as I had fallen so far from God during my marriage to Robert. I was so happily married, attending church with my husband and children, and growing again in my relationship with God. During church services, the altar call was always a special time to take our cares to The Lord and, as the Pastor urged everyone, to "leave them there." Every Sunday, Eric and I went to the altar and said our quiet prayers for our family. I knew that God was real and that He would answer our prayers. I knew He was real because there was no other explanation for my life and the adversities I had overcome. I had my dream husband, children, a great job and a good life. Clearly, the more we yielded to God, the more we began to see how he had moved in our lives. There was no question about God's grace in my life over many years. Whenever things got tough, I prayed earnestly and believed God would make a way. In like fashion, Eric and I prayed about the balance on the Cadillac. Where were we going to get $12,000?

Eric and I were frustrated with our duplex rental and desired to put our earnings toward purchasing a home. The more we discussed this dream, the more the balance owed on the Cadillac hung over our heads. Despite being middle class and having substantial income, Eric's parents had never *owned* their home. In my case, although Big Daddy owned his home, my mother and we girls lived there, with momma paying him monthly rent from her welfare and disability checks. For Eric and me, achieving our dream of owning a home would be a major step forward in raising our children in a stable environment while being an example of setting and achieving goals. We continued to pray and tithe.

Early in the spring of 1996, we received a letter from the insurance company with whom Eric had coverage for his brother. We opened it, and there was a check for $15,000! This came as a shocking and welcome surprise. The letter detailed the status of the insurance settlement for his brother Kevin. According to the letter, there was an additional review of Kevin's murder, and the company had deemed his death an "accident." The finding led the carrier to invoke the policy's accidental death clause. We thanked God, understanding that He had repeatedly shown us favor. We took this as further affirmation that ours was a match made in heaven and that God would come through for us if we followed and remained faithful. We paid off the Cadillac and had a bit of money left over. Receiving this check affirmed our faith and emboldened our commitment to God.

Another Gift

Eric was happily working, and I was happily parenting Jesse and Erica. What a difference a year had made. I returned to work half days after about four weeks following Erica's birth. The judge who granted Eric's divorce had ordered his ex-wife to pay Eric child support since he had full custody of Jesse. Her inability to maintain a steady income resulted in no payments up to that point, more than a year since leaving El Paso. She disappeared and stopped contacting Eric. A year passed, and we filed to have her parental rights removed for child abandonment. We also filed paperwork that would allow me to adopt Jesse. Jesse turned five years of age, and shortly thereafter, we received a date to appear in court. The judge appointed an ad litem to represent Jesse and another to represent his birth mother. Eric and I went to court with Jesse, and after some dialogue and questions, the judge removed the parental rights of Jesse's birth mother. At that exact moment, the judge approved my adoption application.

Our Family Grows, Again

Approximately eight months following Erica's birth, I was pregnant again. It was quite a surprise.

My boss approached me and said, "Well, Sandra, it seems when you birth a child, you birth a new program. What do you think about writing a grant for TRIO Talent Search?" Unlike Upward Bound, Talent Search served many kids, as the minimum program size was six hundred participants. I agreed to take a stab at it and, in preparation, visited a couple of programs in Texas. I determined that the most effective model was to serve fewer schools; this way, there was a greater opportunity to make a difference in student outcomes at the proposed target schools. I visited with the principals of two South El Paso middle schools and their two feeder high schools. After explaining the program's benefits and obtaining the principals' commitment to collaborate and provide the program its needed space and resources onsite, I began the process of writing TRIO Talent Search.

With the Talent Search application completed, the car paid off, and another baby on the way, Eric and I began to look for a larger house. After about five months of research and financial preparations, we were able to purchase our first home. We looked at many houses and decided on a new home in a developing neighborhood just off Resler. The house was located at the top of a cul-de-sac and had a huge backyard, perfect for children playing and entertaining. Realtors had sold only a couple of the eleven homes on the street. When we viewed the house, Eric and I walked through opposite areas and met in the kitchenette. A large bay window with a bench provided a perfect view into the backyard. The yard stretched most of the length of the top of the cul-de-sac. We looked at each other simultaneously and agreed this was our home. Eric was as excited to show me what he had seen as I was to share my observations from the other side of the house. Eric, recalling the move from Ft. Bliss to the duplex on the west side, joked that we were moving again, and I was pregnant.

"You will do anything to get out of helping to move," he said. I certainly could not deny being pregnant, and I appreciated the humor he brought to the process. We needed to buy additional furniture to fill the home. Jesse had a room to himself, as did Erica, at least through the birth of her sister. Our 1800-square feet were more than enough and included three bedrooms, two full bathrooms, a living and formal dining room combo, a den, kitchen, and kitchenette with the bay window nook.

Eric Gets a New Job

Eric was doing very well in his position of manager for the Team Sports Department at the sporting goods store. Not only was he an excellent salesperson, but he was also highly knowledgeable about sports. Having played baseball for so long, Eric also had excellent coaching skills. While working one evening, a man visited the store with his son, an aspiring baseball player. Eric assisted them and answered all of their questions. Eric spent time with the son, demonstrating techniques to assist him with his game performance.

After spending about an hour with Eric, the man explained that he was in the restaurant business and asked Eric about his interest in restaurant management. Eric responded that he had never considered it. The man explained that he could use someone with Eric's dedication and customer service focus.

He also explained that his company would provide Eric with all the training necessary to be a good restaurant manager. Eric then inquired as to the name of the company, to which the man responded by handing Eric his card. Eric explained that he did not want to work at Village Inn. Mr. Viceroy responded that the management position would not be for Village Inn but for Applebee's, a new company they had purchased with plans to expand throughout the region. After finalizing the sale of sports items for his son, Mr. Viceroy told Eric to speak to me about the opportunity and to contact him in the coming week if he was ready to join his new Applebee's management team.

Eric told me about his chance encounter with Mr. Viceroy. We discussed the opportunity with Applebee's as presented by Mr. Viceroy, including the opportunity for growth. We were thrilled that Mr. Viceroy recognized Eric's leadership and customer service and sales ability. Eric was happy at the sporting goods store, partly because of his passion for sports; however, Applebee's presented an excellent opportunity for long-term growth. After exploring the pros and cons of leaving his current job and accepting the new one, Eric decided to accept Mr. Viceroy's offer. Eric confirmed his interest, completed the application and interview, and entered Applebee's management training program. Mr. Viceroy assigned him to Applebee's only location at the time, on Mesa Street.

We were continuing to grow in our roles in the church, and Eric had become assistant manager at the restaurant. The hours were crazy, but his salary was higher than at the sporting goods store. After working months on Mesa, Applebee's transferred him to the newest location on Yarbrough. This location was bustling, and the hours were longer because that location was open until 2:00 am. When closing that location, Eric arrived home at about 4:30 am.

Construction of new Applebee's restaurants was proceeding at a rapid pace. Eventually, Eric was asked to come in as a trainer to assist with opening Applebee's location on Transmountain Road in the northeast part of town.

In the meantime, Eric received a letter informing him that his U.S. Postal Service exam scores would expire unless he took steps to extend them. Eric had completed the test for the Post Office shortly after his discharge from the Army, understanding that his federal time served in the Army counted toward his years to retirement in a federal job. Despite Eric having achieved a high score on his test, the Post Office gave preference points to disabled veterans. It was and continues to be standard practice for the armed forces to evaluate discharged service members for service-related disabilities. If doctors identified a service-connected disability, they assigned a percentage-disabled rate. It could take years to receive a rating. Eric did not yet have a rating. Eric followed up as recommended in the letter from the Post Office and took advantage of the option to extend his test results.

As our small cul-de-sac neighborhood grew and other families moved in, we established relationships and became friends. One of our neighbors was a recently retired Army veteran who served with Eric, and they knew each other well. Another neighbor was also pregnant, and her due date was within days of mine. There was a lot of discussion at our block parties regarding emergency plans when it was time to give birth, especially in my case because Eric worked late hours at the Applebee's northeast location. The distance home would be an issue if Eric were at work when my labor started.

The closer the babies' due dates, the more time we women spent together monitoring our status. One such evening, Eric was working late, and the neighborhood sister wives were at my house, drinking strawberry daiquiris. We devised the emergency plan for who would drive me to the hospital if Eric wasn't home. After everyone left at about 10:00 pm, and it was clear that I would not have a baby that night, I settled into bed. At about 2:00 am, I woke with labor pains. I timed them, and they were about 10 minutes apart. I put the neighborhood emergency plan into action, but my neighbor, whom we had designated to drive me to the hospital, did not answer her phone. I called another neighbor, Barbara. She agreed to stay with Jesse and Erica, and her husband, Al, agreed to take me to the hospital. We called Eric and told him we were going to the hospital. I warned Al that my water broke in Eric's car the last time I gave birth but assured him that we should be okay this time. He sped up a bit. I checked into the hospital, and Al stayed with me until Eric arrived. Al was so awesome that he even drove back to our house and returned with the video camera so that Eric could capture the first moments of Jordan's birth.

It was a full moon, and the maternity ward was overfull. Shortly after arriving, the staff led me to my room and hooked me up to various monitoring devices. Other soon-to-be moms began arriving, and since all the rooms were full, several of them were in chairs in the hall, waiting for others to deliver. Because it was a weekend night, my doctor was unavailable and a different doctor was on-call to handle deliveries. The maternal nursing staff called the doctor and explained that I was ready to deliver. When the doctor arrived, he came to check my status and dilation level. He immediately chastised the nurse and explained to her that I was not ready. The nurse explained my history of quick emergency room delivery.

My labor continued, and I relied on breathing techniques and Kegels to manage the discomfort. I refused medications primarily because I did not use medicinal aids during my prior delivery. I knew it was possible to deliver babies without epidurals. Eric was very helpful (and quite funny), explaining to me when the next contraction was coming because he could see it beginning on the monitor. The monitoring unit tracking my contractions also tracked other pregnancies on the ward, and we could visibly observe their progress. Everyone was amazed that my contractions were very smooth compared to others, even though I was older. Others' contractions had jagged lines and erratic strokes, representing difficulty compared to mine.

Like clockwork, after about twenty minutes, the doctor returned, checked my dilation status and noted that it was time for me to deliver. He had his episiotomy kit handy, ready to cut me if necessary. I looked at it and explained he should not cut me unless it was absolutely necessary.

I continued, "I did not need it the first time, and I believe I will be fine this time; I do not want to be cut." The doctor agreed he would not cut me unless it were necessary. At that point, about eight medical interns in white coats entered the room to be a part of my amazing childbirth experience. During my contractions, someone asked me if I was okay with visitors as rarely was there an opportunity to observe natural childbirth without anesthesia. The body behaved differently under natural circumstances.

I looked around and replied, "Who cares? It's all in the name of science education."

The doctor then told me to push, and a nurse stationed on my left side grabbed my leg from the stirrup and began pulling it back toward my head.

I yelled at her, "Hey! I feel that, and I don't have any anesthesia. Back off!" I then reminded the doctor not to cut me, after saying he would not. In a matter of moments and with only a few pushes, Jordan arrived just after 4:30 am.

The doctor looked at Eric and said, "I am very impressed. I have never encountered a patient like your wife, giving direction to my nurse assistant, conversing with me and telling me what to do while orchestrating the perfect delivery." I felt proud that I had given him such a memorable experience.

After a day in the hospital, Jordan and I returned home. As with Erica, I spent a few weeks at home, bonding with my newborn. My neighbor, Barbara, watched Jordan as I drove Jesse and Erica to school and daycare. This was a massive help as it kept me from packing up a newborn and two other children. Sometimes I would pack up Jordan to drive the others, and Barbara would ride along. After a few weeks, I returned to work, and soon afterward, I received word that the U.S. Department of Education had chosen my TRIO Talent Search Grant application to receive funding. Not only would they fund the program, but also my application received a perfect score of 100, which placed it among the top ten percent of all Talent Search application scores in the nation. Being in the top ten percent set our application apart from others, as these programs would receive five years of funding instead of four. My supervisor was thrilled because receiving the Talent Search grant also affirmed his theory that I birthed a new program each time I birthed a child.

With my oversight of a third TRIO program, my supervisor and I discussed my need for a job title change. The title "Director of Upward Bound" no longer worked with the addition of Talent Search. There was a fourth TRIO program on campus, Student Support Services, which served college-level students who were low-income and first-generation. That program reported to the Dean of Students in the Student Affairs office. Because I did not oversee Student Support Services, we felt that the "Director of TRIO Programs" was inappropriate. Thus, we settled on the title, Director of TRIO "Youth" Programs, as the programs I oversaw were all pre-college initiatives. The new grant and title came with a slight pay increase, and it seemed once again that favor was upon our growing family.

Eric Joins the Post Office, and I Return to School

After waiting almost two years since leaving the Army, Eric finally received his notice of disability from the Department of Veterans Affairs. With this classification change, he updated his file at the Post Office, and the Human Resources Department added five points to his test score. These added points took him over 100, and within weeks of updating his record, Eric received an offer of a position at the U.S. Postal Service. Though he was grateful for the opportunity to manage Applebee's, at that time, there were few benefits or other support for our family available through the restaurant. Eric made the best decision for our long-term growth and resigned from his position with Applebee's. Unfortunately, he would have to start on the graveyard shift with no seniority at the Post Office. Eric began his new position, reported to work at about ten o'clock in the evening, and headed home at about six in the morning. This would be our life for about a year—Eric working nights and me working days. I wouldn't say I liked it, but I believed we were strong enough to survive anything.

Chapter Eleven

GROWING PAINS

In 1999, UTEP gained approval to provide full-time employees who met position and time-on-the-job requirements fee waivers to attend UTEP classes as long as staff took the class as part of a degree plan. Though a tuition payment was still required, the related enrollment fees represented as much as forty percent of the normal cost of attendance. I met the requirements for the fee waiver, and since I had Eric's support and encouragement, I enrolled in graduate school to pursue a master's in educational leadership. Despite having completed seventeen credits short of an MBA from Mizzou, it was clear that education was my field, and the business credits were far too old. The registrar could not consider them as part of my graduate MBA coursework. It seemed illogical to consider a business degree at this career stage.

On the heel of receiving the Talent Search grant and the announcement of the new fee waiver for university employees, I applied and received my letter of acceptance into the UTEP Graduate School's College of Education Educational Leadership program. I had spent my entire time thus far successfully building new programs. Despite my success, I could not shake the genuine concern of a new president pushing me out for my lack of a post-baccalaureate degree. Thus, I moved forward with school and took pride that I would now invest in myself. In the summer of 2000, I began pursuing my master's in education. I took two classes per semester and enrolled in additional courses on Saturdays when the opportunity presented itself.

Eric and I became increasingly active in our church, with my supporting the Youth Ministry and Eric serving as a Deacon and leader of the Brotherhood Ministry. I also joined the "Voices of Zion" choir. Between school, working full time, being the mother of three young children and balancing the demands of wife and community/church leader, something was bound to suffer. I continued to push through with a great focus on my end goal—to complete the master's degree.

Another Grant, But I am Not Pregnant

The national TRIO community began to discuss a new program, "GEAR UP," or Gaining Early Awareness and Readiness for Undergraduate Programs. There was great concern among TRIO leaders because this program seemed to mirror Talent Search but was funded under an entirely new federal line item. I ignored the debate because at UTEP, we had just received the Talent Search Grant, and as far as I was concerned, there was no interest in adding a new pre-college program.

Some months passed, and I attended a breakfast meeting featuring a local elected official as a presenter. Dr. Natalicio attended the meeting as well. Following breakfast, I spoke to her in the restaurant's parking lot.

"Good morning Dr. Natalicio. How are you?"

She responded, "Good morning, Sandra. How are you?" After a few pleasantries, Dr. Natalicio noted, "I heard you will be adding to your empire." Dr. Natalicio was an amazing woman. She overcame significant challenges as she worked to build the University's reputation as a top Hispanic Serving Institution, and she gained notoriety as one of the longest-serving Presidents in the University of Texas System's history. Dr. Natalicio sat on many national boards of directors for various foundations and educational entities, and she had been very successful in forging strong international relationships with the countries of Mexico and Bhutan. She also just happened to be from St. Louis, MO, and was an avid Cardinal baseball fan. Our St. Louis connection gave me an open door to discuss St. Louis as a point of common interest.

I greatly admired Dr. Natalicio. Over time, I learned that *every* word she said was intentional. I could not shake her notion of my "empire building," and I honestly had no clue where she was going with that statement.

She saw the puzzled look on my face and asked, "You *are* writing the GEAR UP Grant, aren't you?"

I responded, "I am?"

She seemed surprised that I knew nothing of this. "Didn't your supervisor speak with you about this, Sandra?" she continued.

I responded, "I am familiar with the GEAR UP Program but have heard nothing relative to my writing for that competition." She mentioned that she had told my supervisor to speak to me some time prior about this opportunity. I told her that I would follow up with him. With that, Dr. Natalicio set the wheels in motion, and before long, I was off to develop another program. Who was I to argue with the President? I made light of things with my boss. "Though I am not pregnant, I will give the GEAR UP application my best shot."

The GEAR UP opportunity put more things in motion relative to my career because, until that point, I was the director of two Upward Bound Programs and the new Talent Search Program. Adding a fourth would require a shift in my leadership role. I would need to hire a full-time Director for Talent Search. Additionally, GEAR UP would require its director. I struggled with the need to hire a director for Talent Search as I did not believe my team at the time had sufficient depth to promote a candidate from within. At the same time, I knew that promoting from within was the expectation of that department's staff. The most likely candidate for director had been the subject of complaints from colleagues. The situation weighed on me. Morale could further suffer and remaining strong staff might seek other opportunities. I knew the employees were unhappy, so I offered the supervisor guidance, development and counsel. I asked God for guidance.

A short time later, I had a dream. As was typical in many of my dreams, a storm was coming—a tornado. Perhaps my dreams reflected my growing up in Missouri, a place known for violent storms and tornadoes. We always prepared for the "big one." There were also the sirens at the firehouse, across the street from Big Daddy's house, which sang out not just for fires but also as a tornado warning. These sirens prompted us to run to the basement for shelter. I lived in a single-story home in El Paso without a basement, so running below in a storm was not an option. In my dream, I saw the giant black storm, swirling and howling, destroying and lifting everything in its path. As the tornado approached, my instinct was to grab my three children and brace myself in one of the foundation points of the home, near a hallway intersection. I had heard a home is strongest at its foundation. I grabbed the kids, ran to the foundation and held tight. I prayed for God to protect us, and we survived the storm. I woke up a bit shaken because I was not too fond of storm dreams. I was glad to have survived. I was also glad to remember what I had learned through dream books. Running downstairs was a sign of losing oneself. I was glad I didn't run down a flight of steps. The dream affirmed my strength and control.

I went to work the next day and thought nothing of the dream. I spent significant time reflecting on my staffing dilemma. I had to finish writing GEAR UP but needed to determine my successor to lead Talent Search in the director role. At one point during the day, I looked around my office and it struck me that the *foundation* of a grant program was the application itself! I looked at the shelf and saw three grant proposals—two for Upward Bound and one for Talent Search. I discerned the three babies in my dream were not my physical kids but the three programs I had *birthed*. I grabbed the Talent Search proposal off my shelf and turned to the section that addressed "Qualifications of Personnel." There, I read what I had written almost a year prior. The Talent Search Director would have attained a bachelor's degree with a master's preferred and would have a minimum of three years in a leadership position. As it turned out, none of my existing Talent Search employees possessed the credentials or experience to earn the director position. With that revelation, I had a frank discussion with the internal candidates, letting them know I would not consider them for the position. I then moved forward with my plan to advertise the position and hire a qualified director. With my Talent Search director dilemma resolved, I turned my attention to writing the GEAR UP grant.

Mom's Illness is Exposed…and so am I

In 1998, I was one of several employees nominated on behalf of the UTEP President's Office for a YWCA Reach Award. The Award recognized local women's achievements in health, business, education, the arts and community service. Criteria included demonstrating how the nominee had empowered women through her work and had overcome challenges in her life. A colleague completed the application on my behalf and called me to obtain additional information about the challenges I had overcome. I shared that my mother suffered from schizophrenia and that, as a result, I spent several of my teenage years in foster care. Reach nominations were extensive and not easy to complete and having the President recommend one for the award was a significant honor.

All nominees received invitations for themselves and a guest to attend the Reach Awards Luncheon, and the award recipients learned of their selection during the program. Eric accompanied me to the luncheon. The YWCA recognized all nominees in the written program booklet and the mistress of ceremonies called each by professional category to receive individual certificates. After returning to our seats, she presented the winner and proceeded to read my bio. I could not believe it. With so many women nominated, *I* was the recipient. Winning the Reach Award was a big deal, and UTEP had more than one employee who received the award that year in different categories.

Never had the University had two Reach winners in one year; thus, the University's News and Publications Department included a story in UTEP's monthly employee newsletter. My picture was on the front page. I read the story and was devastated. There it was, in black and white, "The daughter of a schizophrenic mother." I cried — I had only shared my mother's mental illness with my closest friends. I rarely spoke of my mother's schizophrenia, primarily because I felt embarrassed by it, and I was afraid that people would judge or label me as a result. My colleague who wrote the nomination application had now exposed my secret to the entire campus and University alum community. I called my colleague and explained how upset I was because I had never publicly shared the information she put in print. I was upset that no one asked my permission before printing it. She apologized profusely, but it was too late. Everyone now knew my very personal family secret. I received a few calls, mostly people offering congratulations and a few

> "And we know that for those who love God all things work together for good, for those who are called according to his purpose."
>
> ROMANS 8:28

who offered congratulations with a tone of sorrow that I had to endure my mother's mental illness. Having others pity me was the last thing I needed or wanted. At this point, the only thing I wanted was to crawl under a rock.

Time proved that good things could come from the seemingly terrible. With my closely held secret of mom's mental illness out of the bag, I had the courage to talk more about it and to begin speaking about it publicly. This became a turning point for me. I accepted speaking requests to share my experiences. I mostly shared my story with youth living in foster care but also with women's groups in the community. I found that I had a personal connection with foster kids, and they were appreciative of knowing that I, too, was once in their situation and had overcome it.

Following my breakdown after the printed story about the Reach Award, I refocused my energy on the GEAR UP application. I researched school performance reports to determine the best partner for GEAR UP and I set my sights on northeast El Paso as the target area. The area was notorious for gangs, and there was broad concern in the community for children who resided there, especially those who lived in the area known as "The Devil's Triangle" (later renamed The Angel's Triangle). The Triangle was so named for its three public, low-income housing complexes, which bordered the area as sort of a fortress that "prevented escape," literally and figuratively. Children in this area were at the greatest risk of falling into the gang lifestyle and overwhelmingly lacked exposure to post-secondary educational opportunities. South El Paso was another high-risk area, but because Talent Search was serving six hundred children in that area, I was excited to take GEAR UP to the northeast. In addition, El Paso's African American community was small at some three percent, but the northeast had the largest percentage of African Americans compared to other areas of the city. I was hopeful more Black children would benefit from this program.

My supervisor thought my interest in focusing on the Northeast was well placed and offered to connect me with a colleague who was the principal at a Northeast middle school. I was excited, knowing I did not have to make a cold call to begin the process. The fact that my supervisor had a relationship with this individual and we had $40,000 for a cash match gave me confidence we could quickly secure the support and partners needed to demonstrate a strong proposal relative to institutional and community support.

We visited the school we hoped to partner with, and the principal met us outside. We shook hands, and she and my supervisor greeted one another as old friends. We began our meeting in her office. She smiled as she shared all the great programs and efforts happening at the school. She gave us a short tour, and we returned to the principal's office. I explained the program and related requirements as we sat in the principal's office. I could not shake the odd sense I felt about the principal as she responded with lukewarm feedback; thus, I shared what I considered my ace in the hole. "I am thrilled the University has committed $40,000 as a cash match to support a computer lab and technology center for the school." The principal explained how many programs and grants they were working with and how she did not know if they could manage another initiative. I explained the bulk of the work was on us and that we would provide staff to work onsite four days per week, adding support while building the school's capacity. The principal assured me they would look at the program and get back to me very soon with an answer regarding the proposed GEAR UP partnership, and we ended the meeting and returned to the University.

I drafted grant language and made concerted efforts to keep the principal in the loop. After almost three weeks with no response to my emails or voice messages, I was desperate to know where the principal stood relative to our partnership.

With only two weeks remaining before the submission deadline, I called my supervisor and asked if he had received any word or decision from the principal.

He responded, "Well, I guess no news is bad news." What? I thought... No news is bad news? I was shocked.

I phoned the school again, and the principal took my call. She said there were too many projects in the school and the team could not work with another grant. I accepted that response though I wished I had that answer a week prior. I felt I had been led on a wild goose chase that would make my writing this grant successfully near impossible. I called the University President's Office. She was not available. As I contemplated the task before me, I resigned that without a target school or principal on board, the GEAR UP proposal was immediately doomed.

Not being one to give up, despite a seemingly impossible task, I thought about Guillen Middle School, one of the Talent Search target schools. Guillen's new principal was in one of my classes. I called her and explained my dilemma and the fact I had to write the GEAR UP grant. I further explained its importance to the president and that even though Guillen Middle School

> "Opened and closed doors and opportunities is also a way that God speaks to us, to affirm His will."

already had Talent Search, GEAR UP would function differently. I also explained we would purchase $40,000 in computers and technology to benefit her school. She perked up, and I knew I had her full attention. I asked about potential partners. She provided several names and even agreed to facilitate meetings between us. With her response, "Let's do it," I was back in business.

I emailed all University stakeholders (excluding the president) and explained, "I am sorry to report that our proposed target school has declined the opportunity to partner with GEAR UP. But, where one door closes, another opens, and I am pleased to share that I have visited with the principal of Guillen Middle School, and she has agreed to work with us." I also noted that I would begin the proposal immediately.

Later that afternoon, I received a return call from the UTEP President. I explained the turn of events and that I would do my best. She empathized with my position and noted plans underway regarding my future. I would be promoted to assistant vice president and my reporting supervisor would be the Vice President of Student Affairs. I listened in shock. She continued that the plan was to make this move following the notice of funding for GEAR

UP, but in light of challenges with the grant, she would work on moving things forward sooner.

Before the night ended, Dr. Natalicio shared with me a letter that she would send the following day. The letter noted…

> "Effective immediately, Sandra Braham will assume the role of Assistant Vice President for Outreach Programs, reporting to the Vice President for Student Affairs, and will oversee the following programs: Upward Bound, Talent Search, the High School Equivalency Program, National Youth Sports Program, the Summer Food Service Program, the Summer Youth Employment Program and GEAR UP, pending its successful funding."

I shared the letter with Eric, and we were thankful for this opportunity and recognition of my leadership and grant writing ability. Because I was already being included in meetings with my supervisor and the vice president for student affairs, the transition was smooth, though admittedly, a bit awkward.

My Perfect Marriage Meets My Sixth Sense

With my submission of the GEAR UP Grant and promotion to assistant vice president for outreach programs, my salary increased accordingly. I continued my coursework in the master's program, taking as many as two to three classes per semester while working full time and raising three young children. With Eric working the graveyard shift, we began to experience marital strains that would last for years. Eric also began to coach youth baseball, and our son played on the team with a neighbor's son. I attended the games and felt my neighbor was too attentive to my husband's needs. When he asked for water, she ran to grab it as if he was *her* man. During neighborhood block parties, she flirted, not just with Eric, but with any number of married men. She would call my house for any opportunity to speak with him, and I began to point out to Eric her blatant manipulation and ill intentions. He denied anything beyond a cordial, friendly relationship. The more she called, the more I noted to Eric that she was not calling for me but him. She was not *my* friend, and I told Eric that if she was not my friend, she could not possibly be his friend.

Eric and I loved each other. We knew that God brought us together; however, we had become busy people, passing in the night. He began to hide his friendship with the neighbor and his whereabouts when I could not reach him by phone. There were countless excuses as to why he could not answer the phone:

- I left it in the car.

- It was dead.

- I was with my supervisor and could not answer.

I resorted to leaving angry, accusatory messages because I knew it wasn't true. I was angry at the thought of being a fool. My worst-case scenario was that I remained in a relationship built on deceit, the relationship lasting just long enough for my husband to secure plans to move on with another woman. Thus, I would have to acknowledge publicly that I was a stupid fool.

During those years, we received hard copies of phone bills in the mail, with detailed pages of completed calls, numbers called, and length of time for each call. As these bills were for Eric's phone only, I resisted the urge to open his mail. I felt terrible even at the thought of secretly reviewing the bill because I knew I was becoming *that* woman. You know, the woefully insecure woman who, as a result, becomes the stalker. I wanted to believe Eric, but I gave in to the suspicion and insisted that he show me the bills. There were calls to many numbers that I didn't know—I honestly didn't know hers, so I found myself trying to memorize numbers quickly, always with the plan to test them later. That plan never came to fruition because I could not bear to go through with it even though I desperately needed to know.

Eric and I prayed that God would allow him to move from working the graveyard shift to days. I believed Eric would be more accountable for his hours when I was working if his hours aligned with mine. Eric verbalized if God granted his request for a day job, he would no longer play ball on Sundays and dedicate himself to growing stronger in his walk with The Lord. It was not long before God answered that prayer. Eric knew working the graveyard shift was a major contributor to our marital problems. With Eric switching to the day shift, we strengthened our church involvement. He was tapped to be a Deacon, and I joined the choir. I became the assistant director of the church youth group, our marriage was seemingly back on track, and life was good.

Life continued being good for about thirteen months. Eric had separated himself from the relationship with our neighbor. I sensed something off. I would call the house while on the way from my evening class, and it was apparent from the phone click that Eric was talking on the other line.

When I asked with whom he talked, Eric always responded, "One of the deacons in the church." I never believed it.

I could not shake the feeling in my gut that Eric was again hiding something. At home, when the opportunity presented itself, I went to work when Eric was not watching—trying to review his phone log and see if he was speaking to a deacon from the church. I checked the home phone's call history to see what calls were coming in and going out. Eric knew I was watching and again began to erase logs and keep his phone in sight, even while going to the bathroom.

I continued to stumble upon facts that demonstrated my neighbor was as conniving and manipulative as ever. There were rumors that she and her husband were experiencing issues. Eric was falling for her "damsel in distress" routine once again. Eric was in over his head, thinking this was simply a friendship. I never had to look very far to determine that something was up because the proof seemed to unfold before my eyes.

The situation with my neighbor came to a head one day while I was at work. My assistant told me my neighbor's husband was there to see me. I had no idea what would bring this man to my office, but I knew it would not be good. My heart was pounding. We sat down, and he showed me cards my husband had sent to his wife. He accused his wife and my husband of having an affair. I tried to keep my cool while he was there, and he and I made a plan for the four of us to meet that evening together. We agreed not to give them advanced notice so our spouses would not have the opportunity to collaborate on their responses. Our plan was simply to have them call for a quick visit, and he and I would bring things out of the dark.

That evening, the neighbors came to our house. I shared the cards and blew up. I challenged Eric to own up to the fact that the cards were from him and that my concerns were right. He denied the cards were from him—they did not have his name but were "anonymous." I knew Eric's handwriting when I saw it, and I was further inflamed that he would not admit the truth. Our neighbor told Eric to stay away from his wife. Of course, she denied everything short of a friendship. I gave up.

> "Then I proclaimed a fast there, at the river Ahava, that we might humble ourselves before our God, to seek from him a safe journey for ourselves, our children, and all our goods."
>
> EZRA 8:21

I told Eric that I planned to file for a divorce, and for two days, I slept on the couch and fasted. I prayed to God for clarity. I cried so much my eyes were swollen shut. Eric apologized and finally admitted that he had had an inappropriate relationship with the neighbor but promised that it had never involved sexual relations. I had to believe this in my heart as a fact. Accepting this was necessary if there would be the hope of moving forward. My neighbor and his wife eventually separated and divorced, and she left the neighborhood. She moved on…for a while, at least.

I had come to trust my gut instincts and senses. I remained faithful to God and my commitments to the church. Eric and I began marriage classes at church. I had shared with no one that my marriage was not what it seemed on the surface. I kept praying, trying to regain my trust in Eric. Eric increased his involvement in the church Men's Ministry. I found the more I prayed and depended on God for direction and insight, the more He revealed. I began dreaming regularly and maintained a journal to write my dreams when I woke.

The Female Preacher

As time passed and the girls grew, we could no longer keep them in the one big bed. We decided to redo their room with new beds to create a more open space. We took a family trip to the furniture store. While there, we met a family in the children's bedding department. The family had just relocated to the community and sought a church home. We invited them to our church and offered to help them connect in the community. The wife described herself as an evangelist. She and her husband had two children, a toddler and a pre-teen. The couple visited our church the following week and enjoyed the service. They lived on El Paso's west side, which made it easier for our families to develop a friendship. After just a few visits, the family became members of our church. The more engaged they became in the church, the more time our families spent together. Our kids attended daycares on the same street, so the evangelist and I began to share transportation duties.

It was my week to pick up the kids. Once I had them all, we made our way to my house, where their mom would come to retrieve them. As I neared my street, I had a vision. I was accustomed to dreams but had not paid much attention to fleeting thoughts that occasionally popped into my head. I wrote these thoughts off as simply imagination. This thought was different. It was as though an entire story had unfolded instantly in my mind.

I was inside my house with the evangelist's children in the vision. There was a knock at the door, and when I answered, a case manager or child investigator was there. She asked me if I would be willing to keep the kids until they could notify the next of kin because there was a murder-suicide, and both the evangelist and her husband died. In a flash, I was back to reality. I turned onto my street and asked myself, *What was that?* I was angry with myself and wondered how I could think such a horrible thought. I felt terrible. I wrote the experience off as another episode of Sandra's imagination gone wild. A short time later, the evangelist retrieved her children, and I never shared my fleeting thought with anyone—it would be nothing short of crazy to do that, *right?*

Sunday arrived, and we went to church, as usual. Post-benediction was always a time of impromptu fellowship and discussions about dinner plans. On most Sundays, our family would join other families at a restaurant of choice. We enjoyed our Sunday dinners with the "usual suspects." The usual suspects represented our closest friends, all of them married couples, most of whom were Black. In addition to dinners after church, we spent holidays together, and some of us vacationed annually. On New Year's Eve days, the group expanded to include other close friends, married and single, who did not attend church with the rest of us. On this particular Sunday, the evangelist asked if I could take her children home with me, as she needed to visit with the Pastor. She noted that it was a tough weekend, and she would explain everything to me later. I agreed without hesitation to take the kids.

> "As each has received a gift, use it to serve one another, as good stewards of God's varied grace."
>
> 1 PETER 4:10

Later that evening, the kids' mom arrived at my house and requested to speak with me in private. We went into the formal living room, which we rarely used. She proceeded to tell me the story of her weekend.

Her daughter began to argue with her and, in the course of doing so, noted, "My daddy loves me more than he loves you." This led to the daughter's disclosure that her father would come to her bed to show her love, and she reportedly described the feel and color of semen. However, he never had actual intercourse—only rubbing and ejaculation. The evangelist confronted her husband and threatened to call the police and have him arrested. She then shared something that blew my mind. Her husband got his gun and threatened to kill himself if she called the police. He pointed the gun to his head as she pleaded for him not to shoot. She promised she would not call the police but convinced him to let her call the pastor, as they needed help. He agreed. The rest of the story went as well as her career would afford. She had to report him for child abuse, which she did. He was arrested, pleaded guilty and went to prison. She and the daughter sought counseling. He served his time, she helped with his transition from prison, and eventually, he resumed his role as a father, living across town. The family moved out of state.

I reflected on the scenario, and the evangelist's story blew me away. What she shared was eerily close to what occurred in my vision, short of the deaths. The gun, her husband's threat to kill himself—all of these facts rolled around in my head, and I realized *I could see.* The vision almost mirrored what took place in reality. Realizing my visions might have some basis in reality gave me a new level of clarity regarding my relationship with God. He opens the eyes of those who are to see, know and discern. I felt exceptional and petrified. As much as I longed for answers, a big part of me did not want whatever this *gift of sight* entailed. I started to wonder why I always seemed to attract people in trouble. I reflected upon the friend in Lafayette, Indiana, who I helped to enroll in college. I later learned this incredible and beautiful student had schizophrenia. I saw her on the street, talking to herself and very troubled. I became a resource for her mother, as her mother did not drive. So, I drove her back and forth to the hospital to visit her daughter. I did not understand it, but I found comfort in knowing I could be there in their time or season of need. There were other examples. Finding myself in the middle of the mess with the evangelist was just the most recent.

That Sixth Sense...Part 2

I accepted God would reveal the answers to my deepest questions through dreams or simply by being at the right place at the right time. I started to sense Eric was once again distracted. I began having dreams again. Something was going on, and I knew Eric was keeping secrets. I, too, was distracted, working on a master's degree in the evenings after work and on some Saturdays. Again, I felt like Eric was always on the phone with someone when I called. He would not answer his phone during the lunch hour. He always had an answer, and I did not believe him. We argued that he no longer brought his cell phone bill into the house. I had not seen one in months. The more he denied he was talking to the former neighbor again, the angrier I became, as I knew in my heart that he was. I asked God to reveal the truth.

One Sunday, we hosted dinner at our home in between the morning service at church and a special afternoon church service where I would be singing. Eric's Thunderbird was blocking my car in the driveway, so he suggested that I take his car. I got in the car, backed out of the driveway and as I turned into El Paso's bright and blinding sun, I pulled down the visor on the driver's side.

"Husbands, love your wives, as Christ loved the church and gave himself up for her, that he might sanctify her, having cleansed her by the washing of water with the word, so that he might present the church to himself in splendor, without spot or wrinkle or any such thing, that she might be holy and without blemish. In the same way husbands should love their wives as their own bodies. He who loves his wife loves himself. For no one ever hated his own flesh, but nourishes and cherishes it, just as Christ does the church, because we are members of his body. 'Therefore a man shall leave his father and mother and holdfast to his wife, and the two shall become one flesh.' This mystery is profound, and I am saying that it refers to Christ and the church."

EPHESIANS 5:25-32

Eric's cell phone bill fell into my lap. *Wow*, I thought. What are the odds that after fighting about the phone bill, here it is? It simply fell into my lap, like a gift from above. I arrived at the church, entered a side room, and studied the bill. Countless calls were received from a calling card, and countless were made to an 800 number. What was this? I decided to call the 800 number. Guess who answered. Yes, my neighbor. I was so pissed off—this was the epitome of deceit and cover-up. She provided a brilliant solution to hide their calls to one another: buy an untraceable number so that Eric could use it without detection. The calls took place all day—she talked to my husband more than I did.

Discovering the truth that Eric had once again fallen back into a relationship that nearly destroyed our marriage was more than I could bear. My heart raced, my head felt like it was going to explode, and I wanted to scream at the top of my lungs. I wanted desperately to leave service and return home to confront Eric, but that would have forced me to share that I had a problem, which I could not do without a breakdown. Instead, I called Eric and told him I found the phone bill and knew about the cover-up. I told him my plan to share this news with a church leader because I could no longer handle it. I would no longer protect his image as he had once again made a fool of me. I had enough.

After hanging up the phone with Eric, I called Deacon Lee, a leader in our church who was also a trusted advisor, Bible scholar and very dear friend. A couple of years prior, Lee had begun a series of marriage classes for couples in the church, and Eric and I were regular attendees. Lee knew of our history with the neighbor, and he could not believe that the neighbors' conversations had started again. I explained I was about to give up on my marriage. By that time, Eric was walking through the door, and Lee asked to speak with him. Eric was very angry that I told Lee about the ongoing issue, but I did not care. Eric seemed to have no capacity to put himself in my shoes. I left Eric on the phone with Lee, knowing that Lee would manage the matter. My prayer was that he could help save our marriage. Lee brought in another trusted friend who committed to wrapping themselves around our problems and helping us work through them. With Lee's counsel and my desire to separate due to years of deceit, Eric agreed to marital counseling with Lee. Lee insisted that Eric commit himself to our marriage and weekly counseling, and Eric did. These sessions began almost immediately.

During our first session, Lee explained it is the husband's responsibility to present his wife to Christ and he must be in the position to do so. Eric and I learned so much during that first session, and we were grateful. With each week, we grew stronger. Eric completely severed all ties and communication with our former neighbor (which happened immediately as a requirement for Lee to counsel us). As we reflected on God's creation of marriage and the mysteries surrounding His works, we discussed the many ways in which we knew our marriage was of God. We discussed the steps and manipulation that led to Eric's agreement to participate in the calling card scheme.

Eric shared his belief that I was unique and had a way of seeing what God wanted me to see, to the point of the phone bill falling into my lap. He repeatedly saw how God revealed the things I yearned for and needed to know and understand. It never failed. In my deepest, darkest moments, I cried out to The Lord, and He answered. I began to embrace the gift of hearing God's voice and worked like crazy to have the "right spirit" so I would see and discern more. I dreamed and shared my dreams with Eric. In many cases, my dreams revealed something close to the truth. Eric came to understand that what was in the dark, God would reveal. We got our marriage on track with Lee's counsel. We both grew through the process, and I believed the old neighbor would never be a problem again.

Chapter Twelve

A Major Career Shift

Young Women's Christian Association (YWCA) El Paso del Norte Region

El Paso's YWCA has a long and notable history. By most standards, YWCA leaders recognized it as the largest YWCA in the nation. Established in El Paso in 1909 by a group of prominent women, the YWCA had a solid reputation as a female-led organization that had played a significant role in improving women's lives in the Paso del Norte region from its early days as a western frontier town. The YWCA began to grow significantly with the appointment of Myrna Deckert as its executive director in the mid-to-late 1970s. Under Myrna's leadership, what was a small operation with one main branch grew to five community branches, eight pools and as many as sixteen childcare centers. Included were fifty-five after-school programs, housing for women and their children who were experiencing homelessness, plus an eight-acre camp. Over this same period, the number of staff grew from about thirty to as many as 700 at one time. The YWCA also had a large Consumer Credit Counseling Service and boasted more than twenty distinct programs. YWCA leaders across the United States were awed by its sprawling physical plant and $32 million budget.

My work with youth through the UTEP Outreach Programs placed me in some of the same circles as YWCA employees who worked in its teen leadership programs. As youth advocates in the community began to learn aspects of my story, many asked me to provide motivational speeches to share my story to inspire youth by impressing upon them that they can succeed in life, despite its many hardships. As I made my way about the community, schools and youth groups to deliver speeches and keynote addresses, staff from the YWCA Teen Leadership department asked me to join the YWCA teen advisory committee. This was the start of my volunteering with the YWCA. The YWCA became an essential part of my community service. I participated in their overnight weekend retreats and other workshops and outings. YWCA Board members noticed my engagement in their youth programs. They preferred to bring women onto their board of directors through service on one of the YWCA's numerous committees. My service and receiving the Reach Award made me a good candidate for the Board, and in 1999, the YWCA Board nominating committee asked me to serve on its Board of Directors. I gladly accepted the appointment, as I was enamored with Myrna Deckert and her larger-than-life image and reputation (as were most young professional women). As an organization whose national bylaws mandated a female governance model, the YWCA Board of Directors was comprised of females only. In El Paso, this group of women included the community's most familiar, revered and some of the wealthiest figures in the city. It was an honor to serve alongside these women.

Board members were each required to chair or co-chair a committee, and I became the Teen Leadership Committee chair. After chairing the Teen Leadership Committee, I became chair of the Child Development Committee. After a couple of years there, Myrna asked me to chair the Mary Ann Dodson Science Camp Committee. She warned that the Science Camp Committee would be challenging because Mary Ann Dodson also served on the Committee, representing El Paso's Insights Science Museum, a museum founded by Mary Ann and her late husband, Chuck. In Downtown El Paso, Insights exposed youths to science, technology, engineering, and math careers through hands-on experiences. Years earlier, the Dodson family had significantly contributed to the YWCA, and the YWCA Board named their upper valley camp in Mary Ann's honor. Mary Ann had a sincere interest in seeing two projects she cared so much about working together to support the success of the other. The YWCA Science Camp Committee led school outreach efforts to encourage attendance and overnight science experiences at the Mary Ann Dodson Camp. Insights Science Museum provided the teachers for each camp and a curriculum to inspire children to engage in science.

School districts paid a fee and transported students, and the YWCA and Insights shared the revenues, which offset the costs of maintenance, staffing by the YWCA and Insights, meals and other supplies. As Myrna and the Teen Leadership department staff warned me to tread lightly relative to working with Mrs. Dodson and having a directive to make the joint operating agreement fairer for the YWCA, I spent my first few meetings working to understand the Camp's history, challenges with the Insights partnership, and true operational costs. Mary Ann and I immediately liked one another, and she told me I was very smart. She listened and accepted my proposals to shift the revenue sharing to help the YWCA get closer to covering its costs. I enjoyed working with Mary Ann on the science camp committee, and this work carried me through my first three-year term on the Board.

I agreed to a second three-year board term. Shortly after beginning my second term, Myrna announced her retirement after almost forty years of leading the organization and building an amazing legacy. Members of the Board were shocked and wary of the task before us to search for her replacement. We hired a search firm and began the process. Search consultants tasked Board members with planning and participating in a two-day retreat during which we would lay the groundwork for the new executive search. Our goal was to develop a profile of the CEO we desired and a framework for her job description. We started the retreat on a Friday night. One of the exercises that night was for each board member to write the top three things we wanted to see in our new CEO. Once compiled, the following morning, we were provided a one-page summary of all the different characteristics, skills and qualities we collectively wanted our new CEO to embody.

There was laughter as everyone looked around the room, acknowledging this person did not exist but in a dream. My response was quite different. As I read each criterion, a feeling I cannot describe beyond a "swoosh" came over me. With that feeling, I leaned back in my chair, looked around the room, and thought, *Oh my God, they want me, but they don't know it.* At the same time, I heard a firm and clear voice speaking in my ear. It said, "It's not your time." The swoosh and the voice shook me. I stood up and went to the restroom. I cried silently because emotions overwhelmed me. As much as I felt in my heart this position was for me and I could do it, I understood it was not my time.

I told myself they would never consider me because the Board thought only God Himself could replace Myrna. I also felt that the organization, having never had a woman of color in such a role, was not ready to go down that path despite its motto to "eliminate racism and empower women." I felt this partly because community members had grown to understand the YWCA Board comprised (at that time) so many women of wealth and status. Whether it was my feeling of being *less than* others, others lacking the capacity to imagine a Black woman in this role, a combination of both and something else, it was not my time. I found the whole experience very strange. Myrna and I shared the same birthday which was equally strange. I pulled myself together and went back to the meeting. I had just completed my master's degree in May 2002 and was set to begin doctoral studies in the fall. I did not apply for the CEO position and never spoke to anyone about my spiritual experience during that meeting.

Concurrent with my time on the YWCA Board, I spent years as assistant vice president at UTEP and gained additional oversight of other grant programs. My growing portfolio extended my outreach and engagement in the greater El Paso region. During my first eleven years at UTEP, the folks under my leadership had increased from four to more than eighty full and part-time employees. In the fall of 2002, I began work toward attaining my doctorate in education. My first semester included a full-day class schedule on Mondays, taken with the new cohort of doctoral students. I flexed my work schedule with my supervisor's permission.

It did not take long for life's many demands to catch up with me. Five years had flown by, and it was time for me to write for the new Talent Search grant. I found myself weighing the question of whether to quit the doctoral program to ensure sufficient time to focus on writing a successful grant. I tried to do it all until things came to a head. There was no way I could complete both my end-of-semester school assignments and a good Talent Search application. I took my dilemma to my cohort's faculty liaison, who appealed my case for additional support. Because of my grades up to that point, they agreed to provide me an extension to the due date for my final assignments. I completed my Talent Search application, then focused on my finals, completing them in much less time than my professors allotted. I was so thankful I did not have to quit my studies.

Eric was a tremendous support during this time. For three years, I attended school full-time and worked full-time. I maintained my involvement in the church, as did he. I also took on leadership roles in the church. I sang in the choir and chaired the youth ministry for a period. I was active in Sunday school and attended meetings as a member of the Pastor's leadership team. I was very visible throughout the community. I had many church and community commitments throughout my time in the doctoral program, and I tried to honor them all. Folks often asked how I managed being a wife and mother of three young children. My response was always, "Through the Grace of God."

The longer I served on the YWCA Board, the more Board leaders pushed me to take on "gateway" volunteer roles. Gateway roles were those one must undertake to become qualified to serve as Board President. In the spring of 2005, Board leaders asked me to serve as co-chair of the Annual YWCA Women's Luncheon. Accepting this role meant I would chair the event in 2006. I agreed to serve in this capacity. Anticipating my success, the Board elected me to the position of President-elect. I would become Board President after two years of working and learning alongside the Board President. It was an honor to hold this position as there had only been one other African American Board President in the YWCA El Paso's ninety-five-year history.

At the same time that I was chairing the Women's Luncheon, I was also framing my dissertation and working to finalize my research topic and strategy. I had accumulated months of vacation hours, which usually rolled over into sick leave as I had reached the maximum carryover allowed annually. My accumulated vacation came in handy when I took a two-week vacation to complete a two-week dissertation preparation course that met daily between 8:00 am and 5:00 pm. Though this course was far from a vacation, it helped me to complete my dissertation proposal through the first few chapters, including the methodology.

About Grace

With God's grace, I found that no matter what I set my mind to, if I was doing the right thing or doing something to help others or the church, everything seemed to fall into place. If I put off an assignment to accomplish another task like attending Bible study, speaking to youth, or a women's group, I learned not to worry about the assignments or meeting the established deadlines. The answers for my assignments would seemingly fall into my lap from nowhere. The many pieces and parts of my life seemed to connect like putting together pieces of a puzzle. Getting answers and directions from seemingly random places and people become routine, and I began to embrace my life as living under grace.

My writing skills vastly improved through the master's degree. With each grant, I could see how better my writing was than the one I had written three or four years prior. An example of my life

> "But he said to me, 'My grace is sufficient for you, for my power is made perfect in weakness.' Therefore I will boast all the more gladly about my weaknesses, so that Christ's power may rest on me."
>
> 2 CORINTHIANS 12:9

and work during this time is having a paper due in three weeks. I would spend time thinking about the topic but did not attempt to write anything down as I lacked a clear focus or direction. I continually accepted engagements to speak to youth and church groups and presented academic topics at the state, regional, and national training meetings for TRIO and other programs. During any number of conversations held while volunteering my time to support a cause, someone would mention a resource or some emerging topic, something she saw in the news. At that moment, she unknowingly planted the seed and revealed the topic for my paper. I might jot down a note but continue to let the subject marinate in my mind. Then, more resources would come to me, and I was ready to write. Perhaps three-four days before the paper was due; the topic was all clear and ready to put on paper. This was grace manifested.

I believe the more I focused on God, the more He focused on me and revealed answers or solutions to my most challenging situations. Groups increasingly asked me to speak about my life or present on a subject of interest. Preparing for presentations made me think more about my childhood. Thinking back on my time and life in Detroit always led to my revisiting the events of that night when Momma sent Lorie and me to the store for cigarettes. I never forgot the man who took us home. I often shared this story with schools' "at-risk" youth groups. They were at risk because of poverty, and statistics noted their likelihood of not graduating from high school. According to the social implications of poverty, these kids were less likely to graduate high school and more likely to become teen parents. Growing up in poverty and spending time in foster care, I identified with this group of kids. They touched my heart and drew me to spend time trying to touch theirs. My words seemed to reach them, as shown on their faces. They had hope, and I could see it in their eyes.

Whenever I shared the story of being lost in Detroit and a strange man offering to take us home, I asked, "What do you think happened next?" It never failed that their answers were always horrible… "You were kidnapped" or "you were raped." They never guessed the truth: the tall, white male stranger took us *home*. Being a novice storyteller, I could never keep my composure during those early days of sharing my life, the tears flowed, and I apologized repeatedly. It was hard not to cry. When I recognize I am here today, whole and confident, partly because of this strange man who appeared in the crowd, I acknowledge and accept this man as an angel from God. Any normal adult would have wanted to know what type of parent sends two little girls out after dark, in the heart of Detroit, for cigarettes, of *all* things. This man could not have been ordinary. I have come to the solemn belief that angels are in our midst daily, helping those who cry out to God, seeking His help and mercy.

Nothing has been more impactful in my growth than the awareness that I have more because of my faith, and thanks to the prayers of my ancestors and mother, I am blessed. My capacity to remember and countless impactful memories were given to me for a time such as this to write this book and share that there is more to life than what we find on the surface—we must go deeper. The more I thought about my life, the more revelations unfolded. What drew me to immerse myself in the study of Spanish in high school and college? Was it just because I loved the language, or was it a requirement for God to orchestrate His great plan for my life? That plan included living most of my adult life on the US-Mexico border. Why did Robert receive only *one* job offer at a university that bordered Mexico? He was so smart, and his colleagues all received multiple offers. Though the marriage ended, my life began in El Paso, meeting Eric, remarrying and building a life and family together. Grace has undoubtedly been at the center of it all.

When it is time for a change, God will make it very clear

I neared the completion of my doctoral coursework, but things had to line up perfectly if I was to graduate in May of 2005. The assignments in my dissertation preparation course helped me shape my study topic and research methodology. Also, during that time, I developed my proposal to conduct research involving human subjects and submitted the plan to the University's Institutional Review Board (IRB) for approval. With the IRB approval, I began research for my study, "The Experiences of African American Middle and High School Students in a Predominantly Hispanic Educational Environment." I poured myself into student interviews, transcription, and making meaning of what I learned. It was as though everything I needed and related resources was unfolding before me. I wrote the dissertation in the spring of 2005 and graduated in May. With my doctorate behind me, I could anticipate changes in my career development and path at UTEP.

Meanwhile, a new provost was hired at UTEP. He was in the process of establishing his leadership team and I was asked to join him for lunch. At lunch, we discussed my thoughts regarding the future of Outreach Programs, and I explained these programs were endless, relative to adding a new program. I had developed a schedule of future grant opportunities for discussion purposes. He told me there was an opportunity for me to join his leadership team as they were looking to make changes in entering student programs. It would take some time for them to flesh out the details, but I assured him I was interested in the next step of my career. I was later told that I would be promoted to Associate Vice Provost and responsible for overseeing entering student programs. His plan was for me to collaborate with a colleague overseeing student retention programs and we both would report to the provost. As time passed, the timing of this change became less clear. I also appealed to retain the outreach programs under my supervision, as I had spent years developing and nurturing them. In response to my request to retain the programs, the provost said the burden of these programs, plus my new responsibilities, would be too much. I was so sad. I rationalized this loss by telling myself that I would be able to help the programs more from a higher-level position within the University.

Several months had passed. The provost had settled in and had started regular meetings with his direct reports. I was not included in these early meetings, and I wondered why. I faced a wall as I navigated the winding path to find answers. There was no specific plan, simply an affirmation that the change would happen, and we were moving forward. I received word via the Office of the Provost regarding changes in the provost's plan. Things did not fall into place as I had anticipated. Yes, I would still be a member of the provost's team, however instead of reporting directly to the provost, I would now be reporting to my colleague. The number of people reporting directly to the provost had become unmanageable. Thus, my new report. Though I was neither thrilled nor prepared with the shift in plans, I felt the need to get beyond it to make things work.

On moving day, my colleague and I disagreed by phone. The conversation ended with her telling me I could forget the position and stay where I was. Her tone shocked me. Living in daily tension with my new supervisor would be my new reality. I moved into my new office and attempted to assume what I understood to be my new responsibilities. At best, it was challenging to take on the

> "No weapon forged against you will prevail, and you will refute every tongue that accuses you. This is the heritage of the servants of the Lord, and this is their vindication from me,' declares the Lord."
>
> ISAIAH 54:17

role as there were revelations of internal politics and the expectations of others in the division. I met with one individual who explained that my new supervisor had promised her a promotion and the promotion entailed overseeing much of the work I was tapped to oversee. After about forty-five days, that individual resigned from her position. I found myself immersed in a web of petty power plays, but I committed to try to make the change work. As I sought to make strategic changes, I encountered obstacles at every turn. I felt increasingly ineffective.

I saw my former Outreach Programs staff on campus, and I could not hold back the tears. I felt boxed in a corner. I was far from happy and even farther from professional fulfillment. I began speaking quietly to God in my heart, "God, I know You did not prepare me for *this*. I always said when it was time for me to move on, You would make it clear." For me, it could not be clearer. I could not get through a day without tears. I made up my mind it was time for me to go. God had to take drastic steps to make me see it. God knew how much I loved the TRIO and outreach programs. He also knew I might never leave if I still had oversight of outreach. With that separation having occurred (thanks to the provost), my heart was free to go. Eric and I regularly discussed a potential career change for me as he could go anywhere in the country with his job at the Post Office.

> "Hear my prayer, Lord; listen to my cry for mercy. When I am in distress, I call to you, because you answer me."
>
> PSALM 86:6-7

An Update on Robert

I occasionally bumped into Robert while walking about the campus—he did not look well. His colleagues shared that he "looked like crap like he was sick." Robert had lost a lot of weight, but his weight constantly fluctuated. He earned tenure and remarried a woman he met during her graduate studies in science. I heard she was from Mexico and, after completing her doctorate at UTEP, moved up north to begin post-doctoral work. Robert left the University and took a position at a small Catholic girls' college. This change allowed him the opportunity to be closer to his new wife.

Shortly after I moved into the position of associate vice-provost, Robert phoned me from his new job out of state, and we had a short conversation about Upward Bound. He said that he had a student who was hoping to land a job as a summer counselor for an Upward Bound Program. He wondered if he could give her my number and if I would speak to her about the program. I agreed. We shared small talk, and he joked about being closer to God with his new position. We said goodbye, and I never heard from Robert again.

In Search of a New Job

It was November of 2005. I had not applied for a job in fourteen years and struggled with how much information was too much to provide on my resume. I received the Chronicle of Higher Education online, and job announcements were weekly. One position caught my attention. The requirements read like my resume; it was located in St. Louis, MO. I could not believe it. It involved outreach to schools throughout the state and helping connect youth to the college pipeline. I applied and thought it ironic that this perfect job was in my hometown. I researched background information on the company, and I was surprised that the CEO was so young, about forty years old, and an attorney by profession. It seemed as though it could be a great opportunity.

About a month later, I saw another position. It was with a major foundation in Kansas City, Kansas. It also matched my experience and credentials, so I also decided to apply for that one. This position was for a chief academic officer for the foundation's educational program, overseeing and providing leadership to teachers whose work focused on teaching youth at risk of academic failure. Though I was not a teacher by profession, I believe my initial experience hiring and leading instructors in the Upward Bound Program and my doctoral studies in educational leadership made me a great candidate. I thought, *Wow, God, You want me to return to the Midwest...I'm going back home*. I thought it was time to return to my family and my mother. She was aging, as was my father, and they were both beginning to experience the impacts of age and hard life. I figured that this was where God was leading me.

Shortly after applying for the position in Kansas City, the St. Louis agency made national news. There was a rift on its board of directors over whether and how to use millions of dollars to support infrastructure development among the state's public colleges and universities. The CEO resigned, and there was talk of a legislative battle because a state statute created the entity, and related funds were reportedly for a restricted purpose. The Chronicle of Higher Education reported the controversy and the organization's plight. I realized my "perfect" job was no longer viable. A couple of weeks later, I received an email stating that all agency vacancies were on hold until further notice. I was not surprised. I continued to scan the horizon for other opportunities.

In December, the CEO of the academic division for the Kansas City foundation invited me to participate in a telephone interview. I arranged to take the call at home, and Eric happened to be there. The chief executive officer downplayed my experience and questioned my qualifications to guide educators, having never taught in a public educational setting. I shared my Upward Bound experience.

He responded, "Oh yeah, I'm familiar with little Upward Bound and the TRIO programs." He was very condescending.

Afterward, I told Eric, "I know I did not get that one."

The 2005 Christmas holiday came and went. By then, I had risen in the ranks of the YWCA Board of Directors to the position of president-elect. In this role, I met every few weeks with the board president and the chief executive officer to review the status of the agency, challenges, or other pressing issues. We planned to meet for breakfast on January 3rd. Despite the New Year, simply entering my workspace proved energy-draining. I was tired of dealing with the drama on the job, so I chose to sulk in my office and not attend the YWCA meeting. About two hours later, the YWCA Board President called me.

"Sandra," she said, "you should not have missed the meeting with the CEO today."

"What happened," I asked.

I was not expecting her reply. "The chief executive officer gave me her letter of resignation today." I froze at my desk. She continued, "So I guess we will have to conduct another search. But I think you would be great for this position." I could not believe it. I phoned Lee Hoskinson, a mentor and the Deacon who counseled Eric and me and asked him to join me for lunch. I then shut my door and called Eric. My tears had become tears of joy. This was going to be my new job, and I knew it.

At that moment, I realized every time God planned a significant shift for my life, He made it very clear. His plans were always smooth and flawless, so only God could orchestrate them. Tears flowed like a river from my heart. God kept His promise. It was just three years prior when I sat as a YWCA board member, looking at the full-page list of characteristics of the next YWCA CEO. I recalled

> "Those who sow with tears will reap with songs of joy."
>
> PSALM 126:5

that voice, "It's not your time." I could not believe the turn of events. I was in awe of God's handy work. Never before was my future laid out so plainly. I knew *this job* was now mine, as revealed three years prior. How perfect a divinely laid plan. *Now* was my time, and I was ready to bid farewell to my position at the University.

On the Martin Luther King, Jr. holiday, I was the keynote speaker for the YWCA employees' "All Staff Day." I delayed submitting my credentials for the chief executive officer position as I did not want there to be gossip at the Board or staff level that I was a candidate. I was convinced that with my candidacy known, others would view me differently, which could affect my presentation to the staff. I also did not want them attempting to size me up amid the presentation. After All Staff Day, I submitted my application package. I then shared my actions with my supervisor. Several weeks into the process, my supervisor from the Outreach Programs department approached me and noted his awareness that my current role was not fulfilling my professional goals. He asked that I consider shifting to a different role under his leadership. I was already at the interview stage for the YWCA CEO, and I knew in my heart that God had established the position for me. I told the vice president I would consider it, pending the outcome of the YWCA position, though I strongly felt I would be successful through the hiring process. After several rounds of interviews with the search committee, Board and administrative staff, and reference checks, the YWCA Board offered me the position of chief executive officer, effective May 1, 2006.

> "The heart of man plans his way, but the Lord establishes his steps."
>
> PROVERBS 16:9

On Thursday, April 27, 2006, I had the honor of leading the YWCA Annual Women's Luncheon as the event chair. Jackie Joyner Kersee was our keynote speaker. Jackie was very gracious and gave willingly of her time. She even met with young high school athletes for a special presentation before her formal presentation to the Luncheon's 1,800-plus attendees. Before introducing Jackie, it fell to me to make the formal appeal for contributions. I shared the story of having experienced a period of homelessness, noting how people, even strangers, had opened their homes to me following my emancipation from foster care. Excerpts included, "The YWCA is *your* home. You built it, and every time you give to the YWCA, you make it possible for others to have a safe place—you are opening your home to women and their children who have no other options." Chairing the 2006 Women's Luncheon would be my last official act as a member of the YWCA Board and president-elect. During her closing remarks, the Board president presented me as the agency's new chief executive officer. The next day I boarded a flight to attend the national YWCA meeting in Washington, DC.

I was content and grateful. I met many executives at the national meeting, and the majority were surprised to learn of my role with the El Paso YWCA. There were two camps of women; one camp loved Myrna, and the other did not. My goal was to meet everyone where they were, despite their feelings. I was glad to return home and to my new office. During my first week, I received a call from the Kansas City foundation's representative. She wanted me to come for an onsite interview. I was shocked. Months had passed since my telephone interview. I never expected a callback. Knowing that I was where God wanted me to be, I thanked her for the opportunity and politely declined the offer, explaining that I had accepted another position.

God's Path Brings a New Set of Challenges

There is nothing like knowing that you are doing what God *purposed* you to do. Even though God gives us a path and directs the way, wrought is the journey with twists, turns, and challenges. The challenges unfolding at the YWCA were numerous; I questioned if this was where I was supposed to be. There were unethical, lying employees. One employee's lies forced a showdown with one of our funders. Another employee had a long history of perpetrating fraud, having manipulated operations for financial gains through back-door deals for years. In addition, there were thieves behind cash registers, and thieves "cleaned" our facilities.

Beyond the workforce, operationally, the childcare division was experiencing an $800 thousand deficit, and the fitness programs were equally distressed, operating at a whopping loss of just over one million dollars. Some random vendors and bullies would show up unannounced on Fridays to harass accounts payable clerks, demanding their checks. Despite the need to address these and other significant challenges, there was hope and belief in the eyes of hundreds of employees. Employees hugged me as I visited programs and facilities; some told me they had prayed for a strong leader to clean things up. Others prayed for a Christian leader, one able to bring back the foundational values of the Young Women's Christian Association.

Within the first year, I was able to make needed changes in staffing, including hiring a new chief financial officer (CFO). I was amazed at the new CFOs competence, ethics, and diligence—a real rock star, though uncelebrated. Together we devised structures and strategies to rid the agency of unethical people, set a network of identification protocols in new software programs, detailed procedures for financial operations, and ultimately purchased sufficient technology to identify those employees who abused and neglected financial protocols. As more employees left the agency, I felt increasingly vulnerable to foul play. I was not making many friends. I walked around my vehicle at the end of each day after work and checked for tampering. I had pissed off many people.

Help in the Storm

My administrative assistant retired, and God again blessed me with an amazing woman of God. CJ was insightful and dedicated her life to serving God. There is something about the love of Christ that shines through the heart and soul of His people. CJ came highly recommended, and her references told me that the school district's loss would be my significant gain—indeed, it was. CJ and I became a fierce team, praying together over the many issues and challenges that required my attention. Just knowing that she was constantly praying for me and the YWCA brought a sense of comfort. We loved one another, and I depended greatly on her insight and partnership. She was so much more than an administrative assistant—she was special. Her story, like mine and like that of Dolores (my administrative assistant from UTEP Upward Bound), was a remarkable one of overcoming a difficult childhood that forced her to grow up and care for her siblings when she was a teen in high school. CJs prayers reassured me that I was on God's path and to stay the course.

The YWCA presented me with the added challenge of a balancing act to address the many issues of the agency while keeping its numerous problems close to the vest to ensure not to tarnish its rich legacy. El Paso's small, tight-knit business community also challenged me to identify local mentors and advisors who could offer guidance and expertise as I pondered significant changes. I identified and approached several people who knew the agency, possessed needed expertise and agreed to honor my need for confidentiality. With wise counsel, I was able to verify my concerns and develop thoughtful solutions over time.

In 2009, Eric and I moved our church membership to Coronado Baptist, about three miles from our house. We had been in Bible study with Lee Hoskinson for years, and thanks to his support and counsel, Eric and I grew in our marriage and faith. Lee had joined Mt. Zion when he first moved to El Paso but eventually left to support the ministry of a dear friend who became the pastor of a church in the city of Horizon. Every Sunday after services at Mt. Zion, several families gathered for a potluck dinner and Bible study at Lee's house. Lee was more than a friend, and we went to Lee for everything whenever there was a pressing question about living a Godly life or a funny question about someone's interpretation of a Bible scripture.

After years of meeting on Sunday afternoons for "church following church," Lee announced that he would move back to Washington to be closer to his children. He was already seventy-two years old, and they had pressured him to return. Preparing for Lee's departure was difficult. Where would we find the expository teaching to which we had become accustomed? When we shared our thoughts on changing churches, Lee recommended several visits, and we settled in on Coronado Baptist. Eric and I joined the Sunday school class focused on healthy marriages and met other couples trying to live as God intended. We attended faithfully, every Sunday excluding vacation.

Listening to the Voice of God

I received an email from a strong colleague in the ministry and an author of several Christian books. She noted that she lived down the street from me and that the mail carrier delivered a letter of mine to her house by mistake. She was so excited that we were neighbors and could not believe that Eric and I had been in our house for three years, living on the same street. She agreed to walk the letter to my house. During our visit, she mentioned a woman she wanted to invite to her home for a weekend workshop.

The focus would be on "listening to the voice of God," and she asked if I would attend. I thought this workshop was right up my alley because I had spent a good portion of my life trying to listen to the voice of God. I wanted to do a better job of discerning God's will in my life. I agreed to participate, and we made plans for dinner and an introduction on Friday night, followed by a daylong workshop on Saturday. The session was a few months off as the presenter had yet to confirm the date. I was thankful to have been included in the small group of women invited for such an intimate study and anxiously awaited the workshop.

"For it is by grace you have been saved, through faith—and this is not from yourselves, it is the gift of God—not by works, so that no one can boast."

EPHESIANS 2:8-9

Social Media

In January of 2010, I received a request on the social network LinkedIn. It was from a male named "Larry." Being new to the social networking scene, I ignored the request. I was not keen on the idea of connecting with strangers. About a month passed, and I received a second request from Larry. I wondered why he was trying to connect with me. This time Larry added that his mother had been following my career in El Paso, and she was very proud of what I had accomplished. I looked a little deeper into his profile and saw that he spent time at UTEP and was now a scientist in Oklahoma. His profile lacked a photo, and I thought if I could see him, perhaps I would know who he was and feel better about allowing him to connect with my professional network. With LinkedIn, once you accept someone into your network, they can view and access all others in your network. I was leery of salespeople and folks connected to multi-level marketing companies.

I typed a note to Larry. "Why don't you have a picture?"

He responded, "I'm not as advanced as you are, and I have not gotten that far." I was not satisfied with this answer, so I ignored the request. Finally, another month passed, and I received a third note from Larry. This one stated in a very matter-of-fact manner, "Sandra, you need to call me. It has been a long time. My wife (he named her) asks about you and is doing fine." He provided his number. I looked at the wife's name and thought it was familiar, but I still could not place them.

I decided to call the next day. I asked for Larry and told him that this was Sandra. He was so surprised and glad to hear from me but explained that he was in a meeting and asked if he could call me later that evening. It was Friday, and I had dinner plans with the group of women attending the "Listening to the Voice of God" retreat. I gave him my cell number, feeling a bit more comfortable at that point. That evening, Larry phoned me just before I was to leave for dinner. He expressed how happy he was to connect. He asked about my job and said he and his wife were doing great. I still had no idea who he was, but I did not want to offend him, as he knew me reasonably well.

Larry said, "You know, when you all split up, we all understood why." I listened, still trying to figure out the voice on the other end of the phone.

I responded with interest, as though I knew exactly who he was. "Yeah, it was challenging…."

Then Larry said, "So, when was the last time you spoke to Robert?" At that moment, everything came rushing back to my memory.

Larry was one of Robert's former students who worked in his lab. Larry and his girlfriend would come to our house and hang out, and we occasionally had dinner with Larry's parents. I explained that I had not spoken to Robert since early in 2006 when he called me about one of his students who had expressed an interest in summer work with an Upward Bound program. Larry shared:

> "We never understood why Robert would leave a tenured position and take that position at such a little school. I kept in touch with him as much as I could when I moved to California. He really tried to stop drinking, but he never could. The job did not work out, and he was very depressed because he could not find work. I tried to send him notices of vacancies in the corporate research industry, but he was never interested. Well, the reason I have been trying to reach you is that I am sorry to tell you, but Robert died on December 22nd."

I felt terrible—here was Larry, trying to find me to tell me that my ex-husband is dead, and I ignored the inquiry. I asked Larry how Robert died, and he was not sure. Larry said that Robert's wife had tracked him down through Robert's computer. Robert had always been very secretive, so it was not surprising that he had locked his wife out of his computer, even as he had locked his family out of his life. Even his closest friends' contact information was under lock and key on Robert's computer. Once Robert's widow got inside, she found Larry's email address and reached out to him for help.

Larry continued, "Robert's wife had him cremated, and she needs help locating his family because she never met them. I hope you can help us contact his family so she can pass along the ashes and bring closure. Robert always talked about a lake in New Jersey, and she wants to meet with the family to spread his ashes there." This phone call blew me away! Heck, I *never* met his mother, either. It had been some seventeen years since my marriage to Robert and at least twelve since our divorce. Not only did I not remember his mother's name, but I also did not remember the one sister who came to our wedding. I told Larry it would take some time to see if I could find anything with the sister's name in my shed. I promised to get back to him within the coming week. I had no idea where to begin and felt burdened with the task ahead.

Following my call with Larry, I left for the workshop my neighbor was hosting. I apologized for being tardy and said nothing of my phone call. There were seven-to-eight participants. After brief introductions and reception, we had prayer over the meal and sat down to dinner. During dessert, our host asked what situation we would like covered in our prayers. When it was time to share, I began to tell the story of my phone call and the burden I felt in finding my now late ex-husband's family as they did not know of his death, and his widow needed to give them his ashes. By this point, I could not hold back the tears.

We discussed Robert's salvation. As a Christian believer, I understood that no matter life's sins and mistakes, one could ask God for forgiveness. One can profess their faith and belief that Jesus is the Son of God, that He died and rose again and lives in Heaven. One can ask Jesus to come into their heart, and they are saved through faith by God's grace. I was not sure what happened in Robert's last days, but I knew he was raised Catholic and should have had the opportunity to profess his faith. I also knew Robert passed away seven days after his fifty-first birthday. There was that number seven, again. The retreat leader prayed for each of our requested needs. We completed a few activities in preparation for the day ahead and departed for the night.

When Eric came home, I shared the news of my phone call and explained the burden I was carrying. Eric was supportive and lovingly told me to do what I needed. We went to bed, and I woke up early the next morning, about six o'clock. I lay in bed and prayed to God in my mind, *God, please help me to remember. Please help me to remember.* I continued to plead silently for help in remembering the names of Robert's family members. I was not hopeful about finding names in the storage shed. I lay there quietly, with Eric sound asleep. I began thinking, *What was his sister's name? What was her name?* Minutes passed, and I remembered that her name was Mary. I thought, *Yeah, that's it, Mary, and she was married to a guy named Dan. Yeah! Their names are Mary and Dan Myers.* I sprang from the bed and went to the computer to find them. Twenty years prior, Mary and Dan lived in New Jersey or Philadelphia or somewhere in Pennsylvania. I searched their names, and there were *hundreds* of people by these names and even more with variations. Where was I to begin?

After a few moments, I realized this attempt was fruitless, so I returned to bed. If only I could remember his mother's name. What was *her* name? I thought, *Gosh, her name was so Italian. What was her name? She moved to Florida to work for a phone company after the breakup of 'Ma Bell.' This is where she lived when she called Robert during our time in Columbia.* Then, unexpectedly it came to me—Gabriella Maria Esposito Webb! I jumped from the bed, ran upstairs to the computer, and searched for her full name. Just like that, it appeared. Only one was listed in Florida, and she was seventy-one years old by her public profile. This would make her old enough to be Robert's mother. I wrote down the information and emailed it to Larry, who was out of the country. I felt confident this was Robert's mother. I did not attempt to call her because I did not feel it was my place or purpose to phone her. In all these years, I had never held an honest conversation with Philomena, and I did not believe a relationship needed to start that day.

Chapter Thirteen

A Time to Every Purpose

Life Comes Full Circle

I spent significant time thinking about my life and this turn of events with Robert. What was the point of it all? My entire life, I gave Robert credit for getting me to El Paso. I told everyone his purpose in my life was to get me to El Paso because this is where my life began. If it had not been for Robert's one job offer, I might never have come to live and work in El Paso. More importantly, I would have never met Eric, whom I later married and shared in raising three beautiful children. My career took off in El Paso. I had achieved more than I ever thought I would achieve so many years ago when I first arrived in El Paso and applied for a teen leadership job at the YWCA.

It was obvious Robert's purpose in my life. What I had never thought about was my purpose in *his* life. In science, Newton's Third Law teaches us that every action has an equal and opposite reaction. I have come to believe this law also works in human nature. We meaningfully touch a life, and that touch, positive or negative, reacts. The reaction may not manifest itself immediately, and the originator of the touch may never know or understand the outcome. As much as I believed Robert's purpose was to get me to El Paso, I, too, had a purpose in his life.

Robert's death revealed my purpose in his life. I would like to think my purpose was to make him a better person, but the reality may be simply and profoundly that I was the *one* person on the planet who could timely reconnect him back to his family. Now *that* gave me pause. Here is a family that excluded me because of the color of my skin—a mother who would not open the door to a relationship with the wife of her only son. Yes, it fell to me, this horror of a Black daughter-in-law, to connect the pieces of their fragmented lives. Though I may never know what happened when they all got together to spread his ashes, I am confident my purpose was fulfilled in his death.

Doris and James

Mom and James were perfect for each other. It seemed the longer they were married, the more their lives mirrored that of other long-term married couples. They had their difficulties as any married couple. Whether true or imaginary, Momma believed other women were after her husband. She was certain that women were jealous of her and were out to steal her husband. Momma was also convinced that her social worker wanted to be with James. Though Lorie, Lacy and I often laughed at this thought (we figured no one but Momma wanted James), we recognized in her mind, it was as she believed—that was her reality.

Lorie phoned me and expressed concern that Momma wanted her place. She was sick of living with James and tired of "all of his women." Lorie spent considerable time working with *Places for People*, the agency that managed the care of Momma and James. They found Momma a one-room efficiency she could move into and separate from James. By now, Lorie was frustrated with the timeliness of her request, and Lorie was concerned that Momma was going back and forth about whether she would move. Lorie said Momma was concerned and did not feel safe with James anymore. At the same time, Momma would state emphatically she did not want to move in an efficiency. Lorie did not know what to do to make Momma decide. I asked Lorie why she felt she had to burden herself with this one way or the other. I told her that I would speak to Momma.

I phoned Momma to discuss the efficiency and her interest in separating from James. I explained that if she and James were not together, they could no longer retain the three-bedroom apartment as it was over the limit in the space allocated and subsidized for one person.

Momma was very upset and argued, "I am not giving up my home! Why do I need to move? Efficiency, I am not living in no efficiency!" I explained to Momma if she did not feel safe with James, she would need to move into the efficiency and there was no other option.

As I listened to Momma's rant regarding leaving her home and living in an efficiency, I could not help but think about my own experience with Robert. I lived in an efficiency after leaving him. The efficiency is where I was living when Eric came into my life. That time of privacy and independence afforded to me while living in my efficiency was the best. It allowed me to reflect on my life and to get to the bottom line of what I wanted.

The more I listened to Momma, I realized she was fine with James. She was just angry with him. I thought, *If an efficiency is good enough for me, why is it not good enough for her?* I phoned Lorie and told her that Momma was fine and that she could no longer worry about Momma's housing. The bottom line was if Momma truly felt threatened by James, she would do whatever it took to get away from him. With that, we stopped entertaining conversations about her moving and made it clear that the only option for her was the efficiency.

In December 2011, Lorie informed me that James was in the hospital. She said that he did not look good the last time she saw him and that the doctors feared it might be cancer. James and Momma had completed twenty-three years of marriage. They were lifelong companions and best friends. Though they were both mentally ill, together, they made a life. Test results later confirmed that it was cancer, and James refused chemotherapy. He still needed constant care and monitoring, so hospital staff transferred him to a long-term care facility. My aunts and uncles began to visit him in the hospital and asked my mother to go. Momma refused and continued to decline the opportunity to visit James for almost two months. James became increasingly agitated each time he would greet visitors, and Momma was not among the group. I spoke with Momma to see if she understood what was happening. I asked her why she would not go to the hospital to visit James.

Momma responded, "That's not James in that hospital bed, that's my hair doll." In another voice, she agitatedly said, "I'm not going up there to that hospital! For what? So that I can see a dying man?"

As the weeks passed, James' health deteriorated. I spoke to Momma and softly tried to convince her that she needed to see her husband. She responded that James was fine, he had come to visit her, and *she* was giving him chemotherapy. There was nothing much to say to Momma because the more one probed, the more upset she became.

My Aunt Dean and Momma were very close, and we lived with her at one point growing up. Aunt Dean had a way of reaching Momma that others lacked. Aunt Dean had promised James that she would bring Momma with her the next time she came for a visit. Aunt Dean went to Momma's apartment the day before she planned to take Momma to see James, laid out her clothes, and combed her hair for the next visit. Aunt Dean phoned the next day to let Momma know she was on her way to pick her up and take her to see James. When Aunt Dean arrived, Momma refused to go. Though she was very upset, Aunt Dean decided to continue to the hospital anyway. When she sat down with James, he was upset as usual. Whatever transpired during that visit led to Aunt Dean phoning Momma and putting James on the telephone. James asked Momma why she would not come to visit him. At that point, Momma began to cry and admitted that she would not come because she thought everyone was trying to trick her into going to the hospital to admit her. Momma promised James she would come the next time.

A few days passed, and Aunt Dean went to pick up Momma to take her to visit James. That visit was the last time Momma saw him alive. Lorie and I both lived out of state, so we immediately made the trip to St. Louis, knowing that we needed to plan a funeral, as Momma could not help. James' siblings had planned a cremation because of limited financial resources. James had a large family, and one of his brothers had a friend who owned a funeral home. That friend had taken the body from the hospital and was awaiting final details regarding arrangements.

Lorie made it clear she did not want cremation and we would raise the money necessary to have James embalmed, put in a casket and buried. When I arrived in St. Louis, Lorie followed up on funeral details by calling aunts, uncles, cousins, etc.... on Momma's side of the family. Several of them contributed money, and one of my uncles helped in a major way. My father also assisted, and we three girls made significant contributions. Lacy prepared James' obituary and funeral program. James' brothers and sisters came through, and we were able to work with the funeral home to plan a nice service.

We met James' son at Momma and James' apartment and discussed arrangements. James was a collector of all things electronic, and Momma was the collector of fashionable clothes and purses. Upon entering their apartment, there were two couches on the left and a long makeshift coffee table where they kept three computer monitors, dating back to the dinosaur days of computers. We spent significant time discussing the funeral, and Lacy agreed to make the obituary (she is very good at document management and producing printed programs for special occasions). I asked Momma if James' son could get rid of the monitors because they were no longer functional. She argued they were indeed functional and had the keyboards and everything; we just needed to plug them into an outlet.

I explained to Momma that those computer models on her table had been obsolete for decades. I pulled out my smartphone, "See, Momma, this is how small computers are today. Let me show you what all it can do." I showed Momma my phone and asked again if we could get rid of the monitors, and she agreed. James' son removed three monitors, and while she was not focusing on the monitors, we were able to get rid of three or four old printers, some keyboards, a scanner and a few other items, which were trash. It was a good night's work.

The undertaker told us he would call us when the body was ready for viewing. We settled on a Wednesday morning funeral. Lorie and I met Lacy at the cemetery. We agreed to pay for a double-deep grave jointly, acknowledging that Momma and James were lifelong companions and that her time would come (as will all of ours) and we needed to secure the plot for Momma to be buried with him. Lorie and I then went to Momma's house to get her out to socialize. We went to Daddy's house and spent the entire day laughing, joking, and talking to Momma. Momma decided to spend the night, and we were happy about that.

The next morning, we waited for the undertaker's call from the funeral parlor. We did not tell Momma that we would be going to view the body, as we did not plan to take her, not knowing how she would react. We made trips to pick up money from relatives, buy cleaning supplies, etc...... for what we would eventually do later in the week, cleaning Momma's apartment, which was not pleasant. Lorie slipped up and mentioned going by the funeral home to see the body, and Momma asked if we were going to see James.

Before Lorie could discourage her, I jumped in and replied, "Yes, Momma, would you like to go?" She decided she wanted to go, and Lorie gave me the evil eye, to which I responded that Momma should see him before the funeral. This way, there is time to recover from any unexpected outcomes.

We made our way to the funeral parlor and went inside. The undertaker was very proud of his effort and success in preparing James' body and making him appear as though he was still alive. He escorted us into the little chapel that adjoined the sales office. White netting draped over the casket's open lid and flowed past its front to keep people from touching the body. Momma stood next to the casket and stared. James looked better than he ever looked alive. His smooth caramel skin tone and handsome features shone radiantly through. Looking back, it was clear that life and mental illness had taken their toll. Even so, the undertaker brought him back to his natural, God-given beauty. Mom looked and smiled, and I prayed that she understood. I believed she did.

We gave mom sufficient time with the body, and just as we were about to leave, several of James' siblings arrived. It was quite emotional for them to see their brother in the casket. James was the first of his mother's eleven children to die. Lorie and I understood they needed to see James in a casket like Momma. The siblings all knew Momma and treated her well. Following a brief reunion, we made our way to Momma and James' apartment. She did not want to stay the night at my father's house again, so we spent time at her house and then went back to our routine of finalizing other funeral details.

James' Funeral

On Wednesday morning, we woke early to pick up Momma and bring her back to Daddy's, where the funeral car would meet the family for transportation to the church. Aside from a bit of confusion (which was no surprise) and the fact that we narrowly pulled off the funeral, once the ceremony started, it was very beautiful. Momma sat in the front row with Lorie next to her. James' son and a daughter whom we had never met also sat in the front row, along with a couple of his siblings. I sat off to the left on the second row, which put me on the other side, opposite immediate family members, as sitting in the family section would have landed me near the back row. Momma sat through the service with her hands held together; at times, she raised her hands to the front of her face as though praying. Momma lifted her hands in worship as the pianist sang beautiful, heartfelt songs.

The church Pastor gave remarks, and my Uncle Hut, Reverend David Rice, Sr., was also on the program to give remarks. The Pastor stood to review the order of events just before opening the program for remarks from family and friends. At that moment, Momma stood up and everyone looked and wondered what she was thinking. Exactly *what* was she about to do?

The Pastor, having his remarks interrupted, brushed over it and said, "Well, okay." Then Lorie grabbed Momma's arm and tried to pull her back to her seat. Momma pulled away, walked to the front of the church next to James' casket, grabbed the microphone and began to sing: "When I've gone the last mile of the way, I shall rest at the close of the day. I shall see the great King and His beauty, when I've gone, the last mile of the way." The pianist picked up the key and began to play for Momma. Momma repeated the verse. I broke down at that point. I had not heard my mother sing since we attended Faith Temple Church as a teenager. When Momma completed her tribute, the entire body of mourners stood on their feet, clapping and praising God. If ever there was any doubt as to whether Momma understood that James was gone, it was clear in those moments. Nothing more seemed to matter at that point. The funeral ended, the burial took place, we gathered for a repast and took Momma back to her place for the evening.

I cannot explain all of the past, nor do I know what lies ahead in the future. I pray that I have a lot more living to do and God continues to speak to my heart and move me to act in ways pleasing to Him. During the week of James' death, there were two other deaths of close family friends in El Paso. I was able to attend one of those funerals before flying to St. Louis. None of these individuals had the significant time or warning of their illnesses. For James and my El Paso friend, the time from diagnosis to death was about two months. While attending her funeral and repast the day before I traveled to St. Louis for James' funeral, I sat next to another friend. We had not seen each other in months. After the repast, we said goodbye. Four hours later, she went to the hospital and died. Her death was shocking and unexpected, as she had no known signs of illness. Life is short, tomorrow is not a promise, and our plans may not line up with God's.

Doris the Widow

Months passed, and Momma lived alone in the two-bedroom apartment she had shared with James. Though her case managers thought she should move to a smaller place to avoid further disruption, they agreed Momma would stay in her current situation as long as she was capable of successfully living independently. Momma did not do well living alone without James. She became increasingly suspicious and withdrawn. Case management staff assigned a housekeeper to help Momma, which worked well for a while until Momma became more suspicious that the woman was stealing her things and trying to poison her. Momma reached a point where she stopped taking her medicine for longer periods, and questions increased as to whether Momma was thriving in her efforts to live alone. The answer was a clear no. Momma was not getting better and would not leave the house.

During one visit to St. Louis, there was a dinner at Daddy's house, so we picked up Momma for a visit. We agreed that she would spend the night and enjoy as much time as possible with the family. After breakfast the following morning, we all sat in the formal living room and shared life stories. We laughed and reminisced. As was typical, we gave her money before we said goodbye to Momma and drove her home. Momma then said that she had money in her purse, but someone had stolen it.

Lorie asked her, "Who stole your money?" We never quite knew where imagination and truth began and ended with Momma, so we always took care to explore her conversations and claims. Momma explained she was walking down the street, around the corner from her house, and a group of men approached her and yelled, "Drop it!" She said she was afraid, so she dropped it, just as they told her.

Momma went on to give details as to how they looked and what their hair was like. Momma explained she had $13.47 in her purse, and they took it. Eric told Momma he was so sorry she had lost her money, and he promised to replace it. He asked her again how much money she lost to see if she remembered the number (he was also trying to be funny because it was such an odd number, and he did not believe her story). Momma repeated it. Eric then went downstairs, retrieved his wallet, counted $13.47 and gave it to Momma. She was pleased. I shook my head at Eric and noted, "You are not funny!"

Despite our uncertainty about the truth of Momma's story, we were very disturbed and felt the need to report it to case managers. Momma's apartment key was also in the purse, and we were afraid this put her in the vulnerable position of someone possibly accessing her apartment when she was alone. Because it was a weekend, Lorie jumped through a few hoops to reach an administrator who could see to the lock being changed. Though they could not get to it that day, they agreed to do it first thing Monday. We contemplated and agreed that it was best to keep Momma with us an extra night until we were certain no one would enter her apartment while she was there.

Later that afternoon, Lorie drove Momma to her place to pick up a change of clothes and to take Momma for her daily dose of medicine.

Lorie phoned me. "Guess what?" I feared she would tell me someone had broken into Momma's apartment. Lorie continued, "I found Momma's purse." Lorie said she asked Momma where she was when the men approached her. Momma explained that because staff had made it clear that she needed to get out of the house and do more socially if she was to continue to live alone, and she decided to take a walk. It was during the walk when she encountered the group. Lorie said that something led her to drive to the end of the street, turn right and then turn right on another street where there was a field. Lorie said something led her to go into the field where she found Momma's purse, keys, and deodorant inside, but no money. We were thrilled we would not have to change her lock. We still could not help but question if Momma's encounter was real or imagined—we were happy that she was okay and that Lorie had found her purse.

Following that St. Louis trip, Lorie and I agreed to increase the level of intentional monitoring from afar and to increase communications with her case managers. As time passed, Momma's case manager expressed concerns that Momma had been refusing to take her medicines. The team responsible for her care and oversight also noted she had become increasingly reclusive and paranoid. Lorie and I routinely spoke, sharing our phone interactions with Momma and conversations with Team D staff. Weeks passed, and Momma refused to take her medicines.

The case manager asked Lorie to speak with Momma to convince her to take her medicine lest the team force her to do so at a medical facility. Lorie made calls and implored Momma to take her medicine. Momma finally agreed and began taking her diabetes medicine and occasional doses of psychotropic medicines. Momma's mental stability worsened, and she finally quit retaking all medicines. The care team decided to give Momma a certain number of weeks to comply. If neither they nor we could convince her to take her pills, then they would force her to take them by the authority of The Baker Act. The Act allows forced admittance to a mental health facility if someone is doing bodily harm to themselves or others, usually resulting from mental instability. We understood the situation and prayed that Momma would comply. We hated the thought of her going to the hospital by force.

Doris Gets a New Home

Momma's case manager called Lorie and explained that they did not successfully get Momma to take her medicine. Their only option was to call the sheriff to transport her to the hospital. They asked if Lorie was okay with this. Lorie phoned me, and we had a painful discussion, knowing this was the only way to save Momma from herself, to get her rebalanced and to lessen the risk of greater complications from her diabetes. We also notified Lacy of Momma's pending trip to the hospital, and Lacy agreed to go to the hospital to check on Momma following the sheriff's transport. Lorie telephoned the case manager and affirmed their decision to call the sheriff to transport Momma to the hospital.

Lorie and I were relieved when Lacy phoned and let us speak to Momma. Momma was not "locked down" but stationed on the psych floor. Daddy also went with Lacy to visit Momma. Momma was in a pleasant mood and told Lacy and Daddy that she would be there for a few days.

Work began almost immediately to find Momma a place to live because returning to her apartment was not an option. In many ways, we felt great about this. We knew she could not live well alone. On the other hand, housing options were few for persons living on social security and disability income. Momma was not a good candidate for a roommate. Adding to our concern was facility staff, who noted if Momma failed to thrive while living there, she would have no other option but institutionalization, perhaps permanently. Thoughts of this were unbearable, so Lorie and Lacy asked others for recommendations. Within a few days, Lorie and Lacy secured a private room at the nursing home in south St. Louis.

A Guardian for Momma

With Momma's transition to the nursing home, her old case managers had limited time they could legally serve as her guardian. They explained to Lorie that they could not continue to serve as Momma's personal and financial guardian. They would need to transfer Momma's checks to the nursing home, who would be assuming her care. However, the nursing home staff could not serve as Momma's guardian. They offered us advice on guardianship for Momma moving forward.

As we girls discussed the need for Momma's guardianship to change, Lorie and I were not successful in explaining to Lacy the rationale given to us as to why one of us would need to be Momma's guardian. Despite this, we agreed in moving forward with a guardianship claim, Lorie would be the best person to serve in this role, despite her living out of state. Lacy refused to become a party in our legal case to change Momma's guardianship.

For Lorie to gain guardianship, we needed to hire an attorney who specialized and was sensitive to guardianship issues with fragile adults. I had no idea where to begin the process of hiring an attorney in Missouri. I decided to reach out to Doni Driemeier, my dear friend from high school whose family took me in during my senior year after my emancipation from foster care. Doni and I had kept in touch over the years, and she mentioned her father had a friend who had since retired but had done a lot of work with guardianship matters. She agreed to talk to her dad to see if he could offer guidance. Doni called me with the name of an attorney who might be able to point me in the right direction.

My conversation with the attorney was very helpful, and he provided me with the name of a young woman he believed would be very sensitive to our situation with Momma. She had focused her career on advocating for disenfranchised persons, including adults with mental illness who faced guardianship issues. Sarika was her name, and I contacted her via email. Sarika and I set up a call during which she explained that though she could represent us, Momma would require an ad litem attorney to represent her interests. Sarika also explained we would be responsible for paying the costs of Momma's attorney and that there were potential risks should Momma decide to fight us by exclaiming she is not ill and could therefore take care of herself. Sarika advised if this was the case, a separate psychiatric evaluation might be required, the case would take longer, and it could get expensive. After reviewing Sarika's proposal and costs, Lorie and I agreed that she was the right person.

Momma's Day in Court

Lorie and I made our way to St. Louis. We resigned ourselves to the fact that Lacy would remain disengaged, and we prayed that she would not have a last-minute change of heart, which could do more harm than good because of her lack of prior engagement. Sarika provided copies of Momma's recent psychiatric evaluation that noted her diagnosis of schizophrenia. I found this very emotional. Though we had always known Momma's illness, reading the doctor's notes regarding Momma's capabilities and related commentary made me cry. My tears came like a rushing river bursting through a dam. Momma's capacity, per the doctor, was heartbreaking, and knowing that Lorie and I would face Momma in court was equally heartbreaking. Still, it was the only way to move forward.

On the morning of our court date, Lorie and I went to the nursing home to assist Momma with her wardrobe and hair. We also needed to work toward establishing a calm and cooperative mindset. We had no idea what to expect during court. We had prayed about as much as possible, stopping short of insulting God's power and ability to do all we had already asked. We knew only He could order the day's events for our desired outcome. We told Momma we had to go to court so that Lorie could gain authority to assist her in making decisions about her life. Up to the court date, Momma was uncooperative and argumentative. She stated she did not need Lorie to make decisions for her.

"I'm a grown woman. What do I look like, a child? I don't need Lorie making decisions for me. I can make decisions for myself." She continued, "What? Do I look crazy? You think I'm crazy? You all are the ones who are crazy!" Therefore, with these back-and-forth deliberations up to the court date, we all had our hopes and prayers that God would intervene so we could move forward for Momma's sake.

I dropped Lorie and Momma at the doorsteps of the courthouse and found parking. I quickly joined them after passing through security. We took the elevator to the proper floor and sat on benches in the middle of the hallway, waiting for our attorney. Within minutes, Sarika arrived, and she met Momma and greeted her in a very caring and friendly manner. A short time later, Momma's attorney ad litem arrived. Sarika knew her, and we were delighted with their obvious collegiality and mutual respect. Momma's attorney explained that she needed to spend a few minutes with Momma to explain the court's proceedings and her role in being there to support Momma. Lorie and I hugged Momma and told her we were not going anywhere. Momma and her attorney did not go far. They found another area to sit and talk within our sight.

After a while, a court official ushered us into the courtroom. The atmosphere was very formal and a bit intimidating. Because I was the petitioner, they sat me at the hearing table next to Sarika, in the center of the small courtroom and across from Momma and her attorney. Lorie sat behind us, in an elevated box, almost like a juror. The judge and a court reporter sat in a typical courtroom fashion. Following brief introductions and the judge's naming of the cause of the hearing, the judge noted he had received and reviewed Momma's medical history and the doctor's evaluation.

The judge asked me about my relationship with my mother. I responded, "I love my mother. She raised us with good values and was an excellent mother when she was in her right frame of mind." The judge asked if I believed my mother was capable of making important decisions about her life and health, and I responded, "No, sir." He probed further, and I explained, "My mother has schizophrenia, and she has dealt with it all my life." At that moment, the tears began to flow as I looked into Momma's eyes. I could sense she felt a sense of betrayal, and I watched her expressions change from one of disengagement and occasional smiles for the daughter she loved to confusion.

Momma interrupted me, "How could you say such a thing about *your mother?*" Her attorney urged her to stay calm and assured her she would have a chance to talk to the judge. The judge asked me about my sister Lorie and why I thought she was the best person to take on the role of guardian should the Court rule in our favor. He also noted our having a sibling, Lacy, who resided in St. Louis. I explained that Lorie was the oldest and historically kept in closer touch with Momma, ensuring at minimum weekly calls, regular trips to St. Louis and attending to Momma's personal needs through following up with her case managers and such.

The judge then turned his questions to Momma. He asked her a few questions about her relationship with her daughters. Momma explained, "I love my daughters; they are very blessed." Momma's love for her daughters was clear, but her other incoherent responses made it equally clear, early on, that she was mentally ill. The judge asked Momma if she believed her daughters loved her and wanted what was best for her. Momma replied, "Yes, my children love me." He continued, asking if she believed she would benefit from having someone to help her make life decisions and look out for her best interest. Momma responded, "Well, if it is Lorie, then yes, I don't mind."

Finally, the judge turned his attention to Lorie and asked her specific questions regarding her willingness to serve in the role of guardian. He explained her responsibilities of completing annual paperwork and her rights relative to acting on Momma's behalf. Lorie noted her understanding and agreement with the related responsibilities. After a few more moments of review, the judge granted Lorie guardianship and thanked us for our efforts, noting our clear love for our mother and her best interests. He thanked the attorneys who represented both sides. With the judge's gavel, he concluded the case within less than an hour. Lorie and I thanked Sarika and Momma's ad litem attorney, leaving the courthouse as we came together. Lorie and I commented on how smooth things went, and we celebrated with Momma by buying White Castles, her favorite, and returned to Daddy's house.

A Renewed Spirit

With Momma's case behind us and our having secured her future residency at the nursing home, I returned to El Paso, back to my work at the YWCA. The experience with Momma made me long for the opportunity to visit her more regularly, to assist Lorie and Lacy as much as possible. This would require a larger budget as it was costly to travel to most places from El Paso. I had a few conversations with a close friend and professional colleague, during which I confided my readiness to leave the YWCA. I felt I was starting to experience recycling of some of the issues I had successfully resolved.

The Child Care division, though in much better shape financially, began to experience turnover, and finding qualified leaders at the salary offered was difficult. Technology was significantly improved, but we were now experiencing the need for upgrades and improvements. Facilities and maintenance costs were an ongoing challenge, though significant improvements had taken place thanks to the changes in our contracted agency and oversight of these operations. As I saw my role as CEO rounding a full cycle, I was dismayed at the thought of another full run on the hamster's wheel. I did not want to do the same thing over again. I felt like certain members of the Board lacked appreciation of the challenge of our work and the efforts I had led to bring the agency from the brink of front-page news due to the many fiscal and other challenges I inherited. I was ready for a change.

I then found myself apologizing to God. I apologized because I knew He was the reason I went to the YWCA, to begin with. I recalled my experience in the Board meeting following the announcement of Myrna's retirement, that whooshing feeling that came over me, and the voice in my ear. While praying and apologizing to God, I told him, "Lord, I know you brought me here, and I am sorry I have not fully honored your plan for my life. Though I am ready to leave, I depend on You. If it is Your will that I remain at the YWCA, please give me a renewed spirit." I prayed for a renewed spirit, and God answered my prayer.

My friend remained a steadfast and dependable confidant through many conversations regarding my work at the YWCA. She was insightful and wise.

During one such conversation, she commented, "Sandra, you may be ready to leave but is the agency ready for you to leave? Have you prepared the agency to move forward in your absence?" As I pondered the question, I realized that despite my efforts and accomplishments, there was still work to do. I needed to ensure that the heart of the YWCA was poised to keep beating, ethically and morally without me, when I left. I recognized the heart of the YWCA was its people—our workforce. I thought about the many people who had left the agency. Many of those departures were necessary and were cause for celebration.

In response to my prayer for a renewed spirit, I set out to strengthen the people's hearts. This would be my new thing, carrying me through the next phase of my work at the YWCA. Many projects moved the agenda forward, including developing a new onboarding process for employees. The new orientation would focus on people, their needs, our clients and our values and ensure a meaningful connection between employees and supervisors from day one. Over a year, our orientation shifted dramatically, from a four-hour information session of "being talked at" to an engaging two-day session of immersion in the company culture, programs, locations, tours, meetings with supervisors, etc. Once that project was successfully underway, I established a CEO Leadership Series, akin to the wildly successful leadership programs hosted by community chambers of commerce. The first class comprised up-and-coming leaders and employees across the agency who held front-facing jobs. Other inaugural members included individuals who had demonstrated a passion for the YWCA clients and programs. These also were individuals who were quick to volunteer to help on committees and special projects and who had proven loyal ambassadors for the company's values.

I could not believe how time began to fly when I threw myself into this new body of work. It was as though I was building an army of "mini-me" enthusiasts for our work. All the other projects moved forward as much as possible as financial resources remained challenging. Even so, I found renewed life in this work and prepared the agency for my departure, whatever that meant. I had faith it would be great, no matter what and whenever God willed it so.

A Nail in the Coffin

In June 2014, the YWCA USA held its annual convention in Washington, DC. I attended with several staff and members of the local Board of the

YWCA El Paso del Norte Region. During the meeting, the national staff unveiled its new publication on racial justice. There were many discussions regarding the renewed focus on girls of color, noting that to empower *any* girls, we must first acknowledge the position of African American girls and other girls of color who appeared at the bottom of most progress indicators. The idea put forth by the national staff was that by focusing on increasing opportunities for Black girls, when their lives improve, opportunities for all girls would improve, by default. Many breakout sessions focused on the topic. The national CEO shared progress toward identifying measures by which all YWCAs in the country might contribute data.

I felt that I was slowly disconnecting from the politics of the YWCA. If this became clear, it was during the YWCA USA Business Meeting, held on the last day of the conference. When the floor opened for new business and discussion, someone asked when the YWCA USA would remove the divisive aspect of its history by eliminating the word "Christian" from its name. The YMCA had already taken such a step and now identified itself as simply "The Y." The member who posed the question noted there were many faiths represented among the membership of the YWCA, the YWCA was not inclusive, and it discouraged women of other faiths from taking on leadership roles. This was a battle with debates dating back many years.

I recalled my first national meeting of the YWCA USA in Albuquerque some fifteen years earlier. It was highly contentious as member agencies across the country came together to seek and mandate a change in the national structure. Alongside this fight was the issue of the name and use of Christianity. Member agencies and their delegations from the United States stood and argued late into the night about why the name should or should not change. To move the agenda of a new national structure and priorities forward, the body of attendees agreed to drop the issue of the name to focus on achieving a majority vote on a new national structure.

As I sat in the meeting in Washington, DC, I thought to myself, *Here we go again…* The national CEO commented she had received several letters requesting a name change and the National Board was exploring opportunities to address it in the future. She also noted we had, in effect, already addressed it as we do business as The YWCA USA, noting the organization's formal name was only required for legal documents. I recalled the history of the battles that ensued among the membership every time the issue of a name change arose, and I anticipated perhaps at a future national meeting, the membership would have to debate and vote on the continued use of "Christian."

Some El Paso YWCA members agreed that the YWCA USA should change its name. Our local Board was very diverse and included women of varied faiths and beliefs and others who considered themselves non-religious altogether. Though local leaders occasionally asked about a name change to remove Christian, the matter had not come before our Board. Also, as the YWCA USA had not addressed the name change, there was no urgency or political appetite to address it locally.

In August 2014, the Board Chair of the YWCA El Paso del Norte Region entered her second and final year as president. She worked with the Board Executive Committee to lay out certain goals for the year to ensure she could achieve critical milestones before the completion of her term. Among the year's goals was to develop and present a contract to the CEO, a first for the agency. Having raised the issue of a contract on numerous occasions in years past, I was pleased that they would place a focused effort on this goal. The uncertainty of one's career from one year to the next with changes in Board leadership was unsettling at best. Every time the Board installed a new president, I went through a period of mourning and anxiety. There were so many questions and habits to learn again or develop. Failure to adapt to the new Board leader's style and preferences could immediately lay a path of conflict that could lead to my eventual demise. In such a case, my employment separation would come not because I could not perform the CEO duties but because I could not mold myself into the image and style of my new boss…for the next year or two.

A contract would make clear the circumstances surrounding the termination of the CEO. I was constantly being terminated (in my mind) for reasons such as hurting the feelings of a Board member. The Board could fire me for any petty reason without consideration or compensation. I often thought about what Myrna would jokingly say (though it was no joke), "I am one Board president away from being fired." I believed a contract would lay out the terms of separation from the company and related severance. After many years, a contract for the CEO was now at the forefront of Board goals for the year. After eight-plus years without a contract, I wondered if I wanted to be tied down.

In the summer of 2015, I received the proposed CEO contract for my review. The Board President expressed her hope, I would have a quick review followed by the Board's approval to have the contract executed well before the end of the fiscal year and turnover of the Board president. Together these items—the vote, the contract and a new president on the horizon, created the perfect storm of emotions within me. I completed a quick, cursory review of the contract and sighed deeply. This would take some time. I zeroed in on its tone, which I felt was not reflective of the long-term relationship I had enjoyed with the agency and its Board. Among a few of my concerns about a CEO contract were phrases like:

- Must dress appropriately at all times.

- No guarantee of retaining a company vehicle or vehicle allowance.

- Termination of the CEO without cause and no severance under such termination; however, if the CEO left on good terms, she would be entitled to certain benefits (benefits that had, basically, already been earned).

The more I read, the more discouraged I became— *Who has a problem with my dress, and who is going to instruct me as to whether my dress is appropriate?* Other thoughts included, *Are you planning to take away benefits?* I put the contract aside to work through this.

That same summer, the YWCA USA called for a vote of member associations on the action item of removing "Christian" from its national Bylaws and Articles of Incorporation. Instead of voting in person, as was the case of most controversial votes taken nationally, national leaders sent the matter to the membership via an email with an explanation that each member association would debate the matter internally and determine one position, one vote, to be communicated to the national organization. Voting would be via online submission, with each Association voting individually on whether or not to support the change. I was shocked that our national office would ask for an email vote on such a divisive topic.

To comply with the timing of the vote and meet the national deadline, we prepared the email with as much clarity as possible, sent it to the Board, and awaited responses. Upon receiving the email, several people complained that we needed a special meeting to discuss the issue. In the interim, we began receiving other Board members' votes online. Early votes leaned toward removing Christian from the YWCA USA governing documents. I was very uncomfortable with this potential outcome, as I feared God and the prospect of what could happen when the governing body removed His name. I spoke with God, "Lord, I know the YWCA is not a Christian organization. It has not operated as a Christian organization in the United States for many years. I do not have to work for a Christian organization. I do not want to continue to work for an organization where You have existed, and Your name is intentionally removed."

I was very concerned. I believe people often do not understand or see the protection or blessings of God's cover until it is gone. Because I feared the wrath of God, I prayed to be removed if the national vote passed. The Board president called a special meeting to take place almost immediately. I focused my energies on researching and preparing documents that addressed the history of the World YWCA and its *continued* existence as a Christian-based organization of which the YWCA USA is a member.

During the special meeting, the Board debated the matter of our vote to keep or remove "Christian" in the formal name of the YWCA USA.

There was a sufficient debate on both sides, and someone asked, "What would happen if a non-Jewish participant in a Jewish program asked the program to remove Jewish from their name?" A Jewish board member responded this would never be a question. She added that she puts herself in the place of Christian women, and even though she is Jewish, she would not ask that the Christian organization remove its history by changing the formal name. The Board member noted she had never felt excluded in programs of the YWCA USA and that she would vote against the motion to change the name. With this strong affirmation, the YWCA El Paso del Norte Region voted to retain the Christian in the formal name of its national organization. It would be months before the national CEO disclosed the outcome.

I had plenty to keep me busy, with preparations underway for Jordan's high school graduation, our annual July vacation and our family's drive to Missouri in early August to take the girls to college. Professionally, there was the budget, completing my annual CEO self-evaluation for the Board of Directors, and finalizing the outcomes of our prior-year goals and objectives.

After completing the agency budget, I turned my attention back to the draft contract for the CEO. Again, I pushed the contract aside, which weighed greatly on me and affected my morale. I had to focus on other tasks to make progress toward the end of the fiscal year.

The Board President asked for a timeframe as to when I would return the contract. I knew I could not continue to put it off—they wanted it finalized before the start of the new fiscal year. I also knew there was no way this was going to happen. I had not touched it for about two months. Word finally came down from the YWCA USA regarding the name change. Members' vote were affirmative to remove Christian from its formal name and Articles of Incorporation. The national staff, under the direction of the national CEO, had already begun work with attorneys to change the governing documents. My heart sank further. I believed that the YWCA USA would have to account for this act against the name of Christ, and I did not want to be there to experience whatever would come next. I felt I could not attend YWCA USA meetings and commit myself to work toward a plan without my sense that God was in charge and making success possible. In addition, I questioned how the YWCA USA would reconcile this vote with the World YWCA, where a "commitment to the Christian background and identity of the YWCA" remained integral to expectations of member agencies, per World YWCA Affiliation Standards.

Chapter Fourteen

THE PRAYER OF JABEZ

My Next Career Opportunity

In early August 2015, we packed up Jordan's belongings and prepared for our cross-country drive to take her and Erica to college. Jordan would attend college in Missouri, like her sister Erica. After a few days in St. Louis, we drove Erica to Mizzou to begin her duties as a resident assistant. After unloading, shopping for supplies, assisting with set-up, etc....we took the standard "dropping a kid off at college" photo, posted it to Facebook and made our way back to St. Louis. Four days would pass before we had to return to Columbia, MO, for Jordan. We followed the same routine as Erica, except we were dropping Jordan at Stephens College, about a mile down the road from Mizzou. While on campus with Jordan, my phone rang. The call was from an El Paso colleague assisting with the CEO's search for the local health foundation there.

He asked if I had considered applying for the vacant position, to which I laughed and replied, "No."

"Why not?" he asked. I explained I found the idea of my serving in that role to be weird. It just so happened the CEO retiring from that position was the same one who had led the YWCA for more than thirty years. When she retired from the YWCA, the Board hired a replacement who left the role after three years, which led to my hire.

I explained, "I think it odd I would follow her into another high-profile community job." After a bit of coaxing, I agreed I would apply. I honestly did not feel that this was *my* opportunity. There were no warm fuzzy emotions, no bells going off in my head—it was, at best, an interesting opportunity to watch.

I understood one never knows how God will answer our prayers. I recalled my Pastor's comments from a recent sermon, "We pray and ask God to change our situation or to bless us, and then we want to direct Him in the manner with which it happens." I did not want to be that person who questioned God and missed His blessing because I thought I knew better what was right for me. I decided to keep my promise to my colleague, not because I believed the position was for me at that time, but more out of my sense of obedience to what God might be prompting.

Whenever I sincerely seek a new career opportunity, I pray "The Prayer of Jabez." This is a tiny prayer that appears in 1 Chronicles 4:10. It is odd because it leaps off the pages of what some might consider a boring section of The Bible, where we learn about the descendants of Judah. It is a section loaded with names, names and more names, and then, just like that, out pops the Prayer of Jabez. The Bible introduces Jabez, noting his mother named him Jabez because she bore him in pain. I prayed this prayer while in my turmoil at the university, and I began to pray it daily during this period of reflection while contemplating my future with the YWCA. I only pray this prayer when I am ready for change, with a sincere heart, ready for God to move me to that place where He wants me to serve.

> "Jabez called upon the God of Israel, saying, 'Oh, that You would bless me indeed, and enlarge my territory, that Your hand would be with me, and that You would keep me from evil, that I may not cause pain!' So God granted him what he requested."
>
> 1 Chronicles 4:10

It was September before I would submit my letter of interest for the other health foundation position. I focused my attention on the many tasks that lay before me at the YWCA—the priority was completing my review, followed by providing comments and thoughtful responses to the proposed CEO contract.

Be Thoughtful and Don't Take it Personal

It was as though I was looking at the draft CEO contract for the first time. Line by line and page by page, I made my way through it. Wherever there was a concern, I noted it and provided a rationale for why the Board might reconsider. The more progress I made, the more I felt a spirit of peace and calm over my future. It was becoming clear that the draft contract was neither a statement regarding my performance nor the Board's intent to push me away; it was simply a template. That template was, not surprisingly, slanted in favor of its creator, the Board. My responsibility was not to take it personally but rather to inform the process with a balanced reality check. I found the process liberating, and I increasingly gained a deep sense that I was not doing this review for myself but for a future YWCA CEO.

October came and went. I had heard nothing from the local foundation. I had also shared with my Pastor that I had applied for that job, and he said that he would be in prayer for God's will in our lives. On Sunday, November 15, 2015, I made certain to speak to the Pastor after church.

> "You keep him in perfect peace whose mind is stayed on you, because he trusts in you. Trust in the Lord forever, for the Lord God is an everlasting rock."
>
> ISAIAH 26:3-4

As I shook his hand, he asked, "So Sandra, how was your interview?"

I responded, "Well, Pastor, I don't know if I will receive an interview; I have heard nothing."

Then my Pastor stepped back, looked me dead between the eyes, pointed very matter-of-factly, and said with conviction, "Well, you're getting one!"

I was shocked at the Pastor's statement, and all I could muster to respond was, "Pastor, from your mouth to God's ears," as I pointed to the heavens and looked above.

His Plan Unfolds

On Thursday, November 19, 2015, I received an email personally addressed to me. The sender represented a search firm conducting an executive search for a large non-profit, a Jewish family services agency, in Florida. I glanced at the job description, which read exactly like my job at the YWCA. My natural response was to discard it—what sense did it make to do precisely what I was already doing. In addition, I thought a Jewish agency would never consider a Black, non-Jewish woman to lead their agency. Aware of my workspace, I forwarded the email to my home address and wrote it off as coincidental. I believe I received the note due to my being part of a larger mailing list of random people.

I was glad to finish the week, and on Friday, I went home and commenced relaxing with Eric. At one point, I decided to check my email to see if I had heard anything regarding my application status with the Foundation. In my email was a note from the Foundation. The sender thanked me for my application and noted the many qualified applicants and the committee's decision to move forward with other candidates. I felt a sense of relief as the months-long waiting period had ended. At the same time, I felt a sense of confusion.

But the Pastor said I was getting an interview. If ever there was a man close to God, I knew my Pastor was that man. I believed and trusted him, and I trusted God's use of my Pastor as a vessel to lead His people correctly. My next thought was, *Then what is this email from the search firm?*

I revisited the email that I had received the day before. I read it with new eyes and an open mind that perhaps *I needed* to take a closer, fresher look. The more I read and learned, I realized this was an extraordinary opportunity. I googled the former leaders and news stories and learned that there had been as many as five persons to sit in the CEO chair in about as many years. The agency's founding executive director of some thirty years committed suicide a couple of weeks after leaving the company. A new CEO served three years and resigned. The Board appointed an interim and later hired a new CEO. That individual served less than six months, and the Board then appointed a senior employee to serve as interim CEO. After about six months, the Board named that individual the permanent CEO. Months into her service, in December 2014, she was the victim of a murder-suicide at the hands of her abusive spouse.

This company had experienced bookend tragedies in the executive office over five years. The Board Chair stepped in to stabilize the agency and support the leadership team for a few weeks. The Board then appointed a long-term interim CEO who agreed to remain in the position for a year, during which time the Board would conduct a national search to hire a new President/CEO. After learning all this, I began to see this opportunity as one I should explore. The agency seemed to be where I could make a difference.

In reviewing the agency's list of programs, I was impressed with the number of services focused on vulnerable individuals. There was child welfare and working with kids in the foster care system. There were services for refugees, helping them to settle in the United States. There were programs focused on behavioral and mental health, which included housing, counseling, life skills development and transitional support. Many services focused on the frail elderly and Holocaust Survivors—more than 250 Holocaust Survivors called Tampa Bay home, and this agency provided daily support services. There were programs focused on Jewish families, teen parents, middle school youth and other programs designed to strengthen families, including a unique program that helped non-custodial parents find work and pay their child support. I thought these programs went far deeper in serving people in crisis. I believed this really might be where I was destined to go.

I emailed Sam at the search firm and noted my willingness to discuss the vacant position. We scheduled an appointment and had two conversations before I emailed my credentials and a letter of interest. The following week Sam informed me that the search committee wanted to meet with me. I booked the flight and made reservations at a nearby hotel recommended by the firm.

The YWCA Board held its November-December meeting on the second Thursday in December, and I finally presented the Board with my completed review of the proposed contract. I was happy to get it off my chest. Following the December 10th Board meeting, there will not be another meeting until January 28, 2016. An executive session was scheduled for the December 10th meeting, and though I was not privy to those discussions, I was certain my response to the draft contract was among the items discussed. Following the executive session, I learned the Board empowered several members to work through the details, including my recommended changes, and to bring back a plan for additional review at the upcoming January meeting. My initial interview with the Clearwater non-profit was not scheduled until December 17th. Given the uncertainty of a first interview, I was not compelled to share this initial appointment with the YWCA Board.

I had never been to the Tampa Bay area or looked at the region on a map. I looked for Clearwater and saw it was located on the westernmost coast of

Florida, on the Gulf of Mexico. Water surrounded the city as Tampa Bay itself bordered Clearwater to the east. I thought, *Wow, living on the water could be very nice.* Having no idea of the region or community, I decided to arrive a day and a half early to allow time to explore. All I knew of Florida was flying into Miami and Ft. Lauderdale to board cruise ships and vacations in Orlando. Oh, and there were also the crazy Florida news stories that always made it to the national news shows (the latest being the Florida Attorney General's effort to keep O.J. Simpson from being paroled there). This was simply a place I never envisioned living. Arriving early would allow me to explore the neighborhoods, interact with random people, and determine the community's livability for Eric and me.

By some strange coincidence, my sister Lyn had planned to arrive in Clearwater the same day I arrived. Lyn worked as a professional counselor and therapist and moved from city to city, wherever companies needed her contracted services. Lyn would be in the area for at least a week, so we made plans to connect. She had managed to secure a beach condominium on Gulf Boulevard, and she insisted I needed to hang out at her place because my hotel was right off Ulmerton Road, which was "creepy and dark." I agreed we would connect once I settled in and had completed some necessary prepping for my interview.

I arrived in Tampa on Tuesday afternoon, December 15th, picked up my rental car, set the GPS on my phone and headed west to Clearwater. I almost immediately hit the Howard Frankland Bridge, an eight-to-nine-mile stretch (before an exit) that connects Hillsborough and Pinellas Counties. I was glad I had not chosen an evening flight lest I miss seeing Tampa Bay's impressive body of water. I made it to Clearwater, found my way to the hotel, and walked to an area restaurant for dinner after settling in. I intentionally sat at the bar to connect with random Floridians. I ordered buffalo wings and a margarita and engaged the bartender in small talk. She was very friendly, and the service (as was the margarita) was excellent.

I noticed two men seated at the end of the bar, one in a white collared shirt, clearly a businessperson, and the other in polo. They were having beers, laughing and talking. Sports and random events were the subjects of their conversation, so I jumped in.

I asked, "So, who is doing good work to help people in need in the community?" I wanted to see if they would name the agency where I would interview, as it seemed to have a major presence in the state, per my research online.

The executive noted, "My company is."

I responded, "What is your company?"

He replied, "Duke Energy." He saw the puzzled look on my face and explained all the work that Duke Energy was doing to help families and the work of Duke Energy leaders in giving back to the community. I clarified I wanted to know which nonprofits were doing good work. He named a few, but my agency never came up. I asked him if he knew of the organization, but he did not. I was disappointed he knew nothing of the company I was interviewing with. At the same time, this was very telling—there was an opportunity to work on the agency's profile and image. I finished my meal and drink and bid farewell to the men at the bar.

Before leaving Texas, I had reached out to the Rotary Club of Clearwater, as I was an active Rotarian in El Paso. A visit to the Clearwater club would assist my efforts to gauge the community's livability and gain a sense of the people I might interact with regularly. Rotary met on Wednesdays for lunch at the Belleair Country Club. After breakfast and a period of study, I made my way to Rotary. I entered the clubhouse and found my way to the meeting, where members welcomed me as a visiting Rotarian. I spotted a table and jumped in as I would have done in El Paso.

I met the CEO of another large nonprofit, and noted that they had a large food bank (my potential employing agency also had a food pantry). The member who greeted me at the door joined our table. I was perpetrating as a visitor in town for "business." Then, my welcoming greeter noted he was a realtor. This seemed to come unexpectedly, and as I do not believe in random coincidences, I felt compelled to share with him that I was in town for a job interview and attempting to discover the area and explore communities. We agreed to visit for a few minutes following the meeting as the day's speaker was about to begin.

Following the meeting, I met with the realtor, who showed me an overview of the area on my phone map and suggested I drive to communities where I might find potential housing. I bid farewell and set out to explore Dunedin and possibly Palm Harbor. As I drove toward Dunedin, I stopped at quaint little parks along the road where there were benches overlooking the water. I stopped and started, drove through little neighborhoods, and found my way to Dunedin's town square. The area's Christmas with a Scottish motif presented a great photo-op. I took a few pictures and continued my drive. I made my way to the Dunedin Causeway and came upon an area known as Honeymoon Island. There was a fee to enter, so I turned around and decided to stop at a seafood restaurant, a prominent tourist spot. Again, I attempted to gain a sense of the feel of the people in the area of Dunedin. I sat at the bar, ordered shrimp and grits, a top-shelf margarita and engaged the bartender in small talk. This stop turned out to be another great visit. As much as I dared someone to be nasty to me and give me a reason to say this is not the place for me, it just did not happen.

I decided to turn back as the day was getting late, and I planned to connect with Lyn for dinner. I mapped my route back and decided to follow Gulf Boulevard. This drive led me through Downtown Clearwater, across the Clearwater Memorial Causeway that crossed the intercoastal waterway. I followed this drive around a circle and stumbled upon beautiful Clearwater Beach. This drive led me to the Sand Key Bridge. Another bridge! I was so thrilled and impressed with the amount of water, the beautiful buildings and the scenes of people walking, biking, boating and simply enjoying life. I thought, *I could get accustomed to living in an area like this*. As I continued my drive down Gulf Boulevard, I admired the many condominiums which rose high in the sky—what a beautiful place. I was looking forward to my interview the next day.

Lyn and I made our way to JDs, a local favorite on Indian Rocks Beach. We sat on the back patio where a one-woman band was performing. She was African American, and I was glad to see this, as it confirmed Black people live and share their talents in the area. People were dancing, happy and seemingly possessing no care—it was simply swell. Lyn and I had dinner and drinks. We shared many laughs and enjoyed the time to connect. Having grown up in different households with different mothers, we rarely spent time together outside of large gatherings at our father's house or as children when he would take us all to the drive-in movies. After a while, we returned to her place, and I departed for my hotel to continue preparations for the next day.

The Interview

I studied and researched the company's Board members. I locked their names and images in my brain. I arrived early and made a small talk with the receptionist. She was a very nice woman who had worked for the company for many years. She noted she was a former client and was forever grateful to the company. I sensed she liked my demeanor, and I felt good about this. I thought about how often business leaders ignore their most important people. Those who greet their customers and work on the front line often have to solve many issues their leaders may never see. I wanted to make certain I did not leave such an impression. While waiting for the search committee to escort me beyond the secure door, I recognized people from the images I had studied, board members entering the building and making their way. As much as I felt I knew who they were, it was equally clear that those who entered and walked past me also knew who I was.

As I reflected on the interviewing process, many things came to mind. There was an earlier conversation with Dr. Diana Natalicio, President of the University of Texas at El Paso. During a meeting with Dr. Natalicio a couple of years prior, she advised me that when a search firm is involved, the candidate has already been presented as qualified and worthy, making it much less necessary for the job candidate to put too much energy into selling him or herself at that basic level. In recalling this, I knew that this was the time to demonstrate my leadership acumen and readiness to be their next president and chief executive officer with confidence.

The moment arrived. A figure appeared behind the door, offered a nice greeting, and escorted me to a conference room where a group of about 10 people, including two employees, was waiting. I immediately went to work, shaking hands, calling each one by their name and noting how nice it was to meet them. I sat at the head of the table and shared a moment of light conversation. I was reminded how important it was for the candidate to have a sense of humor—with so much tragedy in the agency's history, I understood the significance of moving forward with a serious but lighthearted leader. I took every opportunity to demonstrate my sense of humor, though the questions were very serious as to my experience and qualifications. Each question brought me closer to *the* question.

There was no doubt I would have to address my experience (or lack thereof) with the Jewish community. Faking expertise would be a huge mistake, which was not my style. I had run the scenario through my mind a hundred times. Then came the question, "Sandra, we see that you have experience with Christian organizations, namely the YWCA, and you have discussed your values align with Jewish values. My next question is perhaps not even fair, but what do you know about the Jewish community?" I took a deep breath, looked around the room and responded:

> "First, please allow me to clarify that the YWCA is not a Christian organization. Though early leaders founded the YWCA based on Christian values, the nature of its existence today as a federally funded non-profit prohibits it from proselytizing, and I imagine this would be the same case as Gulf Coast Jewish Family and Community Services." I looked around and the heads were collectively nodding so I continued, "For me, it is not so much the values an agency represents but do my own values align with them, and I have demonstrated they do. It would be disingenuous for me to say that I know a lot about the Jewish community. I am familiar with the major holidays and some traditions. I have worked closely with Jewish women who have served as President of the YWCA Board of Directors, including my current President. I have attended Seders in the past…" then my brain warned me, 'don't say it, don't and then… "and as you said, perhaps it is not a fair question, so forgive me if I sound cliché in saying that some of my best friends are Jewish."

I paused and looked around the room. There was a collective burst of laughter; I smiled and noted, "I can provide references if needed."

That was it. I had survived (at least, so I thought) the toughest question. After perhaps another one to two questions, the interim CEO escorted me to lunch. After lunch, I met with the two chief operations officers. My day of interviews concluded after that meeting, and I made my way to Lyn's. It was about 3:00 pm, and my flight was after 8:00 pm. Lyn and I debriefed about the day, and I napped for about an hour before making my way across the Courtney Campbell Causeway toward the Tampa airport. I called my spiritual big brother, Lee, and discussed the interview. He asked how I felt, and I responded I did my best and was at peace.

Lee noted, "You're at peace because you feel like the job is yours."

I replied, "To the contrary, I did my best, and I know if not this one, the Lord will put me in the right place in His time."

Lee continued, "They will call you tonight. Just wait and see—you will get a call before 7:00 pm."

I said goodbye to Lee, and within minutes, the phone rang—it was Sam from the search firm. "Sandra, they want you back." I was stunned. It was not until that moment that a question burst forth, requiring an answer.

I asked Sam, "How did you find me?" Sam explained that the search had proceeded for a full year and that a candidate who declined a second interview had been identified. The search committee asked that the firm start over. In starting over, they needed to identify a new crop of candidates. Instead of focusing on health and behavioral health executives, they identified candidates with experience leading "complex" organizations. The search team identified the YMCA as one such organization. Additionally, the search would be limited to the Gulf states, going only as far west as Texas.

Sam made calls to several YMCAs in the target area. Though none of these calls were fruitful, Sam stumbled upon the YWCAs in El Paso and Dallas while scanning Texas. El Paso being the largest, most complex, she reached out to me. I thought if our YWCA in El Paso were just twenty miles west, it would have been in New Mexico, and I would not have been in the new pool of candidates to present to the search committee. We scheduled the second interview for the second week of January 2016. By then, Eric would be able to join me.

With the second interview scheduled, Eric approached his supervisor to obtain advice on when and how he would transfer his job to Florida should the Board extend an offer of employment. Eric's supervisor advised him to immediately begin the process, noting that it could take anywhere from three to six months. Postal employees who desired to transfer into El Paso had been on the transfer list for as long as a year. Eric and I began to study the various Florida postal regions and identify opportunities that offered decent hours and a manageable commute. Each week following the first interview, Eric researched postal opportunities and ranked them as his preferred position, and we waited for the second interview.

Eric and I had served as hosts for an annual New Year's Eve party, and, each year, our closest friends or "the usual suspects" (as we had lovingly come to call them) attended with their families. The 2015 celebration was challenging as we wanted to share the possibility of our leaving the area but knew the fallout from such a rumor was not worth the risk of sharing. We proceeded, as usual, knowing this could very well be our last New Year's celebration in our El Paso home. We welcomed the New Year and once again found ourselves preparing to do something remarkable on January 7th. Again, the number seven was consistently significant in our lives, from the day we met, January 7, 1995, to the day Erica was born, January 7, 1996. Now, twenty years later, Eric and I commemorated this anniversary, and he flew to Pensacola the next day. After a short drive, he arrived in Ft. Walton Beach, Florida, to visit Jesse, his wife and our grandson. I joined Eric on the 9th, and on the 10th, we drove to Clearwater for my second round of interviews. My interview was the next morning.

The search committee accommodated all of my requests. They had planned a full day of activities, including interviews with the search committee, the entire leadership team and some of the community's African American female leaders. There was also lunch with the Board Chair and Chair-Elect, and meetings with staff from two representative agency programs. That evening, there was a reception at the Board Chair's home, and Eric and I had the opportunity to engage with all members of the Board and their spouses. I felt it was a perfect day, though intense and packed with meetings. Eric and I looked forward to our second full day in the area as this allowed us to explore the area on our way and consider the possibility of a new life in the region.

We enjoyed our second day of exploration, randomly stumbling upon neighborhoods and thoughtfully exploring the same route I explored during my first interview. We drove the region to gauge the distance between the various postal facilities and Clearwater. Sam from the search firm reached out and provided a timeline for possible next steps. She asked that I be patient and promised to keep me informed. Thus, Eric and I made the most of our final day in Clearwater. We made our way to the airport, returned our rental car, and hopped on our flight back to El Paso. It was January 12, 2016.

The days that followed included a professional temperament test to ascertain my strengths and work style, reference checks, a credit check, and no doubt, digging into my background like no one had ever done before. Eric continued to check on his transfer job status, and Sam was an excellent liaison between the search committee and me.

Then, mid-morning on January 22nd, Eric phoned me and said, "Well, I have a job in Florida, do you?" I was shocked. Though I was certain a formal offer was coming, I was still in a holding pattern. That afternoon, I received my formal offer along with the opportunity to negotiate a few items I felt were important. Eric and I both received job opportunities in Florida on the same day!

God's Plan is Always Better than Ours

Moving to Florida provided yet another example of God's grace abounding in my life. I have come to understand that there are no *coincidences* for me. I once thought about coincidences, weird connections and "isn't that interesting" moments as something cool that always seemed to happen to me. As I have gotten older, wiser, more reflective and prayerful, I have accepted these times as examples of God's grace and His plan for my life. I have worked to understand it. The more I think about it and how grace has played out in my life, the more in awe I am of the countless blessings God has given me. The true humility of Christianity is instructive, and I can think of many reasons why I do not deserve the level of grace I have received. Rather than consider why I do not deserve it, I have come to accept that I not only deserve it because of my love for God, I can count on it.

Each successive career move builds on the current. One's salary history is a piece of key information requested by hiring officials for administrative and executive roles. It signifies one's value in a competitive market. What will it take to hire the ideal candidate? Is their current salary such that it would make sense to make a career move for the difference? The higher one climbs in corporate leadership, the more significant the salary history. Once an executive hits a certain mark, even an increase of $40-50,000 may prove not worth leaving the current position. When one's current salary does not match the market, it sends the hiring official the message the job may not be as robust, challenging, or complex as the applicant described. I do not profess this as a proven fact, but it is how I have experienced professional growth and development.

Florida has proven to be a great next step. Eric and I have embraced our empty nest and have made strides toward settling into our new community. Everything seems different here, but the one thing that does not change is our commitment to a purposeful life of love and recognizing grace. Our kids continue to pursue their dreams, and we remind them to keep God first in their lives.

Chapter Fifteen

SAYING GOODBYE

I had prayed in years past that my next professional move would allow me to visit my parents more, especially my mother, as she could not get out without assistance. They were both aging rapidly, and there was never an easy or inexpensive way to get to St. Louis from El Paso. Never was the need more pressing to have easier access to St. Louis than the occasion when Lorie phoned me and explained that the nursing home staff had Momma rushed to the hospital. She had a bad fall while outside the residence. Doctors x-rayed Momma's head and discovered a large tumor on her brain. They notified Lorie, and she notified Lacy, who immediately went to the hospital. Lorie was distraught as the doctors suggested they perform emergency surgery on Momma's brain to address the tumor. Lorie insisted I needed to get to St. Louis in a hurry. Hospital staff then transferred Momma to a specialty hospital where they would perform more in-depth tests and offer a more definitive plan of action.

Eric and I were returning from St. Petersburg, about a twenty-five-minute drive from our apartment. I immediately began searching for a flight from Tampa to St. Louis and found a very affordable, non-stop flight leaving about 7:30 pm. I booked the flight and a rental car and quickly packed. Eric drove me to the airport with little time to spare. Lorie informed me about the events as they unfolded. The neurologist would decide as to the need for emergency brain surgery. After a direct flight and picking up my rental car, I went to the hospital where Lacy was waiting.

Momma was awake and happy to see me. We spent the next hour plus visiting and receiving updates from the evening nursing staff regarding plans for the next day, including Momma completing an MRI. Having been through an MRI myself previously, I was concerned as to whether Momma would be able to remain immovable for an extended period in an enclosed area. She had never had an MRI, so I began that night to make small talk about the need for the doctor to look closer at the tumor on her brain. I found I could often help get Momma to do things she might otherwise resist. In recognizing Momma's mental illness, I tried to speak gently, lovingly and factually to her. Momma's paranoia often made conversations about doctors and hospitals very challenging. She generally did not believe she was sick, so we daughters developed a level of expertise in tiptoeing around medical conversations.

The following morning, I made my way to the hospital. Momma was resting but awake. She was happy to see me. She explained, "I don't need an x-ray because the doctor came last night and took the tumor from my brain." With this conversation setting the stage for the day and an MRI planned for later, I knew I had my work cut out for me.

"Momma," I inquired, "when did the doctor come?" I wondered if it was possible that a doctor had come and ordered a late-night MRI. Perhaps Momma mistakenly understood this as them removing the tumor. Momma explained the doctor came and reached over and told her that the tumor was gone.

As I listened, Momma continued, "God came and took it out, just like that!" She gestured with her hand as if grabbing something from her brain. I asked the nurse if the doctor had visited during the night and if my mother had completed the MRI. The nurse explained the doctor would not come until later that day and the MRI for Momma would take place after all emergency MRIs since she was stable.

I returned to the room and told Momma, "It's great that God removed the tumor; I pray it is indeed gone. That was a miracle, and I know God can do it."

"He *did* do it," she said. I continued that even though she believed it was gone, the doctor still needed to perform the MRI to make sure it was gone.

In typical fashion, when it came to doctors and medicine, Momma argued, "I do not need a doctor looking at my brain because there is no tumor; God took it out." I countered that I believed her, but she would not be able to go home until they completed the MRI, and that the hospital had an obligation to verify this. We sat quietly for a while. Hospital staff came and went, running tests and bringing food. I went to get a hot dog, and Momma ate half of it. She loved hot dogs, and I was happy to share them. Later that afternoon, the nurse explained they had her scheduled for an MRI. He was a great nurse, and I loved his bedside manner. He spoke to Momma as if she was a member of his family. The nurse described what would happen during the MRI. Momma liked him and asked if he would be there with her. The nurse explained another nurse, a man like him who was very nice, would be there with her.

Momma then asked, "Is he White too?" I was shocked, and the nurse laughed loudly. He asked her if it mattered, and Momma politely and very properly replied, "Well, I guess it does not matter; I like you." The nurse explained that his colleague was indeed White but that he was also very nice and would take great care of her.

Within the hour, hospital staff came to take Momma for the MRI. As I waited, my Uncle Biggon arrived, as did Lacy and a friend. About an hour passed, and I worried perhaps Momma was having a difficult time with the MRI and the requirement to lie still, immobilized while listening to the varying noises. I called down to check on her, and they said she did fine and would be returning soon. Momma made it back to the room and was glad to see everyone. Not long after Momma's return, my cousin Dollyboo and her husband Henry arrived. We had a full house. We laughed, reminisced and enjoyed photos from the old picture album that Uncle Biggon brought with him. Even Momma participated in the discussions around some of the older pictures, which featured neighbors and family friends from the long past. Lorie called, and we prayed over Momma's brain tumor and the pending results. We sang and thanked God for the good news concerning Momma's prognosis. Because the MRI was taken so late in the day, it would be the next morning before the doctor read and communicated the results. After taking pictures and bidding everyone farewell, I, too, said goodnight to Momma and promised to return first thing Sunday morning. My return flight home was Monday, and Lorie was making plans to come to St. Louis, depending on the outcome of the MRI and related course of action.

On Sunday, I made my way to the hospital. It did not take long for me to see that Momma was in a state of psychosis. As she communicated to people who were not present, she was also asking me the whereabouts of her children. I did not understand the question and assumed she was talking about my children. Momma then asked about Jessica, her niece. Momma wanted to know where her children were and where Jessica was. She made me promise to go and get her kids.

She blurted out, "That man needs to be in jail!" I quietly asked her what man; Momma replied, "Your *father*."

"My father?" I repeated.

Momma clarified, "Yes, your father." As I sat quietly in the hospital chair against the wall in Momma's room, I stared blankly into nowhere. What am I supposed to do with what Momma had said? Who *was* this man, my father? How could he do so many good things for people in need, folks needing work, a loan, a place to live, a musician for a loved one's funeral, a ride out of state, a charming companion? I struggled to balance the multiple views of my father, the good, the evil, the bad, with my views. He was a hard man, a man who worked a full-time job, entered the apartment rental business and played in a band, all to afford the necessary child support to the five mothers of his nine children. He was also our rescuer from Detroit in 1969 as he fought to have Momma's whereabouts disclosed and gathered my aunt and uncle to make the trip with him. Through the good and bad, I forgave. I forgave him, I forgave the foster father and mother for not believing, I forgave my mother for pulling my hair in the back seat of the car, when returning to Big Daddy's house. I forgave myself.

> "For God will bring every deed into judgment, including every hidden thing, whether it is good or evil".
>
> ECCLESIASTES 12:14

The neurologist finally arrived, and I phoned Lorie, who wanted to hear directly from the doctor. He shared what they had learned about Momma's brain tumor. It was very large and sat behind her left eye. It appeared to be slow growing, non-malignant and had likely been growing for ten to fifteen years. The tumor had affected Momma's left eye as it seemingly floated, without function, unlike the right eye. Because she always had bad eyesight, we thought it was simply the normal age progression and its impact. The doctor presented treatment options and explained that surgery would be a considerable risk as there was no way to remove the full tumor (it wrapped around sensitive tissues and vessels) and no guarantee that Momma's quality of life would be any better. There was also the risk of death with such a dicey procedure, and the recovery would be highly challenging. I imagined Momma in a post-operative halo and wondered how she, with her mental illness, could manage such a predicament.

We three girls agreed that surgery was not an option for our mother. The doctor said they would monitor the tumor for change with MRIs every six months. This was the best news we could hope for other than there was no tumor. The doctor would release Momma to return home, following a series of tests and a meeting with the physical therapist. There was a test for eyesight, a test for walking and a test for arm and leg strength. The therapist recommended a walker and a wheelchair in light of Momma's falling tendency. The doctor also prescribed additional medicine for Momma's psychosis. We received Momma's follow-up schedule late afternoon, and the doctor discharged her. After days of running back and forth and just being at the hospital, I was exhausted.

After returning Momma to her residence and transferring the doctor's order to the nursing staff, I returned to Daddy's house to spend a moment with him as my flight was midday. I picked up White Castle on the way, and Daddy was waiting in the kitchen with his girlfriend. He asked about Momma, and I gave him an update. He then asked me if Momma had asked about him. I was not about to discuss Momma's state of mind and commentary about Daddy—especially with his girlfriend present. I responded, "Momma did not have nice things to say about you today." That seemed a sufficient response as Daddy did not pry nor ask for additional details. It was almost as though he knew not to.

Life's Full Circle

In the years following Momma's tumor diagnosis, I was grateful to have had the opportunity to make countless trips to St. Louis. I went as often as my schedule and finances permitted and averaged a visit every other month. It has been a gift to spend significant time with my family. Lorie and I agreed to alternate trips to St. Louis to take Momma to her follow-up MRI and doctor visits. Lacy did an excellent job of stepping in during Momma's emergency hospital trips and supporting her everyday needs. Lorie and I didn't want to task her with taking time off work to take Momma to her scheduled appointments.

After two years, the doctor noted the tumor had not grown, and since we had decided surgery was not an option, they would discontinue the six-month MRI tests. The nursing home also determined that since a geriatric doctor was assigned to the home who made visits and prescribed medicines, Momma could no longer see the senior doctor assigned to her through her prior hospital stays. This news hit us hard, as we also believed the quality of care at the nursing home had deteriorated over the years. We appreciated having an outside opinion as to what was best for Momma.

Goodbye Brian

I continued to travel to St. Louis every other month to spend time with her and to visit my father, whose health had also changed for the worse. While

"The Lord is my shepherd: I shall not want. He maketh me to lie down in green pastures: he leadeth me beside the still waters. He restoreth my soul: he leadeth me in the paths of righteousness for his name's sake. Yea, though I walk through the valley of the shadow of death, I will fear no evil: for thou art with me: thy rod and thy staff they comfort me. Thou preparest a table before me in the presence of mine enemies: thou anointest my head with oil: my cup runneth over. Surely goodness and mercy shall follow me all the days of my life: and I will dwell in the house of the Lord forever."

PSALM 23:1-6

in-between visits, I received a call from my father, who notified me that my brother Brian had died of an apparent drug overdose. This news hit hard as Brian had become a single parent, raising his two children following the death of their mother due to drugs.

My Uncle Biggon visited Momma on Christmas day. He phoned Lorie and expressed concern that Momma was lethargic, and her speech was gibberish. It was noon, and Momma was still in bed. Staff at the home were having a difficult time getting her up. After some time, they could get her up and to the lunchroom, but she would not eat. At Lorie's request, Uncle Biggon tried to get Momma to recite the 23rd Psalm, among Momma's favorite Bible verses. Momma taught us that verse, which has always been a source of comfort. When Uncle Biggon could not get Momma to join in reciting the Psalm, Lacy expressed concern that she might be overmedicated. We were concerned that Momma may have had a stroke. Lorie successfully got Momma to join her in reciting the 23rd Psalm a bit later, which calmed some of our fears. Lacy visited with Momma later on Christmas day, and Momma seemed to have perked up a bit more. I made plans to visit Momma as soon as possible in January. I booked a flight for January 18, 2019, which coincided with the three-day Martin Luther King, Jr. holiday. A couple of days after I booked my flight to St. Louis, Doni Driemeir shared the date for her ordination, having completed Eden Seminary. I was thrilled to tell her that I would be able to attend her ordination because church leaders had scheduled the ceremony during the time I planned to visit. What a coincidence! We were both thrilled.

As I landed in St. Louis, I readied for a full schedule that included visiting with Momma and Daddy, connecting with Lacy and participating in festivities surrounding Doni's ordination to the fullest extent possible. Her ordination took place on January 19 (1-19-19). Doni had asked me earlier to sing with the choir. It was an honor to join the choir, so I humbly agreed and added this item to a busy weekend agenda. After first visiting Momma and Daddy, I headed to the church.

I arrived about two hours early for practice. All members of the Driemeier Family were present for Doni's ordination. Mr. Driemeier's attendance was questionable as he had been very sick and the family did not believe he would survive long enough to attend her service. Fortunately, Mr. Driemeier's health held steady, and he was present with the family.

Following the services and photos, the church hosted a reception in its fellowship hall. There, I had the opportunity to visit with Mr. Driemeier, who sat in a wheelchair, attended by a personal aide. I had prepared a tiny dish of mini desserts, including one tantalizing chocolate brownie with chocolate chips and drizzled caramel. I asked Mr. Driemeier if I could bring him something from the table loaded with options. Doni gave me the side eye, indicating I should not give him sweets. Before I looked away, he reached and grabbed the chocolate brownie off my plate.

I responded, "Well, I guess you know what you want. I will go and replace this one and bring additional snacks for you." Everyone in our vicinity laughed.

Mr. Driemeier reminded me of the time when I sent the family my racial autobiography, a requirement of my dissertation process because of its emphasis on race. He laughed aloud as he recalled my description of the Driemeier family as "the whitest family in America." Then, he began to ask me a series of questions.

"Sandra, when you raised your children, did you eat together at the kitchen table?"

I responded, "Yes."

"And did you have conversations around the dinner table?"

I again responded, "Yes, sir, we did."

Mr. Driemeier then asked, "Did you take your children to church weekly on Sundays, and did you allow them to drive your car?" As I followed the line of questioning, I realized where Mr. Driemeier was going. My family had become the whitest family in America! I acknowledged this, and we laughed heartily. I spent the rest of the reception listening and reminiscing with Mr. Driemeier. I had no idea this would be the last time I saw him alive.

Later that evening, there was a party for Doni at a boutique hotel. I spent my time there visiting Mrs. Driemeier, who decided to hang out with many family members and friends who had traveled for Doni's ordination.

I loved Mrs. Driemeier. She always offered a comforting voice and looked in your eyes when telling you how much she loved you. It was hard not to cry when I was in her presence, as being with her and experiencing her comforting spirit and love had a way of transporting me back to high school. I returned to the moment I found myself at the Driemeier home, sitting on the couch with her while she held me and allowed me to talk and cry it out. That is precisely what I did. All these years later, Mrs. Driemeier had the same effect on me. Perhaps I missed that wise counsel from a trusted adult because of Momma's schizophrenia. Whatever the reason, I could never be in Mrs. Driemeier's close presence nor think or write about her without first clearing my eyes of the flood of tears.

Deciding where I would stay had become the primary issue to resolve when planning visits to St. Louis. In good or bad weather, I could usually make my way to spend time with Momma. During one such stay, my aunt suggested that I apply for a VIP Card at a local casino down rthe street from the nursing home, and perhaps I would receive offers of free room nights. I took her advice and waited for these opportunities for future visits. Shortly after returning to Florida, following Doni's ordination, I began texting with my sisters as Momma's next doctor appointment was April 5, and it would be Lorie's turn in the rotation to travel to take Momma to the doctor. Even though the staff at the nursing home would send Momma via ambulance, we girls preferred to take her. This served multiple purposes, including being onsite to hear firsthand what the doctors thought about Momma's condition and tumor growth and to ensure Momma was not afraid that she was being institutionalized. The three of us began texting about the April 5th appointment as Lorie could not attend due to a work conflict. Lacy agreed to escort Momma for the April 5th doctor's visit because Eric and I had a conflicting event. I began checking flight schedules as I needed to ensure I could visit Momma as soon as there was a break in my schedule. I booked a flight for April 8, 2019.

Goodbye Mr. Driemeier and Goodbye My Cousin, Ann

Doni and I began texting on April 4. She noted that Mr. Driemeier had begun his transition and was declining rapidly. Doni was relieved that her brother and sister had arrived, and that the entire family surrounded him. He was no longer communicating, and Doni felt certain that Daddy Driemeier would die in the next twenty-four hours. I resisted texting during that period out of respect for the family's privacy in light of Mr. Driemeier's final moments.

On Friday, April 5, Lorie, Lacy, and I began texting about my first cousin Ann. She had been in the hospital for about a week. Uncle Biggon visited her and reported that she was terminally ill, suffering from cancer that had spread to her brain and spinal cord. Much of the family was in the dark, as the diagnosis seemed to happen almost overnight. Lorie reached out to other cousins to seek more information. This was an unfortunate and unexpected turn of events. Anne's youngest brother, Darwin and her mother, my Aunt Dean, had both died the year before, leaving the immediate family at a loss, trying to understand God's close timing for three family members in such a short period.

Saturday mornings had become the time I sat aside to work on my book. My friend Nikki joined me as she was also working on a book. We made great progress as accountability partners for the prior two years. I made breakfast on Saturday, April 6, and Nikki came over. Our time together was special when writing, as we were able to share personal stories and insights as to what we felt God was leading us to do. After breakfast, we wrote and shared whatever came to our hearts through our writing. I shared my experiences with the Driemeier family and my concern that Mr. Driemeier may have passed, though I had heard nothing. I then texted Doni and noted my strong desire to be there for Mr. Driemeier's funeral, depending on the family's plans. As I already had plans to be in St. Louis on April 8, the timing was extraordinary that I might be there.

As soon as I texted Doni, she phoned me. I answered and asked her how Dad was, and she explained that he was still holding on. She said they sang and prayed throughout the night, and she did not understand why he might still be holding on. It occurred to Doni that perhaps he was waiting for a final moment with me. She then asked if I wanted to speak with him, noting her belief that he could hear, though he was not very responsive. I asked God to lead me and began to speak to Mr. Driemeier as Doni held the phone next to his ear. Though he could not speak, I heard his pronounced breathing. I told him how much I loved him and how thankful I was that he accepted me into their home. I reminded him of his favorite story he loved to repeat—the story of my dissertation and my racial biography, where I described his family as the whitest in America. Tears flowed from my eyes as I recounted the stories and expressed gratitude for his time in my life. After a while, I said goodbye to Mr. Driemeier and Doni. Mr. Driemeier died before noon on Saturday morning, April 6. Lorie texted at 2:49 am, April 7, that our cousin Ann had also transitioned, less than twenty-four hours after Mr. Driemeier.

With two funerals pending, I changed my flight and extended my trip to St. Louis, with a return to Tampa on April 14. I planned to stay with Lacy, but Doni asked that I stay with her that evening, and I agreed. Doni had asked me to share remarks at Mr. Driemeier's funeral, and this time with the family was important as I reflected upon the right words to comfort them. The following day, April 9, we met at the funeral home, and the family gathered to process to the church. Mr. Driemeier's homegoing service was beautiful. His son Doug sang, the grandchildren shared scriptures, and there were remarks from Mr. Driemeier's lifelong friends and professional colleagues. I, too, shared my remarks about my time with the family. It seemed that each who spoke shared a common theme—Mr. Driemeier was instrumental in improving our lives during critical periods. The stories were as diverse as the storytellers, and it was as though God had connected our paths for such an extraordinary time.

The next few days were a bit of a blur as I went between Lacy's house, the nursing home, and Daddy's and awaited final plans to attend my cousin Ann's funeral. It seemed like a perfect storm of priorities. Earlier in the week, nursing home staff notified Lorie that they could not get Momma to lift her leg. Momma's leg had swollen, and she could not move it. During my visit, they performed an ultrasound on her leg to see if perhaps she may have a clot or other issue. The next day, Momma fell, and the staff found her on the floor. They performed an X-ray on her left arm. Our concerns increased, and Lorie expressed our need to explore a new bed with rails to keep Momma from trying to get up as her mind makes her think she can, without assistance. Lorie insisted we find ways to help Momma with her legs to control swelling and edema. She suggested essential oils, juniper berries, hiring two strong men to help her stand and make steps, magnesium, potassium, compression socks, diabetic socks, rubbing her legs in olive oil and green alcohol…all to get her out of the wheelchair. Lorie reminded Lacy and me that it was "up to us."

After more than a week and two funerals, I was ready to return home to Tampa Bay. After arriving home, I wasted no time looking for airline ticket sales to plan my next trip to St. Louis. I booked tickets for June 5th.

Momma's Continued Decline

Momma continued to have numerous issues at the nursing home. She fell and sustained a golf ball-sized bump on her head, but the x-ray came back clear. The nurse also called and said that Momma could not lift with her leg and that she had been complaining of it hurting. We needed more eyes on Momma on a more regular basis. Lorie spoke with our cousin, Dollyboo, who mentioned her mother (Uncle Sammy's widow) was a certified nursing assistant. We might consider asking her if she had personal availability to begin seeing Momma. Lorie agreed to talk to Lacy and me about the opportunity to have her make routine, weekly visits to check on Momma's health and to note any concerns with her level of care.

Momma's next appointment with the doctor was May 3, 2019. Lacy would need assistance with Momma, but the nursing home staff did not realize she had an appointment and, thus, neglected to contact the ambulance transporter. This required Lacy to transport Momma. Staff helped load Momma into Lacy's car, and the plan was to have assistance from the hospital valet once they arrived to transfer Momma to a wheelchair. While enroute to the hospital, Lacy received a call that the doctor would not be present, and they would need to reschedule Momma's appointment to early June. Since Momma was already in the car, Lacy decided to take her to White Castle. Lacy also planned to take Momma to visit Aunt Lucille, but this did not work out, so after a short drive, Lacy returned Momma to her assisted living facility.

Two days later, Lacy went to revisit Momma and Momma complained that her hip was hurting. Lacy noticed her swollen left thigh and massaged it. Continuing to question the levels of attention to and care for Momma, we asked my aunt to begin her twice-weekly visits. Momma enjoyed the company and added attention. While there, my aunt would put lotion on Momma's feet, arms and legs. She would pray with Momma and phoned to let us talk to Momma. This was great for us, as Momma could no longer answer the phone Lacy had installed in her room years prior. We were also able to video conference through the messenger app. My aunt added to the mix of our visits and those from other family members added peace of mind as we could respond to staff with specific concerns.

A Notable Change

With the cancellation of Momma's visit to the doctor in May, I agreed to step in and take her to the rescheduled appointment in early June. I traveled to St. Louis on June 5th to escort Momma to her June 6th appointment. As was standard, I received staff assistance to load Momma into my vehicle for transport to her doctor's visit. At the clinic, I pulled in for valet assistance. Valet requested a transporter to provide wheelchair assistance and politely ushered me off to a side parking space to wait. It took twenty minutes for the transporter to arrive. He also assisted me in moving Momma from the car to the wheelchair and provided for Momma's use for transport to the doctor's office. Though the transfer was a challenge, with assistance, it worked out. Once we reached the doctor's office, our waiting time was longer, and I was increasingly concerned about Momma's need to use the bathroom. Though she wore a Depends, I was not comfortable with the thought of her urinating and remaining in a wet pull-up.

When the doctor arrived, he reviewed Momma's chart and the updated MRI. He clarified our position relative to surgically removing a portion of the tumor. After Momma's doctor saw her, I asked Momma if she needed to use the restroom, and she replied, "Yes." I was glad she acknowledged this. I was also concerned about leakage in the rental car during the day's heat. I took Momma to the bathroom. After working, straining my body to transfer her to the toilet, she did not go. I pleaded with her to try, but without success, I had to put on her new Depends. This was perhaps the toughest day I had ever experienced with Momma. She was deadweight and could not assist me in any way. I could tell how sad Momma was. After some twenty minutes of effort, I get the Depends on, pull Momma's pants up and move her from the toilet to the chair. All the while, I pleaded with God to help me.

Our ordeal affected Momma as I acknowledged this would be the last time I could personally transport her to the doctor. I tried to make light of the mood by discussing options for lunch and telling her how much I loved her. Momma was sad, and I was sad for her and our family. We waited for the valet to bring the car, and I gave Momma a banana to eat, recognizing that it had been a while since her breakfast and still a brief period before lunch. We drove through White Castle and returned home. After lunch, I left Momma for the day and provided my sisters with a summary of our visit.

Goodbye, Beautiful Momma

Just before Christmas, Lorie received a call from the director of nursing at Momma's residence. The nurse noted that Momma would neither open her mouth, speak nor move, however momma was responsive to push reflex tests. There was concern that Momma may have experienced a stroke, so they transported her to the hospital via ambulance. Lacy met the ambulance. The hospital staff admitted Momma for an overnight stay and gave her an IV and catheter. Several cousins and my aunt met Lacy at the hospital. Momma had reportedly begun experiencing mild seizures and had a urinary tract infection. Momma received anti-seizure medicine and antibiotics for the infection.

After spending Christmas in the hospital, New Year welcomed another transition for Momma. Doctors discussed numerous options, including partially removing Momma's brain tumor. We listened and seriously discussed the option. We were willing to move forward as the noted outcome was relief of the pressure on Momma's brain and possibly extended and improved life quality. After more tests, this proved not feasible. Doctors noted Momma would not improve and recommended we look into Hospice care. Collectively, we saw this as a proclamation of death.

We received a number of options for Hospice providers. I recalled Doni's assignment as a Hospice Chaplain. I asked her to provide insight into what it meant for Momma to enter Hospice and explore providers in light of Mr. Driemeier's recent experience with Hospice. Doni explained that the purpose of Hospice is not to prepare for death but to ensure our mother would spend her remaining time in this life in comfort. She explained the goal of Hospice is that Momma experiences no pain and suffering during her remaining time. Doni shared Mr. Driemeier's experience with Hospice and the family's ability to gather around him during his last days. Hospice would not just care for our mother but us as well, both physically, emotionally, and spiritually. My spirit was comforted because of my conversation with Doni, and she offered to speak to Lorie and Lacy. We agreed never to mention the word hospice in front of Momma, as we did not want her to think we were expecting her life to end. As Momma would not return to the nursing home, she would see all new faces. Thus, we decided that moving her items from the home was a priority. We sensed Momma's fear and wanted to ease her concerns as much as possible.

> "Behold, I stand at the door and knock. If anyone hears my voice and opens the door, I will come in to him and eat with him, and he with me."
>
> REVELATION 3:20

Momma entered hospice on January 8, 2020. We had to answer questions regarding our wishes for her last days. Hospice staff explained the facts surrounding "do not resuscitate" and how such a directive aligned with our desires to ensure Momma was comfortable. After a bit of back and forth, we agreed we should not have her resuscitated with Momma's prognosis and the brain tumor. Lacy and Lorie were there for Momma's transition and first night in Hospice. The nursing staff brought her dinner and placed a cloth napkin atop her clothing. It is surprising how something as simple as a cloth napkin demonstrates the value of one's life and care. We could not recall the last time Momma had dinner with a cloth napkin.

A New Dream Series--Dream One: The Past

I woke up at 2:50 am on January 9. I had a dream that I was doing laundry. I looked down and realized they were Momma's clothes. There were not many items, and I began to fold them. As I folded and placed them in a basket, the need to take care of a piece of weather stripping that was missing from the sliding glass door drew my attention. I passed through the lobby area, took the white weather stripping, kneeled into the doorway and placed the stripping inside the sliding glass door. I stopped just before the cutout where the latch rested. As I neared completing this task, I noticed a small framed white woman enter the building as though she had just gotten off a bus.

At that point, I found myself stumbling toward an area across the street. I continued stumbling while crossing the street as though I had assumed someone in a drunk person's body. As I stumbled further, I observed a dark-skinned man lying on the ground.

The stumbling man asked the other on the ground, "Is it okay?"

The man on the ground responded, "I don't care, man, I'm tired. I'm going to sleep," He then pulled the covers over his head and ignored what was about to happen.

As the other man continued to stumble, he focused on the woman lying in the street. She was recovering from a recent surgery or hospital visit and was highly medicated. At that moment, I recognized the woman lying there was my mother. The man kneeled over her. He noticed that she was out of it and would not fight him. Even though she was deadweight, he was determined. He took out a large knife and began to cut Momma's clothes. He cut the pants from her body. As he attempted to lay upon her, she awakened. She opened her eyes and recognized him—she had been here before. She called his name and said, "No," very quietly, and at that moment, she flashed back in her memory to high school. She flashed back and remembered being in the same position with the same person and two others, a boy and a mean girl. They watched as this man, now a boy from high school raped her. While raping her, the boy stared into her eyes and dictated the words of a rhyme or limerick.

The scene flashed back to the current, and she looked into her rapist's eyes and restated the limerick he had said to her way back in high school. She remembered everything. She knew who he was and what he was doing as she recalled what he had done so many years ago. She was not out of her mind. She could not move and could not fight, so she lay there, closed her eyes, and tears welled over them.

I woke from my dream and noted the time. Once again, the number seven presented itself—2:50 am. I thought to myself, God wanted me to see something. As I thought about the dream, its clarity, darkness, sadness and abuse—all the things my mother had endured throughout her life—He was preparing her for a better place. Hospice is simply the first step of her transformation. I shared the dream with Lacy and offered her comfort that God wanted us to know that our mother has suffered dramatically. Even so, she was His child, and where she was going, there would be no more suffering. It was time.

Lacy agreed the dream was very dark and acknowledged that our mother had suffered much throughout her life. Lacy noted, with certainty, that people had taken advantage of Momma over the years. We agreed that I should not share the dream with Lorie—we did not think she would understand the dream as we did, and we did not want to upset her.

I could not wait for my next visit. Not knowing how much time Momma had left to live, I needed to spend as much of it as possible with her. I booked a flight for January 24-28. I planned to stay with Lacy for two days and to take advantage of two free room nights at the casino. Jordan, having been away from the family since our Thanksgiving cruise, was not managing well with the thoughts and emotions of losing her grandmother. I looked at flight costs and found a reasonable, non-stop from Phoenix to St. Louis, and she planned to join me for my two nights at the casino hotel.

When I arrived after 9:00 pm in St. Louis, I picked up my car and went straight to Lacy's house. Jordan's flight arrived about 10 am Saturday, so I picked her up and drove to pick up breakfast for Daddy and us. Knowing my priority was ensuring we spent time with Momma, I wanted to get my visit with Daddy out of the way. We had a lovely visit, and Jordan and I then went to the new nursing home to visit Momma.

Momma was glad to see us though she was not talking. We updated her on Jordan's time in the Air Force, watched television, listened to music and received several visitors. I was able to feed Momma lunch and dinner before saying goodnight and returning to Lacy's. Jordan had her mind set on getting braids while in St. Louis, understanding access to Black hair salons and products was more likely there than in Phoenix. I thought it a good idea to help her find a stylist as I knew it would also make her happy. Our quest to identify a salon that could get her in on Sunday after church or early Monday, before Jordan's afternoon flight, was successful. The salon assured us that they could see her Monday at 9:00 am and that they would finish in four hours, three hours before Jordan's 4:50 pm return flight to Phoenix.

I was determined to go to church Sunday morning, but I woke up with a sore throat. I also felt restless and decided to sleep a bit longer. Jordan and I later returned to the nursing home to visit Momma. Jordan became restless during the second day's visit. Jordan commented that she could not stand to see her grandma in her condition. Jordan had never been to a funeral nor experienced the death of a loved one, apart from Lee Hoskinson's mother, who loved our kids as if they were hers. Even still, I reminded Jordan of the purpose of her trip, to spend time with her grandmother—not to get braids in her hair. Lacy came before dinner to feed Momma, and Jordan and I left to check in to the hotel.

Upon our arrival, signs greeted us with promotions about the night's activities. I had no idea that River City Casino was the headquarters for St. Louis' Chinese New Year Celebration. After settling in, I ordered my usual Asian chicken wings from one of the casino restaurants. There were now hundreds of Asian people dressed to the nines, attending events in the hotel. I had never seen so many people at that casino. There were live performances, a parading dragon and other highlights. I wanted to hang out but lacked the energy. I took a few Snapchat videos and returned to the room with our wings.

The weekend went very fast. Jordan and I woke early to ensure we were on time for her braids' appointment. We arrived at about 8:45 am and waited for someone to arrive at 9:30 am. Once Jordan was inside, I went to Walgreens to buy cough and cold medicine as I was beginning to cough and did not want to take a cough into the nursing home. I spent the morning with Momma, checking on Jordan's progress. At 2:00 pm, they were barely finished with the top of Jordan's head. I thought she was joking and assured her I was on my way, whether she was ready or not.

I arrived and walked into the salon only to find Jordan sitting in a chair with a toddler on her lap while *one* woman was braiding her hair and carrying on a conversation. It was 2:30 pm, and Jordan was nowhere near ready. By now, my head was hurting and I felt very sick and furious. I reminded them of their promise to complete Jordan within four hours and told them I did not care what they did, but they had thirty minutes to increase the thickness of the braids. I was even angrier as I looked at their length— down to the middle of her back! How much time they had wasted, having made the braids twice the length they should have been. All the while, Jordan babysat and gabbed with the stylist.

I walked out and went to sit in the car. The longer I sat, the more I fumed. I was sick; I had chills and a splitting headache. I mapped the route to the airport to gauge travel time and watched the clock tick away. As angry as I was, I convinced myself to remain calm when Jordan came out, to not concern myself with whether she missed her flight (I had previously looked at alternate flights while waiting just in case she missed this one). My chills increased, and I asked Jordan to feel my forehead to see if it felt warm. It did. I drove Jordan to the airport, said goodbye, and was relieved to make my way to the nearest Urgent Care. I had not felt so sick in a long time. My return flight to Tampa was about 8:00 am the following day, and I needed to clear my sinus to ensure my ears could remain open.

Fortunately, I was the only one at Urgent Care. The weather prediction was for snow starting the next day, and temperatures were dropping. They quickly took me in, and I had a fever of 102.3. They decided to test me for the flu, and my test returned positive for Influenza A. The doctor advised that I should not travel but rest for the week and avoid contact with others. I weighed my options and knew I could not remain in St. Louis. I did not want to spend sick days at Lacy's or additional money in a hotel, possibly snowed in for unknown days. I had to get home.

After picking up prescriptions and fluids, I bought the last box of masks from behind the pharmacy counter. I found it odd that all the masks were gone. I recalled recent news stories about a new virus, coronavirus, which was spreading worldwide, having started in China. I figured even though the

President of the United States told Americans not to worry as there was only one case in the country, in California, perhaps people bought them, just in case. I knew that having decided to fly home, I needed the mask to protect those around me from exposure to the flu. I returned to the hotel, saddened that I would not see Momma before I left.

Back at the hotel, I ordered soup from room service, took my medicine, and went to bed by 7:30 pm. I stayed in bed, sleeping and resting until 5:00 am. My temperature had dropped to a normal range with the medicine, and I was good to travel. I showered, packed my bags and took my time as I made my way to the airport. I felt better and was confident I could make the trip without issue. I was not surprised that I was the only person in the airport wearing a mask. People looked at me as if I was strange, but I knew it was for their good and was not concerned about their thoughts. I boarded the plane early and chose my seat. No one dared to sit with me thanks to my mask, and I enjoyed a row to myself. I was grateful to land in Florida. I had informed my staff of my situation with the flu and of my plan to spend the week in bed.

February 8 came too quickly, and I was on a flight back to St. Louis for three additional days. The following week, I had two days of meetings in Tallahassee and drove from Tampa with a colleague. Two weeks later, I was back on a flight to St. Louis to visit Momma. It was already March 6. Time seemed to pass very quickly. There were increased news reports about coronavirus, but at this point, it still seemed far removed from my world and something happening elsewhere. The media warnings were growing, but Florida and Missouri were not the focus of national news stories, which remained focused on California and New York. I had a mask with me this time but did not wear it.

My visits with Momma were longer, which was nice. Uncle Biggon declined to visit because he heard on the news that senior citizens should stay inside due to their vulnerability to the coronavirus. At first, I thought this was extreme, but I respected his need to feel safe. I also had the opportunity to go to church with my aunt. After church, I visited Daddy for a moment and then spent the rest of the afternoon into the evening with Momma. I texted Doni to check on her and to see if she might be up for a late visit. Of course, she was. Thus, after seeing Momma sleep, I dimmed the room lights for comfort, said goodbye to Momma, told her I loved her and kissed her forehead.

I was pleased to have an opportunity to visit with Doni, who was still recovering from knee replacement surgery. I made my way to Doni's. Her mother and niece were both there. Mrs. Driemeier was excited to see me (Doni wanted to surprise her). After hugs and a short conversation, Doni offered me dinner, Imo's pizza and salad. I did not realize how hungry I was. We also shared a bottle of wine, reminisced about our theater days, and discussed the success of Doni's nephew as a show choir performer. After a couple of hours, I said my goodbyes and made it back to the hotel.

Morning came quickly, and I made my way to the airport. I was pleasantly surprised when the woman behind me offered me a sanitizing wipe to wipe down my table and the arms of my chair. The need to be more thoughtful about germs was beginning to sink in. I thanked her and cleaned my area. I landed in Tampa and went directly to work. After a few days, I began getting sick again. The more I heard about the coronavirus, the more I feared I might have it. I had no fever, though I was dealing with a chronic cough. By now, we had deemed on my job that employees who presented signs of a cough, fever, or cold should stay home. In light of my cough, I was home again, treating myself for a cold.

A few days later, Erica arrived home. Her university was entering spring break week and had canceled all classes for two weeks, pending further notice. I quietly kept my distance from family members and wore a mask, even around the house, because of my cough. I attended meetings via conference and video calls, and as I spoke, I realized how cloudy my thoughts seemed and how out of breath I was. I became more concerned but did not want to let on that I was terrified. Then came the announcement that nursing homes across the nation would close their doors to visitors because of elders' significant vulnerability to the coronavirus. I learned that Momma's nursing home had also closed its doors to visitors. I wondered when I would be able to see Momma again.

Now that Erica was home, she and Eric made light of keeping me at a distance. I thought I might try to obtain a test for the virus. I called the Doctor on Demand to see if they might prescribe a potent cough suppressant to help me sleep. Though I was accustomed to waiting no more than five minutes to speak with a doctor, they told me the wait was approximately fifty-five minutes! I waited and waited, and finally, after close to an hour, the doctor arrived. After a series of questions, she suggested that I should get a test for the coronavirus. After some forty-five minutes on the call with the doctor and public health officials (who gave me mixed messages about allowing me to test at an approved location), the doctor prescribed cough medicine. She also wrote me a prescription wherein she referred me for a COVID-19 test. Even though Pinellas County officials had declined to authorize the test, I called the County Department of Health back and noted my prescription. After the standard series of questions…1) have I traveled overseas to Italy or China; 2) Have I had direct contact with someone who had the virus; 3) do I have a fever…As I could not answer all the questions affirmatively, officials declined to offer me the test.

I continued my self-medicating regimen with cough medicine, an albuterol inhaler, Nyquil, Dayquil, lots of fluids and nasal spray to keep my ear canals open. I stayed home from the office for a few more days until the cough subsided. During this time, I learned that a local hospital had begun offering drive-through testing for coronavirus if one presented a doctor's prescription. Erica, now home indefinitely and weeks away from completing her master's degree in public health, thought that we should test the system to see if, indeed, as President Trump had noted, "Anybody that wants a test can get a test." We took my prescription from Doctor on Demand and drove to the testing center. After about forty minutes in line, we reached the front. The nurse asked me the same screening questions as the Department of Health officials. Then she told me that I did not qualify for testing. I explained that I had traveled to St. Louis and did not know whom I might have encountered during my trip, which may have been positive.

I asked her, "What if I am positive, am I supposed to go home and die simply?"

She responded, "Pretty much, as there is no treatment or cure." Erica and I returned home, frustrated and angry that the systems were not working. I added Mucinex to my cycle of meds to loosen phlegm and get it out of my chest. I continued to rest as much as possible, mainly working from home.

Dream Two: The Trip

I was very concerned about my health and not knowing if I might be positive for coronavirus. The night of our visit to the drive-through test site, I got out of bed, kneeled and prayed to God. I prayed that God would heal my body, whatever was wrong with it, and that He would make me better. I prayed for my children and Eric. I prayed for others in my family. I returned to bed.

I later had a dream, and Momma and I flew upward, fast into the sky. It was dark outside, but the most brilliant stars flew past us in the night skies. As we held hands, I felt the presence of another spirit. We continued upward, "Momma, look how beautiful! Do you know where we are going? Oh wow, we are going to heaven!"

At that moment, a voice said to me, "You cannot stay." My hand separated from Momma's instantly, and I was moving quickly back to earth. I awoke and realized God had given me a glimpse of Momma's journey to Heaven. Even though the voice told me I could not stay, it would be a few weeks before I accepted it was not my time.

The coronavirus continued to haunt me as I became anxious about my health. Our workforce continued to work remotely, and I went to the office several days weekly. I was so afraid of coronavirus I did not need coaxing to stay inside unless for a necessary trip to the grocery store. I even tried ordering groceries for pickup and delivery and wasted time building an online order, only to reach the checkout page and learn that many of the items I needed were not in stock, nor did they have staff to do the shopping. This meant it would be four days before I could pick up the few available items. I gave up on online grocery shopping and continued to do my shopping, buying no more needed but ensuring my freezer was full at all times.

I awoke on April 1, 2020, with a spirit of great concern. April would prove to be a difficult month. Though I could not predict what these challenges would be, public health experts predicted a surge in coronavirus cases, and I observed media reports on what the surge looked like in Italy and New York. I committed to dedicating the month to prayer and sacrifice, expecting God to protect my family and keep all from harm. I wanted to be certain for as much as I wanted God to do for me, He knew I was equally committed to Him. In sacrifice, I committed to refrain from consuming all alcoholic beverages for the month.

I received a call April 2, 2020, from Lorie and Lacy, who were on the phone with the doctor at the hospice facility in St. Louis. Momma received a diagnosis of coronavirus. She was one of the twenty-two residents and five employees who contracted the virus. The doctor expressed that Momma was shallow breathing and that the doctor expected her to die within the hour. The doctor gave Lacy the option of suiting up and visiting and acknowledged the inherent risks of doing so. We debated whether Lacy should take the doctor up on her offer and visit, acknowledging the risk of exposure. I told Lacy I was at peace and did not want her to risk her health—only if she felt the need to do that for herself. Lacy also noted she was at peace, content in knowing she had done all she could for Momma, having had a video conference with her just a few days prior. Lorie, on the other hand, was not at peace. She advocated we remove Momma from Hospice and have her transported to the hospital for treatment, including hopeful placement on a ventilator. Lacy and I disagreed. Lorie noted she was praying for a miracle and did not want to give up on Momma.

Recognizing that Lorie was not being fully rational (Momma was already in Hospice due to a terminal brain tumor), I explained the current, terrible situation in hospitals and emergency rooms as medics worked to treat the growing number of coronavirus patients. Media reports across the country and health care officials advised Americans to avoid going to the hospital if sick. In addition, there was no treatment for coronavirus. Even if one were sick and arrived at a hospital, there was no cure, and any treatment was an experiment. Patient waiting conditions in emergency rooms were horrible, with sick people crammed into waiting areas. The medical staff was under stress and overworked. With Momma's prognosis, she could die while waiting in a scary, less-than-ideal situation, whereas she was at least comfortable in Hospice.

There was also the realization that if God wanted to perform a miracle for our mother, He could do so while she lay in hospice.

The doctor offered the opportunity to arrange a visit via FaceTime but did not understand fully how it might work to connect with multiple people. Thus, we decided that Lorie be the one to participate in the call—the call we believed would be our last opportunity to tell Momma we loved her, and that God had her in His arms. Lorie left the conference line, and Lacy and I continued to speak. We phoned Uncle Biggon, who had attempted to phone Lacy while we were on the call with the doctor. We explained the situation, and he began to cry. We reassured him how incredible a big brother he had been to Momma, visiting her weekly, singing with her, sharing photos and holding her hand—all the things to affirm though she may not be able to speak, she was alive inside and knew that he was there. Uncle Biggon visited Momma until they closed the nursing homes to visitors and advised senior citizens to stay inside.

Uncle Biggon planned to call Uncle Hut, and I urged him to make sure nothing was posted on Facebook, noting Momma's condition. I clarified that Momma was not gone and we did not need family and friends calling us because they may have thought Momma was deceased. We were not ready for calls, though they may have been well-meaning. We had no idea what would come next and did not want to begin discussing a funeral before the three of us could get our heads collectively around what a funeral would look like amid the coronavirus pandemic. There were many restrictions on group size and public gatherings. By now, many states had also imposed safe-at-home orders that placed restrictions on out-of-state visitors.

After saying goodnight to Uncle Biggon, Lorie reconnected, and amid that call, Aunt Lucille called, and we conferenced her in. Aunt Lucille prayed for us, that we would be able to deal with whatever was to come. Her prayer brought us comfort. Momma made it through the night, and we waited for an update. Momma had not eaten for days. We knew that if she did not eventually eat, this would contribute to her demise. It was three days before I had the opportunity to FaceTime with Momma. Nurse Grace connected us following a FaceTime visit with Lorie. I acknowledged if Lorie was on a call, I was certain she had lifted Momma in prayer. Therefore, I wanted to use my time to tell Momma how much I loved her, to affirm how great a mother she was, and how God had her. She was quiet, but her eyes were open. She appeared a bit tired of the struggle. I noted the major sacrifice of nurse Grace to expose herself to the coronavirus by spending extended time allowing us to visit with Momma. No one knew how much time Momma had left, but we took advantage of our time. I sang Momma a version of "My Guy," substituting guy for "God" as sang in the movie "Sister Act." She seemed to like it. I snapped an image of the two of us on FaceTime as I did not want to lose the moment. I thanked Grace and said goodbye to Momma. That would be the last time we spoke.

A few more days passed, and we waited for updates about Momma's condition. We learned that Momma ate some food, not a full plate, but she ate. That was more than she had done in almost a week, and we were hopeful that she might pull through her bout with coronavirus. Our hopes were short-lived. We learned late afternoon on April 8 that Momma had lost her battle with coronavirus and the brain tumor, just after 3:00 pm that day, seven days after I began my period of prayer and sacrifice.

Our hopes of Momma's recovery from coronavirus ended. Uncertainty set in as Lorie and Lacy tried to map our next steps. We spoke to the nursing home staff, and they explained that they had cleaned Momma, washed her body and that she remained in the bed in her room. They said her eyes were open, and she looked peaceful. Lorie asked that they close her eyes. I thought she must have been looking into the face of Jesus as He welcomed her.

We spoke to our Hospice representative, and they assured us that they were working with the nursing home to remove Momma's body. They had already contacted the funeral home of record to notify them of Momma's death. It seemed forever until the funeral home received Momma. It made for a long evening as the word spread and family members began to phone, expressing condolences. We could not provide any details of the arrangements, pending a conversation with the funeral attendants. I also could not plan my trip to St. Louis. With coronavirus, I did not want to travel, but there was no way I was not going to attend my own mother's funeral!

Dream Three: The Hype Woman

Momma's death left a gaping hole in my heart, and we ended the night of her death with no answers as to the next steps. I sat downstairs in the living room, watching TV for as long as possible. I did not want to go to bed. I knew I would have a dream and was wary of what that dream would show me. Would it be another dark dream? Might Momma visit me? That was the scariest thought, even though I knew in my heart Momma was not a scary person. One can never tell nor control what happens in a dream, and I did not want to put myself in that vulnerable space of being at the mercy of just my mind in the cosmos.

I fell asleep (no surprise) and found myself in a great assembly hall. There was a very long head table facing the audience, which I was an observer of. The head table had one large, tall back chair with a pattern of carvings and adornments. The chair was empty, and women were seated and dressed in all white on each side. There was great praise, testifying and excitement as they awaited the arrival of the main person sitting in the large chair, front and center. In the dream, it was clear to me that the individual everyone was awaiting and for whom the praise and worship were about would enter from the left side. Then I looked off to the right, and there was Momma! She led the praise and worship, preparing the crowd to receive Him. I watched as she testified and encouraged others to praise the Lord. As Momma made her way to her seat, folks in the assembly anxiously awaited. Then Momma sprang to her feet again, shouting and testifying, lifting praises to God and urging others to praise and worship Him.

I awoke from my dream, and peace and joy overcame my spirit. My mother was a "hype woman" for God! What I saw in the dream completed the series of dreams about Momma and her life. First, there was the dark dream, whereby I saw Momma's life of hurt, abuse and pain. That dream affirmed what I had always known, mental illness did not rob Momma of all sanity. She knew what she knew and saw and understood far more than most would ever give her credit. In reality, through it all, Momma loved her daughters, and she never left us—taking us to Detroit, Michigan, to join her as she answered Stevie Wonder's call.

Second, there was the trip to Heaven that God blessed me to take with Momma shortly after my final visit to St. Louis. There was comfort in knowing that Momma's fate was sealed and her life, after her earthly death, would be far greater than anything imaginable on earth. I felt so special to have received the gift of gaining a glance. When I think about Momma's path to her heavenly home, there are no words to describe its beauty. I can only pray and find comfort in knowing I, too, will someday be there.

Lastly, there was the final scene of Momma being God's hype woman… It put me in the mind of a song that Lorie did not want anyone to sing at Momma's funeral, "Walk Around Heaven." All the while growing up, Momma loved that song, and she would sing it on special requests by her Pastor or simply if the Spirit moved her to do so. The lyrics describe a place, "Where there is nothing to do but sing and praise His Name," and "every day will be Sunday…" Seeing Momma's life through the dream series was an incredible gift. I knew the tasks, which lay before my sisters and me, were simply that of ensuring Momma a proper memorial service and burial while honoring those who did so much to honor her while she lived.

April 10, 2020: God Speaks

I brewed my morning cup of coffee, poured a bit of blueberry granola into a small bowl and added strawberry yogurt. It was day three since losing Momma. I thought a bit of soft music would start the day just right, and set the tone for a productive, perhaps partial, day of work. Perhaps a bit of Jazz, Nick Coliongne, would be nice. I looked at my list of options, glanced past James Cleveland, and zeroed in on Aretha Franklin. Anticipating a bit of R&B classics, I pressed play, and it cued to Amazing Grace, live. I thought, *Wow, God knows what we need even when we think we need something else.* The affirmation of Momma's presence with The Lord continued, and I thanked God for His goodness, His amazing grace.

Lorie reminded Lacy and me that following James' death, we paid in full for a funeral plan for Momma. With her death, we needed only to determine which mortuary would manage her remains and the funeral service. Austin Layne was our choice as this company had managed many Rice family funerals through the decades. The founder was still involved though his children now managed the day-to-day operation. After a couple of missed opportunities to establish a smooth connection after the mortician retrieved Momma's body from the nursing home, we discussed having a friend in the funeral business pick up Momma's body and take over the arrangements. Lacy was required to meet the funeral planner at Austin Layne. We advised her to go with her gut. If she did not have a much better

> "Let not your heart be troubled: ye believe in God, believe also in me. In my Father's house are many mansions: if it were not so, I would have told you. I go to prepare a place for you. And if I go and prepare a place for you, I will come again, and receive you unto myself: that where I am, there ye may be also."

JOHN 14:1-3

feeling regarding them managing the funeral, we would support the decision to move Momma and her funeral services to another mortuary.

Lacy pulled into the mortuary parking lot, and one other vehicle was present. She stepped out of the car, as did the other person. I was on the phone with her, and Lacy called his name: "Is that you? What are you doing here?" Lacy knew the person in the other car—it was our cousin. They spoke for a moment, and he explained that he worked for Austin Layne, and he promised her that they would take great care of Momma's arrangements and that he would let them know she was family. With that, Lacy was immediately at ease, and the three of us knew this was God's will.

Once inside, Lacy phoned me, and we worked through the funeral details, casket color flowers, and other details. We had more than enough to take care of Momma's arrangements. The value of the prepaid plan in today's dollars was enough for upgrades on their basic plan. Due to limits on crowd size and gatherings instituted to curb the spread of coronavirus, we agreed to host the wake and the service in the same chapel. In addition, because we would not be using funeral cars to transport the family, we eliminated those costs. This allowed for added touches, including additional funeral programs and a memento. We discussed the date, and as Lorie and I had to travel, she requested that it coincide with a weekend, preferably a Monday. I agreed and booked travel to arrive on Sunday, April 19, returning on Tuesday, April 21.

It had been several days since Momma's death, and I had not spoken with Daddy. I think, perhaps, I intentionally avoided the conversation. I knew that Momma was very disturbed by him in her final months and when he visited Momma, he brought his girlfriend. Even though we loved her, and she was a very kind, generous and loving person, we three daughters did not feel right about it. In addition, Daddy's negativity permeated the room, and we did not want Momma to endure it. During one such visit, Daddy mentioned what we girls should do to prepare for Momma's death. We did not want to hear it and did not want Momma to have people in her room, discussing death and making plans for such a time over her living body.

During a conversation with Lorie and Lacy, Lorie noted that she spoke with Daddy. He noted that he has dialysis on Mondays and wanted us to schedule the funeral on a day when he did not have dialysis. We had gone through so much trouble to finalize the date. Deaths increased due to coronavirus, so funeral homes faced increased service demand. I reminded Lorie that she requested we hold the funeral connected to a weekend day due to her work schedule. We agreed that this was not about Daddy. We proceeded with our list of primary invites, starting with Momma's siblings, to create a list of people who should be among the ten people allowed. It was a small group as we focused on siblings and Momma's nieces and nephews who spent years regularly visiting Momma and loving her no matter where she was. It was a short list. After determining who among those wanted to attend, we continued to build the list and the program. We aimed to include many who wanted to attend the funeral service. We finalized the program and had no problem accommodating family members.

I was a bit surprised Daddy had not called me already, by the third day or so, to express his condolences. I received many calls and emails from my aunts, uncles and cousins. Daddy waited for us to call him. When I did, he was on edge, I could feel it. He asked about the funeral arrangements, and I provided details. I explained that we had to limit the guests to ten, including me, Lorie and Lacy, due to coronavirus restrictions and that we checked with Momma's siblings first to gain a count.

"Well, *I'm* one of the ten," Daddy noted. I sat in silence, as I did not know how to respond. Daddy reiterated that he was one of the ten and that we needed to plan accordingly. I was not up for a fight. I neither agreed nor disagreed, I simply chose to change the subject and move on.

As we neared the day of the funeral, Daddy asked us to let him know if we needed anything, but we did not. We were proud we took good care of Momma in her latter days and could take care of her arrangements without financial assistance. Even so, we needed the family's help with other details, and they stepped up to support us. Big stores were closed, so family members provided burial clothing and jewelry for Momma's final dressing. We turned our attention to the funeral program and obituary with the funeral details finalized. We each contributed our talents to that process—Lacy with design and layout, Lorie with poetry and me with the written obituary itself. Together, we chose scriptures and family photos. With so many family members, our goal was to include photos of Momma's siblings, her children, my father and photos highlighting her twenty-five-year marriage to James. We also included a handful of pictures of cousins and family who routinely visited Momma through the years.

I made plans to stay with Lacy since the trip was short. I was unsure what hotels were doing relative to sanitizing with coronavirus ravaging the country. I found comfort knowing that Lacy lived alone with her dog and was not allowing people in and out of her home. Lorie made her usual plan to stay at Daddy's house with her friend, who planned to drive from Alabama with her. We arranged for a two-hour wake immediately preceding the funeral. This would allow anyone who wanted to pay their last respects to enter the chapel in couples and smaller family groups, though not attend the funeral. We also learned that the funeral staff would broadcast services via the internet, and anyone accessing their website could view them.

Momma's Homegoing

I arrived Sunday morning, and Lacy met me at the airport. I chose not to bother with a car rental, figuring anything I needed to do, I could do with Lacy. We went to the grocery store to pick up items for Lacy to make her family famous mostaccioli. She planned to make enough to deliver a batch to Daddy's house that evening. I picked up a couple of bottles of wine, knowing I would want a glass over the coming days, if not a few.

Lorie explained that Daddy planned to attend the funeral after all and that he changed his dialysis to an early morning appointment, which would allow him time to make the wake. I was concerned after seeing the effect of Daddy's dialysis treatments on his body and energy. Daddy was exhausted after his treatments and typically rested the remainder of the day. I did not know how he planned to endure Momma's service after dialysis, but I did not comment. Daddy demonstrated his capacity over the years to do everything he set his mind to do, and to question would undoubtedly lead to an argument.

Lacy and I spent the day talking and making the mostaccioli. While she cooked, I pulled together a playlist of background music and songs for Momma's funeral. It was important to include Momma's favorite artists and the songs she repeatedly played on her record player—albums she ordered C.O.D. (cash on delivery). As I carefully reviewed each song, I made sure Lacy agreed. The one song I regretted not including was "Walk Around Heaven," performed by the Mighty Clouds of Joy, another of Momma's favorite gospel groups. Lorie did not want that song sang or played. I believed she still had not fully grasped Momma's death, and this song made it too real. Lorie suggested other songs Momma had sung, but this was *the song* to me. To ensure good feelings about the musical selections, I left it off. I am pleased to share Momma's Playlist (see Appendix 1).

We finished the mostaccioli and packed a batch to deliver to Daddy's house for everyone to enjoy. We arrived at Daddy's about six o'clock in the evening. Lorie's friend from Alabama and Daddy's girlfriend was also there. We enjoyed Lacy's dish, had a lovely visit and friends' presence helped keep the conversation light. After a couple of hours, Lacy and I returned to her house, talked, watched television and called it a night.

Monday morning came quickly. I was anxious, as I did not want to be late, and Lacy and Lorie were notorious. I made coffee and we had microwave breakfast sandwiches. We understood that wearing black was in order, and there was little discussion about this. The greater conversation surrounded masks and hairdos. Because of COVID-19, state officials across the country closed hair salons due to associated transmission risks. I wore a black hat and boots, and Lacy wore her hair natural, as she had worn it for many years.

The wake started at 10:00 am, and when we arrived (a bit tardy), several family members were already present, parked in their cars on the lot. Lorie arrived shortly after us. As we went inside to speak with the funeral staff, I greeted family members and friends who waited in their vehicles. Inside, we had time to view Momma's body. We read cards attached to the beautiful white and red flowers adorning her casket and said our final goodbyes.

Daddy and his girlfriend arrived and sat a few rows from the back of the church. I greeted them both. A short time later, funeral attendants brought Momma's obituaries. We divided them, delivering some to family members who had already viewed the body and returned to their cars. We kept some on the front pew for me to hand out as loved ones passed the casket and stopped, socially distanced, to give condolences to me, Lorie and Lacy.

Though Daddy was exhausted, he put on a good face for the funeral and for family and friends who came to the wake. He enjoyed the music and commented on the selections. I told him they were many of Momma's favorite songs. He even commented on the Doris Day selections. Daddy held up well, considering he was coming off his dialysis treatment. However I could tell he was unhappy about something. He had no role in the funeral, and, as he was accustomed to being the center of attention, this got under his skin. Under ideal circumstances, Daddy would have found a way to bring attention to himself—he was too tired. Whatever was bothering him, we would soon know, as Daddy was not one to hold his tongue.

Both the wake and the funeral were live streamed. After a hymn, led by Aunt Wilatrel, and readings from the Old and New Testament, led by my cousin Dennis, we read the obituary and my remarks followed. I began by reading Ecclesiastes 3:1-8:

> For everything, there is a season, a time for every activity under heaven. A time to be born and a time to die. A time to plant and a time to harvest. A time to kill and a time to heal. A time to tear down and a time to build up. A time to cry and a time to laugh. A time to grieve and a time to dance. A time to scatter stones and a time to gather stones. A time to embrace and a time to turn away. A time to search and a time to quit searching. A time to keep and a time to throw away. A time to tear and a time to mend. A time to be quiet and a time to speak. A time to love and a time to hate. A time for war and a time for peace.

I honored Momma's life and her love for us, her daughters. I honored the many family members who took us into their homes when Momma was not well or when she needed a place to stay. I also honored the Boyd family and Daddy and thanked him for never giving up on his children. Lacy and Lorie's remarks followed, and another song and the eulogy were given by Uncle Hut, Momma's youngest brother. He shared several stories about his "Baby Sister" and noted other funerals of family members he officiated in years past, including Big Daddy's. This one was like no other. Uncle Hut noted the closeness of our family and the sadness in our inability to gather.

He noted, "It's not but a few of us here, and we can't touch each other, but I know somebody who can touch us, for He's not affected by the virus. He has control over everything." Uncle Hut's remarks comforted us, and he did a great job reminding us about God's power to protect and heal broken hearts.

Later, we followed attendants out of the sanctuary to find almost twenty vehicles that belonged to family members. They had remained after the wake and watched the services online from their phone or another device. They remained, out of respect for Momma, though they could not come inside. We were surprised that Aunt Lucille insisted on attending her Baby Sister's funeral and burial, despite poor health. We ensured she had a seat under the canopy at the burial site. Again, attendants permitted few to gather for the interment, and others remained in their vehicles. I was so touched that they stayed with us, even though they could not get out of their cars. This further demonstrated their love and respect for our mother and us, Momma's "miracle children," as many family members had come to refer to us. Through the years, they witnessed our lives, faith in God, and success despite our many challenges and Momma's schizophrenia.

Knowing that Daddy had dialysis earlier that morning gave me peace of mind that he was not expecting company. We needed our time. We had our little repast. We reminisced, laughed, sang old songs, told jokes, drank wine and ate Lacy's most excellent mostaccioli. Hours passed, and I said my goodbyes, knowing I would not see Lorie before catching my flight the following day. Lacy and I made our way upstairs and I fell asleep watching a movie.

Chapter Sixteen

ANGELS ARE EVERYWHERE

There have been many miracles and dreams since the passing of my mother. God finds ways to show me His wondrous powers and I am continuously reminded of His grace. Today, people are suffering and seeking answers, but don't know where to turn. They turn to cults, to gangs, to drugs and self-destruction. If today's parents are not introducing their children to God, how are the children to learn themselves? I am so grateful to my Momma who taught me The Lord's Prayer at a very young age. I taught my children. Faith gave me hope and confidence, and faith and hope led me to cross that street in Detroit.

People ask me why the title, An Angel for Detroit, instead of An Angel in Detroit? My response, "Angels are for everywhere." There are angels for Detroit, Indiana, St. Louis, El Paso, Tampa Bay, Alabama and anywhere they are needed. I believe God uses even everyday humans to carry forth His will. I am hopeful that those who read my memoir will find there's hope in the midst of sadness and a calm after each storm. My life has been full of miracles and wondrous blessings. My sisters' lives have been equally blessed. I believe everyone can tap into this powerful grace by seeking God.

I have learned to listen, to quiet my spirit enough to hear and see what God wants to tell and show me. If too much time passes, God gives me one more extraordinary experience, just so I am reminded that He is always there. I pray by reading this story, readers' hearts will be touched in a manner that compels them to look back on the good and bad in their lives and connect the dots that reveal the bigger picture and purpose. Not everyone will see it at first, but keep living. I have been so blessed to have reached this stage of my life and be in a grateful place. I could look back, focus on the bad and make excuses for where I might be if it had not been for life's circumstances. Still, I look back and acknowledge I am where I am, fulfilled and steadily growing because of those same circumstances and the opposite reaction they had for good. To God be the glory for the things He has done.

"Write therefore the things that you have seen, those that are and those that are to take place after this."

REVELATION 1:19

Appendix

Momma's Playlist
(As Played During Doris Edmond's Funeral Service)

	Name	Artist
1	Changed	Tramaine Hawkins
2	I'll Take You There	The Staple Singers
3	Ain't No Way	Aretha Franklin
4	What is This?	Walter Hawkins
5	Take Me Back	Bishop G.E. Patterson
6	Lord Help Me to Hold Out	James Cleveland
7	Best Thing That Ever Happened to Me	Gladys Knight and The Pips

	Name	Artist
8	Break Every Chain (Live)	Tasha Cobbs Leonard
9	A Place in the Sun	Stevie Wonder
10	My Cherie Amour	Stevie Wonder
11	Yester-Me, Yester-You, Yesterday	Stevie Wonder
12	Heaven Help Us All	Stevie Wonder
13	As	Stevie Wonder
14	Praise is What I Do (Live)	William Murphy
15	Center of My Joy	Ruben Studdard
16	Whatever Will Be Will Be (Que Sera, Sera)	Doris Day
17	I Say a Little Prayer	Aretha Franklin
18	Bridge Over Troubled Water	Aretha Franklin
19	How I Got Over (Live at New Temple MB Church)	Aretha Franklin
20	Climbing Higher Mountains	Aretha Franklin
21	Goin Up Yonder	Tramaine Hawkins
22	Amazing Grace	The Clark Sisters
23	Walk Around Heaven All Day	The Mighty Clouds of Joy

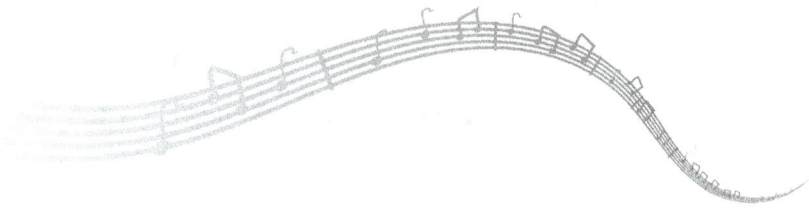

Big Daddy

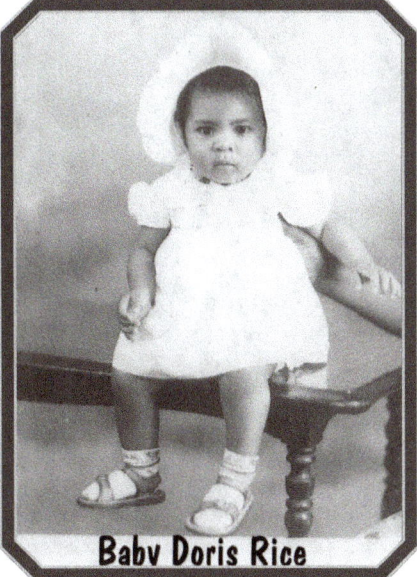

Baby Doris

Kinloch History

Doris, Big Momma, and Baby Sandra

Doris (High School)

Big Daddy's Solid Rock Church

Daddy Samuel

Sandra as a Child

Malcolm Bliss State Hospital

1960s Greyhound Bus

Boaz Apts - Kayci Merritte

Sandra and Doni Driemeier

Doris and Husband James

Eric in BDUs

Sandra with Sisters Lorie and Lacy

Mom's Wedding

Sandra and the Driemeier Family

Mom and Dad Outside Big Daddy's Burnt House

Eric and Sandra

Sandra and Dollyboo

Eric and Sandra

Eric

Doris and Daughters

About the Author

SANDRA E. BRAHAM, EdD

Sandra is President and CEO of Gulf Coast JFCS, a $50 million human social services agency with 550 employees. Under her leadership, the company has added $15 million in revenues. Program services cover child welfare, adoption, elder services, housing, behavioral health and workforce development. Additionally, services for Jewish family services, refugee resettlement and related services.

Prior to her role at Gulf Coast JFCS, Sandra served for 10 years as CEO of the largest YWCA in the country, in El Paso, Texas. She spent the first 17 years of her career in higher education, beginning as a recruiter for a two-year vocational technical college in Indiana, and ultimately reaching the level of associate vice provost at The University of Texas at El Paso. This at a time she noted God's plan for her life and career to shift.

Sandra completed Leadership Texas, Leadership America and Harvard Business School's Strategic Perspectives in Nonprofit Management executive education program. She also completed a Jewish leadership course, which culminated in a 10-day trip to Israel.

Sandra is currently the 2022 Board Chair of the St. Petersburg Area Chamber of Commerce and is the first African American female to serve in this role. She is also active with the national Network of Jewish Human Services Agencies, serving as co-chair for its DEI affinity group, co-chair of its national executives' conference "PowerNET". Sandra is also a member of the national DEI Committee. She has received numerous awards and honors. She loves to golf and was featured on a cover of African American Golf Digest Magazine, following an historic trip to Scotland.

Sandra has been married to her husband Eric for 27 years and they have three adult children.

ANANGELFORDETROIT.COM

#AnAngelForDetroit